Staging art and Chineseness

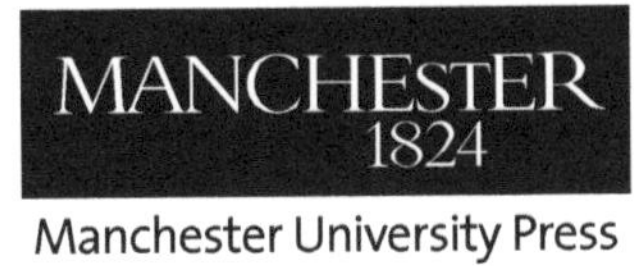

Manchester University Press

rethinking
art's histories

SERIES EDITORS
Amelia G. Jones, Marsha Meskimmon

Rethinking Art's Histories aims to open out art history from its most basic structures by foregrounding work that challenges the conventional periodisation and geographical subfields of traditional art history, and addressing a wide range of visual cultural forms from the early modern period to the present.

These books will acknowledge the impact of recent scholarship on our understanding of the complex temporalities and cartographies that have emerged through centuries of world-wide trade, political colonisation and the diasporic movement of people and ideas across national and continental borders.

Also available in the series

Colouring the Caribbean: Race and the art of Agostino Brunias   Mia L. Bagneris

Performance art in Eastern Europe since 1960   Amy Bryzgel

Art, museums and touch   Fiona Candlin

Travelling images: Looking across the borderlands of art, media and visual culture   Anna Dahlgren

The 'do-it-yourself' artwork: Participation from fluxus to relational aesthetics   Anna Dezeuze (ed.)

Empires of light: Vision, visibility and power in colonial India   Niharika Dinkar

Fleshing out surfaces: Skin in French art and medicine, 1650–1850   Mechthild Fend

The political aesthetics of the Armenian avant-garde: The journey of the 'painterly real', 1987–2004   Angela Harutyunyan

The matter of miracles: Neapolitan baroque sanctity and architecture   Helen Hills

The face of medicine: Visualising medical masculinities in late nineteenth-century Paris   Mary Hunter

Glorious catastrophe: Jack Smith, performance and visual culture   Dominic Johnson

Otherwise: Imagining queer feminist art histories   Amelia Jones and Erin Silver (eds)

Addressing the other woman: Textual correspondences in feminist art and writing   Kimberly Lamm

Above sea: Contemporary art, urban culture, and the fashioning of global Shanghai   Jenny Lin

Photography and documentary film in the making of modern Brazil   Luciana Martins

After the event: New perspectives in art history   Charles Merewether and John Potts (eds)

Women, the arts and globalization: Eccentric experience   Marsha Meskimmon and Dorothy C. Rowe (eds)

Flesh cinema: The corporeal turn in American avant-garde film   Ara Osterweil

The ecological eye: Assembling an ecocritical art history   Andrew Patrizio

After-affects|after-images: Trauma and aesthetic transformation in the virtual Feminist museum   Griselda Pollock

Migration into art: Transcultural identities and art-making in a globalised world   Anne Ring Petersen

Vertiginous mirrors: The animation of the visual image and early modern travel   Rose Marie San Juan

The synthetic proposition: Conceptualism and the political referent in contemporary art   Nizan Shaked

The paradox of body, building and motion in seventeenth-century England   Kimberley Skelton

The newspaper clipping: A modern paper object   Anke Te Heesen, translated by Lori Lantz

Screen/space: The projected image in contemporary art   Tamara Trodd (ed.)

Art and human rights: Contemporary Asian contexts   Caroline Turner and Jen Webb

Timed out: Art and the transnational Caribbean   Leon Wainwright

Performative monuments: Performance, photography, and the rematerialisation of public art   Mechtild Widrich

Staging art and Chineseness

The politics of trans/nationalism and global expositions

Jane Chin Davidson

Manchester University Press

Copyright © Jane Chin Davidson 2020

The right of Jane Chin Davidson to be identified as the author of this work has been asserted by her in accordance with the Copyright, Designs and Patents Act 1988.

Published by Manchester University Press
Oxford Road, Manchester M13 9PL

www.manchesteruniversitypress.co.uk

British Library Cataloguing-in-Publication Data
A catalogue record for this book is available from the British Library

ISBN 978 1 5261 3978 8 hardback
ISBN 978 1 5261 7060 6 paperback
First published 2020
Paperback published 2022

The publisher has no responsibility for the persistence or accuracy of URLs for external or any third-party internet websites referred to in this book, and does not guarantee that any content on such websites is, or will remain, accurate or appropriate.

Typeset by
Servis Filmsetting Ltd, Stockport, Cheshire

This book is dedicated to David, my one and my only

Contents

Plates and figures

The plates can be found between pp. 122 and 123.

Plates

1 Patty Chang, *Configurations*, 2017, still from video installation (photograph courtesy of the artist)
2 Patty Chang, *Configurations*, 2017, still from video installation (photograph courtesy of the artist)
3 Cao Fei, *RMB City Opera*, 2009, film still of live staging at Artissima Art Fair and Teatro Astra in Turin – the world premiere on 7 November 2009 (photograph courtesy of Cao Fei and Vitamin Creative Space)
4 Cao Fei, *RMB City Opera*, 2009, film still of live staging at Artissima Art Fair and Teatro Astra in Turin – the world premiere on 7 November 2009 (photograph courtesy of Cao Fei and Vitamin Creative Space)
5 Zhang Huan, *My New York*, 2002, the artist wearing a suit of raw meat, presented at the Whitney Biennial (photograph courtesy of the artist)
6 Patty Chang, *Shangri-La*, 2005, video still, mirrored mountain on truck (photograph courtesy of the artist)
7 Patty Chang, *Shangri-La*, 2005, video still, monks entering oxygen pod (photograph courtesy of the artist)
8 Patty Chang, *Shangri-La*, 2005, video still, cake decorated with mountains and pod (photograph courtesy of the artist)
9 Patty Chang and David Kelley, *Shangri-La*, 2005, video, staged in Taiwanese-style wedding photography (photograph courtesy of the artist)
10 Patty Chang, *The Product Love (Die Ware Liebe)*, 2009, still from video installation, Hu Huaizhong as Walter Benjamin and Yi Ping as Anna May Wong (photograph courtesy of the artist)
11 Yuk King Tan, *Limits of Visibility*, 2012, still from single-channel HD video loop (photograph courtesy of the artist)

Figures

Acknowledgements

I have been thinking about the issues of identification examined in this book since I emigrated with my family to the United States from Hong Kong. This writing has been a long time coming, and I want to thank a diverse and often disparate group of colleagues and associates whose influence was essential to my process. Words could never convey my appreciation for Amelia Jones, since this book would never have been conceived without her brilliant insight and genuine care. The feminist consortium developed by Lisa Adkins and Nicole Vitellone at the Cultural Theory Institute, along with Laura Doan and the Institute for Gender and Sexuality at the University of Manchester was a point of inception. Since then, Emily Cuming has been a true support, along with Tony Crowley. Donald Preziosi's important work has guided this book. I want to thank the British Economic and Social Research Council and also Tony Bennett, Nikos Papastergiadis, Lynne Pearce, Helen Rees Leahy and Nicholas Thoburn, and Cordelia Warr. The artists whose work constitutes the primary engagement of this study have been personally inspirational, and the earliest representatives in relation to this book were Zhang Huan (for whose generosity, along with Junjun's, I am deeply appreciative), Yin Xiuzhen, Song Dong, and Ai Weiwei in association with those at Reed College, Tsao Hsingyuan and especially Geraldine Ondrizek. I am indebted most of all to the important contributions from Patty Chang, who is amazing in the way she reframes the world of contemporary Chinese art. I am also grateful to artists Ho Siu Kee, Lin Shumin, and Cai Guo-Qiang; and also Wu Mali, Yuk King Tan, Cao Fei, and Wong Hoy Cheong. I am grateful for the support of Adriana Scalise at ASAC and Venice Biennale Archives, The Getty Research Institute, and The Margaret Herrick Library in Los Angeles. My colleagues at the Research Network for Modern and Contemporary Chinese and dear friends from the Chineseness symposium in Lisbon (2015) have played an important part in this book. I must also thank Shreerekha Subramanian, Marsha Meskimmon, Emma Brennan, and Alpesh Patel. The archivist Camille Sui Lin Davidson and photographer David Davidson have contributed so much. The research support of California State University, San

Bernardino was essential to the completion of this work and I am thankful to my colleagues Olga Valdivia, Matthew Poole, Teodora Bozhilova, Tom McGovern, Sant Khalsa, Alison Ragguette, Kathy Gray, Ed Gomez, and Juan Delgado, as well as the amazing students at CSUSB who deserve mentioning. There are countless others who I have not named. But most importantly, this book is dedicated to David, Mei Leah, Camille, and Lucas.

Introduction:
staging art and Chineseness

This is a book about the politics of borders in the era of global art, specifically the borders ascribed to Chinese contemporary art and the identification of Chinese artists by locations and exhibitions. Globalization in the twenty-first century has re-drawn the landscape of art and art history, transforming the cultural mapping, the ideologies, and methodologies for the study of contemporary art produced by cultures that were categorized as 'non-Western' during the twentieth century. The period of the 1980s and 1990s has come to be seen as a turning point for the new global art category that emerged with global expositions as the new art institution – biennials, triennials, artfairs – appearing across the globe in places such as Guangzhou, Taipei, Fukuoka, Gwangju, and Busan, to name just a few in the regions of Asia. One of the most oft-cited examples of global art is Chinese contemporary art, and significantly, the phenomenon of China's *shiyan meishu* experimental art also appeared on the stage of exhibitions in Europe and the United States during the 1980s and 1990s. The most notable example is the 1993 inclusion of fourteen artists from China in the Venice Biennale for the first time in the exposition's 100-year history. The year before, curator Lu Peng had assisted in organizing the 1992 Guangzhou Biennial, the first-ever biennial-type art exposition held in China.[1] But writing in reference to the landmark Venice Biennale show, Lu asserted 'the global "historical passage" that began in 1993 was not only Chinese contemporary art history but an integral component of global art history.'[2] China plays a remarkable recurring role in the political leitmotif of global art and global expositions, providing the impetus for this historical study on *Staging Art and Chineseness: The Politics of Trans/ Nationalism and Global Expositions*.

The underlying political inquiry of this book is in regard to both the temporal spaces and physical borders of transnational capitalism. If indeed the period of the 1980s and 1990s experimental art in China represents the paradigmatic shift to global art, then China's transition during the same period to the market economy that ended Mao's socialist alternative to capitalism can be viewed as a major historical development in both 'global art history' and *critical theory.* The 1992 Guangzhou Biennial functions as the opening act for the *mise-en-scène* of political contradictions – as Lu explains, 'since the 1990s, the only support for Chinese contemporary art has come from the market and the international resources that it brought.'[3] The entrepreneurial force of an inchoate capitalism permitted him to stage the 1992 Biennial in Guangzhou, when just three years earlier, on 4 June 1989, the Chinese Communist Party via the People's Liberation Army literally took aim at the Tiananmen Square protesters who were seeking the same sort of freedom of expression as Lu. But the curator's statement at the time was in defense of criticism by Westerners who thought China's avant-garde artists had sold out to the politics of capitalism: 'All of these critics should know, however, that sales, capital and profit have been chasing the tail of the Venice Biennale since its first installment. Except for the "storm" of anti-capitalist sentiment and protest that swept through several European countries in 1968, capital and the market have never left art.'[4] Lu cites the misreading of China's anti-capitalist position by the West, stemming from the events of revolution in the 1960s, when the European avant-gardist ideal for art aligned with Mao's anti-bourgeois appeal – Mao's 1942 'Talks at the Yanan Conference for Literature and Art' would establish his avant-garde bonafides in the West. And as reiterated by theorist Liu Kang, Mao's influence on the development of Marxist structuralism was integral to the European resistances in 1968, represented chiefly by Louis Althusser who 'identified the critique of capitalist modernity as a central problematic in his deployment of Mao's theories and practices of socialist revolution.'[5] Paradoxically, art history's relationship to critical theory – the Frankfurt School since the 1930s – was defined by an artistic praxis of capitalist resistance that functioned also to combat the fascism of Hitler and the authoritarianism of the likes of Mao during the twentieth century.[6] The point, however, is that the philosophical premise of Marxism was a shared conception during the 1960s and was an outcome of both Maoist and Althusserian analyses.

Raising the specter of Althusser and the impact of Maoist philosophy on his work, my argument for this book returns to his formative concept that 'contradiction is inseparable from the total structure of the social body,' which is particularly resonant for the contradictions of globalization in art and exhibitions. The stakes have been raised by the current cycle of multinational-petro-capitalism and the anthropocenic (or capitalocenic) distinction that is nonetheless inextricable from the earlier industrial model.[7] Althusser's theorization of the 'past *images* of consciousness' suggests that the greater impact of capitalist structures is produced through '*echoes* (memories, phantoms of its historicity) of what it has become, that is, *as anticipations of or allusions to itself.* Because the past is never more than the internal essence (in-itself) of the future it encloses.'[8] The structure of twentieth-century industrial capitalism continuing into twenty-first-century global capitalism constitutes a renewed social apparatus for the ideologies of global art – the radically 'new' biennial in Guangzhou stages the phantom of its historicity from the Venice Biennale. *Staging Art and Chineseness* addresses the new global art ideal by acknowledging the multiple *contradictions*, the paradoxes, and the repetitions of history engendered by status, nationalism, and capital in the globalization of art and exhibitions.

The book's primary inquiry, however, is on the paradoxical subject of *Chineseness*, which begins with the question, what does the term *Chinese art* mean in the aftermath of the globalized shift in art? Ever since experimental artists in the 1980s visualized the epochal change in the advent of Deng Xiaoping's political reforms, the emergence of China's *xiandai yishujia* (contemporary artists) has largely been the defining focus of Chinese art. The term in the twenty-first century evokes the vast and profitable production of China's artists who are currently represented in exhibitions and auctions (along with the curatorial and scholarly texts that inform them) in China and in countries worldwide. Recognizing the difference in representations of Chinese artists who live and work outside of China, the word Chineseness has come to be associated with those who circulate transnationally among the Chinese states of China, Hong Kong, and Taiwan, and diasporic places elsewhere. Since the 1980s and 1990s, when Rey Chow published her influential essay 'On Chineseness as a Theoretical Problem,' the word has also meant something inimically different in its association with the objectification and appropriation of Chinese culture based on the lack of representation by the Chinese themselves under Western methods for displaying cultures.[9] According to this latter definition, the most nefarious example of Chineseness was displayed as an ethnographical subject, one that began with the 'human showcases' and Chinese villages run by anthropology departments in the nineteenth-century world's fairs, continuing into the 1930s with the exotica Chinese female subject of misogyny in transnational cinema. As visual representations viewed on a worldwide scale, these are among the various stereotypes ascribed to the Chinese subject during the twentieth century. The most insidious are the miscegenist depictions of Chinese women in film and popular culture, and one of the underlying feminist motivations of this book is to expose this stereotype specifically. The exotica distinction of Chineseness is inextricable from a history of cultural imperialism, one that aligns with Said's explanation of Orientalism as not simply 'an airy European fantasy about the Orient, but a created body of theory and practice in which, for many generations, there has been a considerable material investment.'[10] To many, Orientalism's capitalist investment in an *inauthentic* Chinese culture had established the 'phantoms of historicity,' the stereotypes of Chineseness that continue to haunt conceptions of Chinese culture today.

In the twenty-first century, however, the concept of cultural authenticity has been problematized, and in the advent of China's assimilation into the global market economy, the expressive differences among artists from China, Hong Kong, and Taiwan, as well as among diasporic artists living in all parts of the world, put into question whose Chinese culture in particular should be considered as 'authentic.' Chineseness in the general definition today refers to the diverse subjectivity of Chinese artists wherever they reside. Thus, the term *Chinese art* in contemporary culture refers first to the inscription of the artist as representative of Chinese states and second to the classifications of exhibitions by national affiliation, such as the pavilions for China, Taiwan, and Hong Kong at the Venice Biennale (as a very obvious example). The new challenge taken up by *Staging Art and Chineseness* puts to the test the very premise of the genealogical inscription for Chinese contemporary art and the ways in which cultural objects are attributed to territories, usually through the status of residency, homeland, or citizenship of their makers – the artist determines the category of Chinese art more so than the object's affiliations by cultural tradition, style, or practice.

As a discourse, Chineseness has meant different things in different contexts, as shown by theorists such as Gao Minglu and Ien Ang, who provide various perspectives on the term's use in defining Chinese exceptionalism, stereotype, and status. During the 1990s, *shiyan meishu* experimental artists such as Gu Wenda and Xu Bing often addressed the synthesis of culture through re-envisioning language and Chinese characters. For his ongoing *United Nations Series* begun in 1993, Gu created unreadable letters and characters in different languages by using the material of hair collected from barbershops in the different countries where he exhibited his installation. Curator Gao Minglu suggests that the project initiated a 'model of universalism' for cultural expression.[11] In contrast, media/cultural studies researcher Ien Ang explains the meaning of the term subjectively as a 'label more than anything else' from her experience growing up in Indonesia. 'Even though my father was a *peranankan* Chinese who never spoke any Chinese, his family had not spoken any Chinese for generations, for some reason his family was still called a "Chinese" family.'[12] Not unlike Édouard Glissant's theory of creolization, Chineseness is useful for re-conceptualizing the mundialization of Chinese identity. Glissant describes 'the mutual mutations generated by this interplay of relations' that contribute to what he calls the 'principles of creoleness.'[13] The principles of Chineseness share mutual mutations in an interplay of relations that circulate around Chinese exceptionalism as well as Orientalism. Wang Gungwu published his 1991 book *The Chineseness of China* to continue his inquiry into the exceptional Chinese identity defined by Chinese tradition and values as opposed to the 'disloyal expression of Chineseness.' Those who assimilate overseas would lose their distinction, much like his own experience since he was 'born in Indonesia, trained as an historian of China in England, teaching first at Kuala Lumpur and then at Canberra, finally ... becoming Vice-Chancellor of the University of Hong Kong.'[14]

Allen Chun explains further the shifting belief in the Han ethnic unity that had changed under 'the term *chung-kuo* [*zhongguo* in pinyin or middle kingdom]' as distinct from 'Chineseness as *hua-hsia*,' which signifies a 'metaphorical defense of a traditional past that contrasts with the extreme radicalism of a communist worldview.'[15] The authenticity of Chinese identity has been a complex subject of debate in China's long history, and from 1949 to 1976, it was irrevocably transformed by Mao's revolution – the Soviet influences in the 1950s could be seen in the impact of socialist realist painting until Mao's death in 1976. While the emergence of China's contemporary art in the 1980s may seem to mark the sudden change from a 'genuine' Chinese artistic tradition, the cross-hybrid fusion of Western and Chinese influences in the arts had begun much earlier, even before socialist realism, since industrialization after the Opium Wars resulted in modernist expression amidst the 1860s internationalism of Shanghai. Nonetheless, the *shiyan meishu* experimental movement of the 1980s and 1990s in China established the contemporary shift in the development of tradition and style, reflecting the mutual mutations of cultural expression.

Chineseness is a changing concept that functions in this book to confirm the problem of identification by viewing through the lens of Chinese artists as they address the misconception of the cultural 'self' in the social sphere. Not unlike other inquiries into cultural/ethnic syncretism in globalization, the theoretical connections of Chineseness are conceived by identifications according to movements across geographical borders and embodiments of citizenship. In the aftermath of the political events of 2016, identity by national borders and citizenship has become highly political, as exemplified by Brexit's anti-globalization position in parallel with the election of Donald Trump, who closed the US borders to asylum seekers and many other immigrant groups. The meaning of the term globalization has changed from positive notions of the far-reaching connections of the worldwide web and the advantages of a global economy. To the anti-globalists, the idea of 'internationalism' appears as a nostalgic term for the 'good, old days,' when the world was enfranchized and mapped according to Europe and North America. The internationalism of the museum world during the 1980s and 1990s when contemporary artists from China were first presented in American and European exhibitions has now been transformed by the global development of museums in metropolitan cities such as Shanghai. As explored in Chapter Five of this book, museums have become important civic centers and tourist sites and about a thousand museums were built in China during the first decade of the twenty-first century.

In the context of art, however, those connections across borders were never easy propositions because subjects of identity in relation to artistic expressions have always been problematic – the representation of a person, a community, a culture through material and immaterial objects (including photography and film) could never be fully accurate portrayals. This book focuses on embodied representations of Chinese artists in order to address the problem through performance and video manifestations, as represented in the work of Patty Chang, Zhang Huan, Wong Hoy Cheong, Cao Fei, Yuk King Tan, Wu Mali, Lee Ming-sheng, Lin Shumin, Ho Siu Kee, Stanley Wong, and Cai Guo-Qiang. As artists who identify as residents of China, Hong Kong, Taiwan, the United States, and other diasporic locations, their use of performative, embodied, and video expressions provides a way to engage the subject of the artist's 'self' as an open and apparent representation of nation, immigration, citizenship, and transnationalism – in this way, they provide a particular opportunity to represent identity artistically. This book's study of Chineseness is therefore represented by the artists themselves as their video performances help to clarify the paradoxical meaning of the term. The explicit focus on the role of film, screen, performance/body in individual and collective ways underpin the critical analysis in the first three chapters, which eventually leads to the focus on the analysis of exhibitions in the last two chapters since the structures of biennials and triennials have long represented nations and locations.

While this book seeks to make sense of Chineseness in relation to the global art shift since the 1990s, the ecofeminist portrayals of the artists Patty Chang, Cao Fei, Wu Mali, and Yuk King Tan provide an activist approach as their transnational endeavors transform the function of global contemporary art. The term *ecofeminism* is attributed to 1970s feminist advocates such as Francoise d'Eaubonne who connected the domination of the environment to patriarchal oppression. The movement has since developed into a global advocacy, and the ecofeminist strategies adopted by the artists in this book are ones that actively address environmental issues by transgressing the patriarchal conventions of capitalist nationalism with its domination over land and resources. They provide a clear example of the expansion of *trans*nationalism in the terminology of the transgressive, the transformative, and the translational, since their focus on issues affecting the ecological borders of the planet are those that are inextricable from the political borders of the nation.

But even as artists themselves confront the larger issues of migration, citizenship, and exile through presenting their own bodies as the subject and object of art, the engagement with the viewer can never be fully accounted for through artistic representation. The perfect example for this dilemma is conveyed by the bodily-oriented performances of two comparative artists explored in Chapter One of this book: China-born artist Zhang Huan and

Chinese American artist Patty Chang. In his project *My America* (1999–2002), Zhang confronts issues of migration and assimilation related to his own experience relocating to the United States by enlisting members of his new American community to participate in his performance events.[16] As one of the experimental artists of the 1980s–1990s generation, his early work resonates for Chineseness at the end of the 1990s explicitly – Zhang's use of his own naked body (along with the participants' naked bodies) as the subject and object of the viewers' gaze places the focus on the live, human subject of the artist in the midst of his configured social body. The juxtaposition of naked bodies has the potential to disrupt the stereotypes and assumptions surrounding the Chinese 'immigrant.'

In contrast, Chang's video performances, such as *Minor* (2010), can be viewed as the Chinese American counterpart to *My America*, since she travels to inner and outer parts of China, including the Xinjiang autonomous region in the northwest where she engaged with the Muslim Uyghur community. Chang's focus through her video lens projected onto her peripatetic Chinese American self juxtaposed with her Uyghur and Han Chinese subjects in Xinjiang puts into question the 'ethnicity' of being Chinese, one that is openly disavowed by many of the Uyghur population. Chang represents the contradictions of Chineseness in the reverse of a history of immigration acts forbidding movements to the United States from China. The conditions of power that exist in Uyghur-Han relations are different from the white heterosexual norm in the United States; however, the patriarchal hierarchies of nationalism continue to inform both Chang and Zhang's works. The underlying *transnational* feminist position of this book is one that recognizes the historical structures of nationalism as patriarchal formations. However, all feminist studies are specific in the ways in which they provide a particular context and perspective, and this study aligns with Aihwa Ong's ideal for 'narratives of nation and community [that] position women within special conditions for expressing their moral agency,' proposing a resistance to 'the hegemonic project of nationalism.'[17] Through performance and video, both Chang and Zhang embody the ontological concept of the 'self' as a product of ethnic borders, nationalisms, and legislated citizenship. Because the artists are problematizing the concepts of authentic and inauthentic Chinese identity, they ultimately disrupt the hegemonic norms of nationalism since the body cannot fully divulge the inscriptions of ethnicity or nationality. Feminist theorists, notably Amelia Jones, have addressed the body's unique failure in identificatory-art practices, and as Peggy Phelan wrote in her analysis of performance, 'identity emerges in the failure of the body to express *being* fully and the failure of the signifier to convey meaning exactly.'[18] According to Phelan, artistic engagement with identity requires a relationship with the viewer in an artistic exchange that is ultimately inextricable from 'self-seeing' and 'self-being.'

Moreover, in the digital currents by which photography and video have become essential for any artistic practice in the understanding that all artworks will end up on the computer screens of social media, the 'screen-based' discourse that pertains to Chang's video work requires further study into the diversity of practices invoked by performance. As Claire Bishop points out, while most art today 'deploys new technology at one if not most stages of its production, dissemination, and consumption,' the lack of cogent responses to digitization in contemporary art has been 'striking ... so little of it seems to address the way in which the forms and languages of new media have altered our relationship to perception, history, language, and social relations.'[19] Taking after the objectives and strategies of film theorists such as Rey Chow, Shu-mei Shih, Kwai-Cheung Lo, and Sheldon Hsiao-peng Lu, this book acknowledges the differences in the visual field of representation and seeks to clarify the use of *video performances* to express embodiments in relation to the locations of Chinese culture. The medium is unique because of its usefulness for the analyses of film interpellation and Chinese identity, which is often the focus of the aforementioned film theorists. The conceptualism of the visual art practice is different, however, from the movie/cinema representation, especially in regards to the performance/bodily-oriented works that constitute the primary artistic subjects of this book. The intervention of video changes the live art performance but functions to expand the cultural vocabulary of the film form in the Youtube age – the liveness of Chang's performance in *Minor*, for instance, connects to the extemporaneous sensibility of capturing an event, a moment. Added to this, the metaphysical meaning that contemporary artists have developed for the individual media of performance and video, *Minor* is able to convey multiple complex ideas in a transnational context. Notwithstanding the potential discrepancies and misrepresentations of identity in the performative/video engagement, both Zhang and Chang exemplify the embodiments of the subjects, issues, histories, and inquiries explored in this book through their bodily-oriented works.

The theoretical objective of *Staging Art and Chineseness* is therefore to connect the performance video subjects of Chineseness to the greater historical scope of 'geographical consciousness' and assumptions of culture by location and nation. While works by global contemporary artists are still representative of their respective geographical territories, the ideals ascribed to their artworks and exhibits can be understood as reflexive of the *continuities* of analyses of social consciousness, particularly those established by historical Marxism for industrial capitalism, which Althusser considers as 'phantoms of historicity.' A study of the historical matrix of *global expositions* can provide the structural connections among art, culture, capital, and nation. The book therefore acknowledges the system of representation in which global art expositions such as the 1992 Guangzhou Biennial inevitably carry the structural tendencies of the Venice Biennale, the world's fairs, and the long European history of cultural management, including the way in which global expositions themselves construct the imagined communities of China, Hong Kong, and Taiwan. Acknowledging this system of exhibition as an important form for identifying culture, the book's interconnected case studies function to define, interpret, and exemplify the concept of Chineseness in contemporary and historical contexts for art. The discourses of the colonial, the post-colonial, and the subsequent decolonial processes are at the center of these contexts, and they are also played out in the curatorial subjects, exhibitionary ideals, and organizing principles of global expositions.

As Walter Benjamin once wrote, 'world exhibitions are places of pilgrimage to the commodity fetish' because their organizing principles 'glorify the exchange value of the commodity. They create a framework in which its use value recedes into the background ... Its ingenuity in representing inanimate objects corresponds to what Marx calls the "theological niceties" of the commodity.'[20] Benjamin went on to explain that Marx's 'theological niceties' were manifested by the '*spécialité* – a category of goods which appears at this time in the luxuries industry' – and fine art objects were exactly the kind of luxe objects that could fulfill the secular role for the worship of special things in capitalist modernity.[21] When the Venice Biennale was inaugurated in 1895, nearly every metropolitan city in the world had hosted a world's fair, and Venice's artfair would take as its model the competition among industrial nations for displaying Benjamin's 'theological niceties' of the commodity. The aesthetic essentialism of the fine arts, showcased in palaces attributed to European and North American nations, would be contrasted with the display of artworks considered as ethnographical artefacts attributed to 'non-Western' cultures at the world's fairs.

As denoted by the very first inclusion of China's artists in the 1993 Venice Biennale, China was not among the nations represented at the 1895 Venice Biennale, and it would take another 100 years before the country would be invited by Biennale director Achille Bonito Oliva to exhibit for the first time in the international group show titled 'Passagio a Oriente.'[22] In the decades to come, *official* pavilions would also be dedicated for the first time to Taiwan in 1995, Hong Kong in 2001, and China in 2005. Lu Peng attributes the success of the first inclusion of Chinese artists in the Venice Biennale to the attention garnered from the 1992 Guangzhou Biennial. The important role of the curator in the globalized shift of biennials and triennials informs the case studies in the final chapters of this book. As curatorial forerunners in China, the leadership of Lu Peng, Wu Hung, Huang Zhuan, Feng Boyi, Gao Shiming, Sarat Maharaj, and Chang Tsong-zung was highly influential in the rewriting of Chineseness. This study also acknowledges the *trans*national contributions to the development of global expositions in the larger scope by curators such as Okwui Enwezor and Adam Szymczyk for Documentas 11 (2002) and 14 (2017) respectively.[23] As the first African curator at the quinquennial exhibition held in Kassel, Germany, Enwezor's 2001 curatorial premise was built on five political 'platforms,' in which the third platform foregrounded Glissant's globalized identity of the 'Creolite and Creolization' as an exploration for Documenta 11.

As the counterpart to the world's fair trajectory of the Venice Biennale, Documenta's history as a political event began in 1955 through its well-known role as a 'corrective to the infamous 1937 Nazi exhibition Entartete Kunst ('degenerate art') in order to construct a rehabilitating narrative of modernism for the German people.'[24] While the quinquennial serves as a prime example of the twenty-first-century *global* art exposition, Walter Grasskamp argues that 'documenta in its beginnings was not really an international show. It was not even a proper European one, but in fact a very German event.'[25] Of 148 artists on the inaugural official roster, 58 were German participants, with the rest consisting of artists representing France, Italy, Britain, Switzerland, and Holland. Ultimately, the 1955 Documenta subscribed to the organizing principles of the 1895 Venice Biennale in a cartography described by Grasskamp as a 'surrealistic world map of "twentieth century art" ("kunst des XX. Jahrhunderts"), which was what the first documenta claimed to cover; as surrealistic a map as the national pavilions in the Venice Giardini in winter.'[26] Even the 'unofficial' exhibitions of artists ascribed to 'nearly every Western European and Central European country' at the first Documenta followed in the hierarchical nationalism of the Venice Biennale.

The formative period for the global art shift is attributed to the late 1990s, but if indeed the biennials, triennials, and artfairs are representative of the 'new' exhibitions of global art, then how do they relate to the longstanding biennial models, such as the Venice Biennale begun in 1895 and Documenta's emulation in 1955? The fundamental legacy handed down from the Biennale is that the 'staging' of the *artist* in the context of the exhibition is always-already representing nation and culture through the biennial's entrenched meanings, categorization, signifiers, and symbolism of display. In this way, Chineseness has been represented as both a national and cultural identity at the global art expositions, both in China and in the historical European biennials/triennials.

Chapter overview

Chapter One's study, 'Chineseness as a theoretical, historical, and political problem in global art and exhibition,' sets the stage by introducing and defining the discourse on Chineseness with its particular history of political debates instantiated by Rey Chow's influential 1998 essay. Chow had established the important dialogue through addressing the problem raised by Said's analysis of the hegemonic West in *Orientalism,* which she reads specifically for her analysis of the fetishization of Chinese 'subject-races.' Her interpretation of Chineseness acknowledges the paradox of the cultural logic of European exclusivism coexisting with the narcissistic, megalomaniacal fantasy of China as an unattainably superior culture. In art-historical terms, these inauthentic forms of Chineseness can be understood as perpetuated through European elitism in art and its domination of art historical narratives – seen in the absence of Chinese representation in the history of Modern Art, while on the other hand, the blockbuster exhibitions of '5000 years of ancient Chinese art' confirm the megalomanic fantasy of Orientalism. In this context, 'Chineseness' was negatively viewed by its attachment to the Orientalist inscription, and as late as 2005, the term was considered contentious because it signified appropriation, reductivism, and inauthentic forms of representation.

This chapter explains how Chineseness has moved away from its controversial meaning and has been used by theorists and historians to specify the shifting, variable, unfixed meanings attached to Chinese culture. Conceptions of Chineseness are nonetheless contingent on many authentic and inauthentic factors for identity and identification. In the advent of Stuart Hall's analysis of race as a 'floating signifier' and Judith Butler's questioning of gender performance, the subjective instability of identity is the only conception that can be consistently attributed to Chineseness.[27] In mainstream representations, however, the word has come to be used to distinguish the difference among the Chinese in China, Hong Kong, and Taiwan, and among the diasporic Chinese generally. Film theorists, including Chow, Sheldon Hsiao-peng Lu, and Shumei Shih, were some of the first researchers to have used the term in this way as Chineseness became a subject of *interpellation* in movies and documentary film. Chow denoted the structuralist concept originating from the dialectical theories of Althusser, which remarkably were also influenced by his reading of Mao. Interpellation is not simply the practice of self-recognition by viewers of film, but is a form of political recognition of human beings who are made into subjects through historical economic and social conditions. The remarkable changes of those conditions in China has brought Chineseness into the forefront of the socio-political economy of representation.

Althusser's exploration of Maoist thought was developed later by his students, including Jacques Rancière and Alain Badiou, both of whom have contributed significantly to contemporary art discourse while conserving in varying degrees the use of Maoist alternatives to capitalism through discourse.[28] The fragments and traces of historical materialism in the structural philosophies for art, affecting representation and identity, can be seen as continuing in Rancière and Badiou's approaches to the discourse. Their position is compatible with this book's study on contemporary art as Chineseness functions to acknowledge the synthesis of philosophical discourses, not unlike the shifting and variable syntheses of cultural influences on the notion of Chinese identity. Perhaps Marxism's greatest contribution was its global and intellectual reach across cultures and languages through its analytical framework for understanding class consciousness. As the theoretical focus of Chapter One, the discourse on Chineseness engages interdisciplinary aspects of intellectual thought, and its representation is therefore connected to the different subjects of this book including ecofeminism, art history, and global expositions. The chapter's explanation of Chineseness functions overall to situate the different approaches to transnationalism as they relate to video performances and exhibitions.

The artists chosen for this book are primarily those who evoke the gendered and raced body explicitly in order to define and examine the subject and object that pertains to geographic origins and movements. But ultimately, these artists were chosen because they have in some way or other challenged the norm of representing cultural boundaries. The most important among them are artists who address the feminist subject, which is a key investigation of this book exemplified by Chapter Two's study on 'Patty Chang and the transnational cinematic subject of Chineseness.' The examination of three video performances in which Chang addresses the very *subject* of cinema and its historical impact on Chinese stereotypes is a reconceptualization of three different transnational films and movies from the 1920s and 1930s. Chang's retrospective focus on early film acknowledges the constructions of gender and race in the diverse world of ethnography, Orientalist fantasy, and miscegenistic desire in twentieth-century cinema. At the same time, Chang is peripatetically traveling to the 'real' places in China as a Chinese American.

In this way, Chapter Two defines transnationalism as the key concept for this book, and through Chang's diverse Chinese subjects, especially in the autonomous outer regions of Turkic-Uyghur Xinjiang in the north and the Diqing Tibetan Autonomous Prefecture in the south, the study presents a foundation for Chapter Three's Chinese subjects in Hong Kong, Taiwan, and China. Chapter Two's close analysis of *Minor* (2010), for instance, will show how Chang emulates the travelogue of ethnographic film as the artist retraces the expeditions in the 1920s and 1930s of Sven Hedin, the Swedish explorer, to Xinjiang and the Lop Nor region of northern China. The journey was documented by Paul Lieberenz, Hedin's cohort, whose 1928 anthropology film titled *With Sven Hedin Across the Deserts of Asia* depicts his caravan with no less than 300 camels. Hedin's scientific objectives were just as ostentatious. Trained as a geographer in Germany, the explorer was part of the *Lebensraum* school of geography and anthropology in the service of empire, and his scientific worldview was shaped by Aryan racial determinism as an ideology of the German National-Socialist movement.[29]

Chang's video project shows a radically different approach to her 'ethnographic subjects,' including her video's discovery of an exhibition of mummies in which the female mummy, the *Beauty of Loulan*, is among the eight others she discovers in a local museum. Chang offers an embodied sensibility for viewing objects of ancestry and ethnicity as she seeks to connect the mummified past with the vanishing present. Meeting a young Uyghur girl in Xinjiang, who could potentially be a descendant of the Beauty of Loulan, she creates her 'ethnographic video' by staging her in the same embodied pose of the mummy artefact laying prone. This embodied gesture pays homage to the ethnographic intervention that James Luna first presented in *Artefact Piece* (1987), his famous performance at San Diego's Museum of Man, whereby he staged his own living breathing Luiseño Native American self by laying prone in a vitrine in the anthropology museum.[30] Luna challenged the ethnographical stereotype that characterized his Native community as dead and extinct due to primitivism. Chang's presentation of the embodied female subject of the Muslim Uyghur community shares the same sense of live human representation since the Uyghur inhabitants of the autonomous region of China are often viewed by similar stereotypes of primitivism and extinction. The fact that the Han Chinese are discriminating against the Uyghur community re-defines cultural hegemony as a concept that encompasses much more than Eurocentric power.

The second work explored in Chapter Two is Chang's 2005 project *Shangri-La*, which brought her to Zhongdian in the southwest province of Yunnan and the Diqing Tibetan Autonomous Prefecture. The local government won a national contest to change the name of Zhongdian to Xianggelila (Shangri-La) in order to capitalize on concepts of paradise from James Hilton's 1933 novel *Lost Horizon*. Through her video installation, Chang reproduces the film fantasy that Frank Capra interpreted for his 1937 movie version of *Lost Horizon*, the story of a plane crash in the Himalayas that led to the discovery of Shangri-La, an ethno-fantastic place of immortality run by a Buddhist lamasery. Through her conceptual video, Chang literally re-constructs the elements of lore from Capra's Shangri-La while working with the community of Xianggelila to build the sculptural replica of the awe-inspiring mountains made from angled pieces of mirror, as well as to recreate the Shangri-La cake that Capra presented at the cast party at the closing of his 1937 film. Chang's subject is the concept of *fabrication* itself, emphasized by a screen shot of the enormous billboard welcoming visitors to the fabricated town of Xianggelila. But overall, her video juxtaposes the illusions of fantasy with the overwhelming sense of the *real* place of Diqing's mountainous terrain at the Tibetan border of China.

Die Ware Liebe (2009), Chang's third and final work explored in Chapter Two, reconceives the cinematic subject of the 1930s film star Anna May

Wong, the most well-known Chinese American actress in Hollywood, who was always cast as the illicit love object for white men in film fantasies of miscegenation. Her characters usually died at the end of the film to exact the penalty for her 'immorality.' Chang writes Wong a new cinematic script based on Walter Benjamin's 1928 essay titled 'Gespräch mit Anne May Wong' (A Conversation with Anna May Wong, also subtitled 'A Chinoiserie Out of the Old West'), which was Benjamin's provocative interview with Wong. Chang's complex project engages the viewer in the production of her movie, allowing the viewer to see behind the scenes in the company of Gu Bo, the Chinese director hired by Chang. We watch as the director instructs the two characters Walter Benjamin and Anna May Wong played by the Chinese actors Hu Huaizhong and Yi Ping as they engage in a pornographic love scene.

Die Ware Liebe's script for Wong's character ultimately re-writes the scene of race and miscegenation by re-conceptualizing the historical form of Brechtian alienation. Chang's video visualizes Rancière's 'emancipated spectator' and his use of Brecht to 'dismiss the opposition between looking and acting and [to] understand that the distribution of the visible itself is part of the configuration of domination and subjection.'[31] Chang returns to 1920s and 1930s film to re-distribute and reconfigure the historical domination and subjection of Chinese people and places, as *Minor* emulates the documentary real of Lieberenz's *With Sven Hedin Across the Deserts of Asia* only to upend the historical impact of Hedin's vision for geographical empire. But then in *Shangri-La* Chang uses the documentary form to compare a past and present transnational construction of a fantastical Chineseness. Finally, her rewritten script for Anna May Wong is a critique of the transnational practice of movie-making itself, exposing the profound effects of 1920s cinema on the construction of race and gender by visualizing what it might mean to see the celebrated Marxist philosopher in a Chinese body. The distinct ways in which Chang uses video to conceptualize a radically different understanding of cinema in relation to the Chinese subject reveals the unique advantages of video performance as a medium.

Chapter Three's study on 'Environment, labor, and video: (eco)feminist interpellations of Chineseness in the work of Yuk King Tan, Cao Fei, and Wu Mali' provides further exploration of performance and the videographic form as used by these artists to address the twenty-first-century problems facing Hong Kong, China, and Taiwan. Focusing on the concept of *ecofeminism*, their works representing the places of their respective Chinese states share the aesthetic engagement in which the viewer is staged to know themselves as the 'human' who is responsible for the anthropocenic shift. The term, of late, has been used to define global warming and climate change as ecological conditions that result from human interference in natural processes. Viewed as ecofeminist interpellations, however, the issues of labor and environmental crises expressed by Tan, Cao, and Wu are representative of the patriarchal drive for power and domination that constitutes the very foundation of global capitalism. It is important to acknowledge that the historical norm of capitalist power was always associated with the colonialist conquer of native lands (extended now to the conquer of the planet), which was consistently fueled by the patriarchal desire for material wealth that has led to the twenty-first-century depletion of natural resources, pollution, waste, and ecological disasters. The final colonialist occupation of territories as the means to profit from natural resources can be viewed as the power to conquer the earth itself.

The primary factor driving man-made ecological disaster is the expansion of global capitalism, by which the industries of Hong Kong, China, and Taiwan serve as textbook examples for industrial cycles of boom and bust economic crisis under Marx's theory of surplus value.[32] The 1970s manifestation of this theory can be perceived in the 'Taiwan Miracle,' which refers to the exponential economic growth of the small island nation of just 23 million people, built largely on high tech suppliers, microelectronics, and textile manufacturing.[33] The rate of industrial growth peaked in 1980, around the time that Deng Xiaoping introduced his reforms on the mainland, but has steadily tapered off in Taiwan since then. Taking its place, China's industrial boom was initiated in 1990, when the Shanghai stock market reopened for the first time since 1949, and was solidified by 2001 when the country became part of the World Trade Organization. Amidst the economic boom on the mainland, however, the economic interdependence of Taiwan, Hong Kong, and China has grown. As Peter Chow argues,

> if Hong Kong is grouped with China, Taiwan's trade dependency on China's markets accounts for nearly 40 percent of its total exports, and outward foreign direct investment has been increasing steadily, with more than 60 percent of capital outflows destined for China. Industrial clusters in the Yangtze River Delta, the Pearl River Delta, and other parts of China were created through foreign invested enterprises, many of them from Taiwan, and have accounted for a substantial percentage of China's total exports to the world.[34]

The cycle of boom and bust in the economies of Taiwan, China and Hong Kong are now interrelated; the primary social shift that occurred in the booms of Taiwan and China was the migration of workers from the agricultural centers in the countryside to the newly formed manufacturing districts. As explored in Chapter Three, artists Wu Mali and Cao Fei address the impact of this migration on the lives of women. Wu's 1997 video installation, *Stories of Women from Hsin-Chuang*, documents the narratives of textile workers in Hsin-Chuang, Taiwan, who left their farming villages at a very early age to work in the factories. As young women, they were sent as laborers by their parents in order to support the university education of their brothers, an opportunity not traditionally given to Chinese girls. Wu does not offer a typical documentary film to recount the women's experiences; instead, her conceptual expression engages the viewer through a montage of words, voices, and images projected onto textile screens embroidered with the aesthetic sense of the women's stories. The interpellation through this fragmented sensibility imbues the viewer with emotional knowledge rather than offering a detached and linear report.

Viewing Wu's 1997 video today, *Stories of Women from Hsin-Chuang* provides a record of the aftermath of Taiwan's economic boom, as her video captures in hindsight the impact of the factories on the life of the workers who convey the loss of their youth. The experiences of the Taiwanese women connect them to the subjects of Cao Fei's 2005–6 video project *Whose Utopia?*, a work that sent Cao to spend six months in the German-run Osram light-bulb factory located in Guangzhou and the Pearl River Delta. Acknowledging China's economic boom as an outcome of globalization, Cao states that she saw the industrial changes transforming her hometown in the Pearl River area into what is considered as 'the world's factory.'[35] The recurring theme, however, of the migration of workers to China's factories such as the Osram plant reproduces the déjà vu of young women who leave their homes to support the education of their male relatives in exactly the same way that the women of Hsin-Chuang explained their motives for working in the textile factories during the 1970s. Cao suggests that 'in traditional families boys are considered to be more important' and therefore receive the privilege of education.[36]

But overall, *Whose Utopia?* is politically different from Wu's expression of Taiwan, as Cao's video project portrays the irony of China's capitalist dream after decades of proletarian revolution under Mao. To create her video, Cao enlisted the performances of the Osram workers, much in the way that Mao's wife, the actress Jiang Qing, staged the workers and soldiers as the subjects of revolutionary operas during the Cultural Revolution. Cao also films them dressed up and dancing on the floor of the warehouse, originally the socialist place of labor. But the new role of the worker looks like a fantasy of capitalist individualism in Cao's video, in opposition to the very ideals of Mao's Communist utopia and the dream of equality for the working class. In the post-socialist reality of China, Cao's fantasy fiction on film, inextricable from the 'real' workers staged at the actual Osram factory, challenges the viewer's engagement with both the cinematic and documentary qualities of the film. Cao illustrates Rancière's concept of 'documentary fiction', which he describes as hailing from a Maoist theatricalization that deploys the 'fragments of the intermingled history of the cinema.'[37] Similarly, film theorist Kwai-Cheung Lo uses the term 'interpellation beyond interpellation' to define the questionable identities represented in today's media, and his model of subjectification derives from the conventional use of Althusser's theory to explain how film confers an identity.

Environmental crises and labor issues are important feminist subjects – they are matriarchal subjects in the ecofeminist cause. Yuk King Tan depicts these issues in visually arresting ways through video works that focus on the city of Hong Kong. Her 2012 video, *Limits of Visibility*, captures the voluminous landscape of recycling materials located at the Hong Kong harbor but headed for the long barges to be shipped to less-developed countries. Tan's 2008 video performance titled *Scavenger* was the initial inspiration to *Limits of Visibility*, in which Tan follows the recycling trail of the present-day *Ragpicker*, Lam Po Po, an elderly Chinese woman who hauls cardboard on her trolley cart across the streets of downtown Hong Kong. Her destination is the Sheung Wan weigh station, where she is paid for her labor and where the cardboard ends up in the landscape of recycling at the harbor site of *Limits of Visibility*. On this particular excursion of the *Scavenger*, Tan supplies Lam Po Po with a stack of cardboard that is laser-cut to resemble the bronze lion statues that have guarded the HSBC banks since they were first made for the 1923 inauguration of the Shanghai branch. The performative act in which the elderly Chinese matriarch literally carries the symbol of global capital from the HSBC downtown location to the recycling center represents an ecofeminist disruption of patriarchal power. However, the performance has even greater resonance when viewed from the authority of the Buddhist teaching, the famous *Jin shizi zhang*, the Treatise of the Golden Lion as the original lion symbol in China's political and philosophical history.[38] The seventh-century teaching was a lesson for Empress Wu presented to her by the Buddhist monk Fazang who explained the laws of the cosmos by using the example of the lion statue in the Empress's palace to reveal the dharma of material manifestations of gold as a contrast to the concept of *emptiness*. Tan's paper lion is simply another manifestation of material properties, given value and meaning by the consumer today who must inevitably reconcile with the laws of nature and the pollution of the planet.

The last two chapters of the book, Chapter Four's 'The dialectical image of empire' and Chapter Five's 'The archive of Chineseness – the global exposition and the museum' are studies that pivot to the subject of global expositions in the greater scope of Chineseness in modern history and the geographical consciousness of global capitalism. Through their structural premises, the new proliferation of biennials and triennials associated with global contemporary art can be viewed as a repetition of the principles for art and nation as descendent from the model of the Venice Biennale based on the nineteenth-century world's fairs. By the late 1890s, fine art palaces had been built for world's fairs held in metropolitan cities such as Paris and Chicago to extol the heritage of European and American art. The 'world expo' was a showcase of industrial nationalism, once described by Benjamin as the 'universe of commodities,' the fairs having established the cartographical model for biennials and triennials.[39] The very first exhibition of the fine arts at the Venice Biennale in 1895 was a celebration of the artistic production of European nations, and their pavilions heralded the Western artistic heritage. The organizing principles for displaying art and cultures were deliberated here, at the fairs, and as noted earlier, China's art was not included in the fine arts in the Venice Biennale until Bonito Oliva invited Chinese artists to the group show in 1993.

Timothy Mitchell in his essay 'Orientalism and the Exhibitionary Order' describes the critical components of this 'new apparatus of representation' that provided a 'central place [for] the representation of the non-Western world.'[40] China's status as an Oriental culture meant that Chinese artistic production was granted 'anthropological' rather than 'fine-arts' classification, exemplified by the displays of 'non-modern' cultures in the world's fairs. As investigated in this chapter, the institutionalization of this divide explains why it took a hundred years for the first *official* pavilion dedicated to the Republic of China *on Taiwan* to be included in the Venice Biennale in 1995. The Chinese Village at the 1893 Chicago World's Fair organized by F.W. Putnam from Harvard University, for example, provides an important historical context for understanding the formative divide between the art historical and anthropological staging of cultures. The fairs' representation of the 'Oriental' body had particular pertinence within this exhibitionary context, with significant ramifications for later deployments of the Chinese body. For the colonial displays were extrinsically a part of the world's fairs, often staged as 'human showcases' of native peoples exhibited in their 'natural' habitats of huts and primitive architecture. The two types of exhibitions – defined loosely as those displaying culture as *art* versus those foregrounding culture as *ethnography* – would establish the binary between Western art history and cultural anthropology. Mitchell goes on to argue that the importance of this powerful system of knowledge in which the non-West was constructed was to serve the 'manufacture of national identity and imperial purpose' during the late nineteenth century.[41] This knowledge production would support the cause of explorers such as Sven Hedin and legitimize the anthropological displays of the Beauty of Loulan. The validation of showcasing bodies dug up from graves was given authority by the universities and scientific parties conducting the ethnographical and archaeological study.

Chapter Four provides the theoretical foundation for Chapter Five's study, acknowledging the significance of the first inclusions of the separate states of China, Taiwan, and Hong Kong in the Venice Biennale between 1993 and 2005. The paradox in which the new global biennials and triennials are considered as the innovative break from the institutional order dividing

Western art history from cultural anthropology can be viewed by the forgotten lineage of the Venice Biennale as the institutional standard for today's biennials. Its inaugural moment in 1895 for European nations was just two years later than the opening of the Chinese Village at Chicago's 1893 World's Columbian Exposition with its display of Chinese 'artefacts.' But the twentieth-century management of cultural objects by anthropology museums took up where the worlds' fairs left off by institutionalizing the displays of huts and habitats representing 'primitive' cultures. One of the major reasons why global expositions, biennials, and artfairs appear as 'new' global institutions is due in part to the museumifying permanence of objects reflecting the manufacture of the art/ethnography divide. Throughout the twentieth century, it was the *museum*, not the biennial/triennial, that inscribed the artwork and the artefact according to the categories of the modern and the primitive.

Chapter Five addresses the knowledge production of museums in relation to artfairs by tracing the colonialist provenance of two seventeenth-century Ming vases in the collection of one of the oldest anthropology museums, the Pitt Rivers Museum at Oxford University. The study of these artworks provides a different perspective, one that disrupts the museal norm for looking at Chinese art, since the vases were exportware made in China for the collection of the Rajahs of Sarawak in the Malaysian state of Borneo, where a Chinese and Malaysian population resides to this day. The most celebrated of Chinese art, the Ming vase can be viewed by its status as a work representing diasporic Chineseness. The way in which objects are categorized by nations, culture, or ethnicity in both of the systems of the museum and the artfair proves to be insufficient for the processes for identifying Chinese cultures. Chapter Five situates the vase in the performance of Malaysian rituals in connection to Chinese contexts of diasporic difference. The conceptual work of contemporary Malaysian Chinese artist Wong Hoy Cheong, staged in the Pitt Rivers Museum, provides a contrast to the historical object of Chineseness. But specific to the realm of the museum, the Ming vase is more readily associated with the collector and the art market as the determinant of national or cultural value. For instance, the Chinese vase hailing from the Qing dynasty court that sold at auction in 2010 for 69.5 million dollars was newsworthy for breaking all previous records, raising the stakes for Chinese art.

In 1995, Ai Weiwei presented his performance photograph, *Dropping a Han Dynasty Urn*, not only to reflect the loss of tradition (and the illustrious heritage of the Han in 207 BCE) but also to question the value and worth of art objects. Bodily oriented artists in China such as Ai have recognized the remarkable ability to address artistic traditions, ideals, and the value of human life itself through embodied expressions that can function to perform those traditions and ideals. Chapter Five closes with a study of bodily-oriented works at the Venice Biennale presented between 1993 and

2005, acknowledging the differences in national and cultural representation by Chinese artists representing China, Taiwan, and Hong Kong for the very first time in the Biennale's hundred-year history. Together, they embody the *event* of representation, as the global artfair illustrates the metaphorical geography, the 'cognitive maps' that Alberto Toscano describes as the varying and recombinant 'axes of class, race, gender, sexuality and more; they [are] affected by the vicissitudes of praxis.'[42] Toscano's study on art and visual culture acknowledges the 'problem of visualising or narrating capitalism today.'[43] Since Documenta 11 and director Okwui Enwezor's groundbreaking effort in 2002 to use the art exposition as a political platform, the artfair event has now been politically effective in re-focusing art toward world issues such as the plight of refugees and the economic conditions of a nation. As discussed in the Postscript in Chapter Four, these issues were important for the development of Documenta 14 as the 2017 artfair was staged in the second site of Athens in addition to its traditional location in Kassel. The political scene for curators and directors of biennials and triennials is usually connected in some way to issues of global capitalism. And as a decolonizing process, the historical premise of the global exposition enables organizers of biennials/triennials to utilize its inherent organizing principles, symbolism, and nationalist signifiers to serve a new political advantage.

In summary, the five chapters of this book define the concept of Chineseness through the study of bodily-oriented artists in video works that function to show the mediation of the gaze in the practice of identification. Among the different explorations in this book, the feminist and ecofeminist positions taken by artists are important to their use of the medium of video performance as a specific form of interpellation – the viewer is implicated in the videos' reflection of the detriment to the environment made by humans. But the showcase of their expressions in relation to the timeless role of the *exhibition* enables the use of metaphors in which the 'staging' of bodies serves to represent both culture and nation, particularly when staged in the biennials, triennials, and global expositions. The nationalism that exhibitions of cultures function to serve has long contributed to the problem of the oversimplification of difference, which has only increased in the classification of global art as the new movement of contemporary art. The ultimate aim of this book's close study of the works of Chinese artists from China, Taiwan, Hong Kong, the United States and other diasporic locations is to provide a more specific analysis of the complexity of Chinese artistic expression. Overall, these works are integral to the larger theoretical study of Chineseness and the concentrated examination of 'geographical consciousness' in the context of world expositions. In the era of transnational capital, the contemporary work of art can only be understood through the historical structures for staging art, culture, and nation.

Notes

1 Lu Peng, *Passage to History: 20 Years of La Biennale di Venezia and Chinese Contemporary Art* (Venice: Biennale Arte, 2013), foreword. The first Guangzhou Biennial, sometimes under the title *Oil Painting in the Nineties* was held 3–28 October 1992.
2 Ibid.
3 Ibid.
4 Ibid.
5 Liu Kang, 'The Problematics of Mao and Althusser: Alternative Modernity and Cultural Revolution,' *Rethinking Marxism*, vol. 8, no. 3 (1995), 2. Liu cites the Maoist-Marxist essays by Althusser, 'On Contradiction and Overdetermination' and 'On the Materialist Dialectic' published during the 1960s.
6 For instance Clement Greenberg and Meyer Schapiro were among the Marxist art critics and historians who adopted this position.
7 See my study on the Capitalocene in 'Performance Art, Performativity, and Environmentalism in the Capitalocene,' *The Oxford Research Encyclopedia of Literature*, ed. Paula Rabinowitz, 2018, http://literature.oxfordre.com (accessed 1 March 2019).
8 Louis Althusser, *For Marx*, tr. Ben Brewster (London: Penguin Press, 1990), 101–2. Emphases in original.
9 Rey Chow, 'On Chineseness as a Theoretical Problem,' *boundary 2*, vol. 25, no. 3 (fall 1998).
10 Edward W. Said, *Orientalism* (New York: Penguin, 1995), 6.
11 Gao Minglu, 'Seeking a Model of Universalism: The *United Nations* Series and Other Works,' in Mark H.C. Bessire, ed., *Wenda Gu: Art from Middle Kingdom to Biological Millenium* (Cambridge, MA: MIT Press, 2003).
12 Sharmani Patricia Gabriel, '"Migrations of Chineseness": In Conversation with Ien Ang,' *Inter-Asia Cultural Studies*, vol. 12, no. 1 (2011), 123.
13 Édouard Glissant, *Poetics of Relation*, tr. Betsy Wing (Ann Arbor: University of Michigan Press, 1997), 90.
14 Wang Gungwu, 'Greater China and the Chinese Overseas,' *The China Quarterly*, no. 136 (December 1993), 932; John E. Willis, Jr, 'Review of *The Chineseness of China: Selected Essays*, by Wang Gungwu,' *The China Journal*, no. 35 (January 1996), 214.
15 Allen Chun, 'Fuck Chineseness: On the Ambiguities of Ethnicity as Culture as Identity,' *boundary 2*, vol. 23, no. 2 (summer 1996), 116.
16 Zhang Huan's project *My America* began with the performance titled *Hard to Acclimatize* presented at the Seattle Asian Art Museum, Volunteer Park (Saturday 20 November 1999). *My New York* was presented in the Sculpture Court outside of the Whitney Museum for the Biennial (7 March–26 May 2002).
17 Aihwa Ong, *Neoliberalism as Exception: Mutations in Citizenship and Sovereignty* (Durham, NC: Duke University Press, 2006), 32.
18 Amelia Jones, *Seeing Differently: A History and Theory of Identification and the Visual Arts* (New York and London: Routledge, 2013); and Peggy Phelan,

Unmarked: The Politics of Performance (New York: Routledge, 1993), 13. Emphasis added.

19 Claire Bishop, 'Digital Divide,' *Artforum* (September 2012), 436.

20 Walter Benjamin, *The Arcades Project*, tr. Howard Eiland and Kevin McLaughlin (Cambridge, MA: Harvard Univiversity Press, 1999), 7.

21 Ibid.

22 The 45th International Exhibition of the 1993 Venice Biennale (13 June–10 October 1993) included fourteen Chinese artists in a section named 'Passaggio a Oriente' (Passage to the Orient), together with the Japanese Gutai group, as well as artists Shigeko Kubota and Yoko Ono, among others. https://aaa.org.hk/en/collection/search/library/45th-international-exhibition-of-art-1993-venice-biennale-cardinal-points-of-art-xlv-esposizione-internationale-darte-1993-la-biennale-di-venezia-punti-cardinali-dellarte/search/events_id:21032/page/1/view_as/grid (accessed 10 December 2017).

23 Documenta 11, 8 June–15 September 2002. Director Okwui Enwezor explains that 'Documenta 11 rests on five platforms which aim to describe the present location of culture and its interfaces with other complex, global knowledge systems.' www.documenta.de/en/retrospective/documenta11# (accessed 8 September 2017); Documenta 14, 8 April–17 September 2017, was held in Athens and Kassel under director Adam Szymczyk.

24 Kristian Handberg, 'The Shock of the Contemporary: At the 1893 World's Columbian Exposition in Chicago, the Kwakwaka'wakw created a and the Louisiana Museum,' *On Curating*, no. 33 (June 2017), 37. Arnold Bode was the director of Documenta 1, 15 July–18 September 1955, Kassel, Germany.

25 Walter Grasskamp, 'Becoming Global: From Eurocentrism to North Atlantic Feedback – Documenta as an "International Exhibition" (1955–1972),' *On Curating*, no. 33 (June 2017), 97.

26 Ibid.

27 Stuart Hall, *Race, The Floating Signifier Featuring Stuart Hall*, DVD transcript, Media Education Foundation (1997) and Judith Butler, 'Performative Acts and Gender Constitution: An Essay in Phenomenology and Feminist Theory,' *Theatre Journal*, vol. 40, no. 4 (December 1988).

28 See Alain Badiou and Bruno Bosteels, 'The Cultural Revolution: The Last Revolution?' *Positions: East Asia Cultures Critique*, vol. 13, no. 3 (winter 2005) and Jacques Rancière, *Althusser's Lesson*, tr. Emiliano Battista (London and New York: Continuum, 2011).

29 See Sarah K. Danielsson, *The Explorer's Roadmap to National-Socialism: Sven Hedin, Geography and the Path to Genocide* (London: Routledge, 2016).

30 See my essay 'De-Territorializing Bodies: Body Art and the Colonial World Expositions,' in Jonathan Harris, ed., *Dead History, Live Art? Spectacle, Subjectivity and Subversion in Visual Culture since the 1960s* (Liverpool: Liverpool University Press, 2007).

31 Jacques Rancière, 'The Emancipated Spectator,' *Artforum* (March 2007), 277.

32 As laid out in his 1848 *Communist Manifesto* written with Friedrich Engels.

33 Chen Been-lon, 'Inside the Taiwan Miracle,' *Taiwan Review* (1 June 2011).

http://taiwantoday.tw/news.php?unit=8,8,29,32,32,45&post=13965 (accessed 18 November 2018).

34 Peter C.Y. Chow, *Economic Integration Across the Taiwan Strait: Global Perspectives* (Northampton, MA: Edward Elgar Publishing, 2013), viii. See also Lawrence J. Lau, 'The Long-Term Economic Growth of Taiwan,' working paper for the Institute of Global Economics and Finance, the Chinese University of Hong Kong (December 2012), 4.

35 Izabella Scott, 'Interview with Cao Fei,' *The White Review* (June 2016), www.thewhitereview.org/interviews/interview-with-cao-fei (accessed 15 August 2017).

36 Ibid.

37 Jacques Rancière, *Film Fables*, tr. Emiliano Battista (Oxford: Berg, 2006), 18.

38 See Wing-Tsit Chan, *A Source Book in Chinese Philosophy* (Princeton: Princeton University Press, 1963), 409.

39 Walter Benjamin, 'Paris, the Capital of the Nineteenth Century,' in *Walter Benjamin: Selected Writings, Volume 3, 1935–1938*, ed. Howard Eiland and Michael W. Jennings (Cambridge, MA: Harvard University Press, 2002), 37.

40 Timothy Mitchell, 'Orientalism and the Exhibitionary Order,' in *The Art of Art History: A Critical Anthology*, ed. Donald Preziosi (Oxford and New York: Oxford University Press, 1998). See also Timothy Mitchell, *Colonising Egypt* (Cambridge: Cambridge University Press, 1988); Timothy Mitchell, *Questions of Modernity* (Minneapolis: University of Minnesota Press, 2000).

41 Ibid.

42 Alberto Toscano and Jeff Kinkle, *Cartographies of the Absolute* (Alresford: Zero Books, 2015), 15.

43 Ibid.

1 Chineseness as a theoretical, historical, and political problem in global art and exhibition

The California-born Chinese American artist Patty Chang is well known for her bodily-oriented artworks, exemplified by performances on video such as *In Love* (2001), *Eels* (2001), and *Melons at a Loss* (1998). Since the late 2000s, Chang has continued her bodily-oriented exploration through video, adopting the transparent, self-reflexive form for expressing the act of crossing borders transnationally as an aesthetic experience. She has traveled to the outer regions and metropolitan areas of China in order to create a series of complex performative and peripatetic engagements, including works such as *Shangri-La* (2005) based on her trek to the Diqing Tibetan Autonomous Prefecture in Yunnan province; *Minor* (2010) exploring the ancient Silk Road area of the Turkic Uyghur region of Xinjiang; *Letdown* (2017), and *Invocation for a Wandering Lake, Part II* (2017) representing her travel to Muynak and the Aral Sea in Uzbekistan. The more recent projects were part of the collection comprising the retrospective exhibition at the Queens museum titled *Patty Chang: The Wandering Lake, 2009–2017.*[1] Included in the show was the video project *Configurations* (2017) (see plates 1 and 2), whereby Chang tracks the South-to-North Water Diversion Project and the development of the three aqueducts redistributing the waters of the Yangtze, Huai, Yellow, and Hai rivers. The water had been transferred through the Danjiankou Reservoir in central China to purportedly 53.1 million people in Beijing and Tianjin since it opened in 2014.[2] The extent of Chang's work located in China is significant, and while Chapter 2 is devoted entirely to her transnational embodied expressions, the introduction of her work here in the beginning of this chapter emphasizes her role as a US citizen in China who is ethnically Chinese. The ability to reconceptualize diversity in Chinese identity is made possible by Chang's use of her Chinese self as a subject and object of video in her continuing bodily-oriented and performative practice. In this way, the artist often functions as a metaphysical representation of her own video observations.

As the counterpart to Chang's border-crossing, the more conventional concept of transnational movements was expressed by artist Zhang Huan,

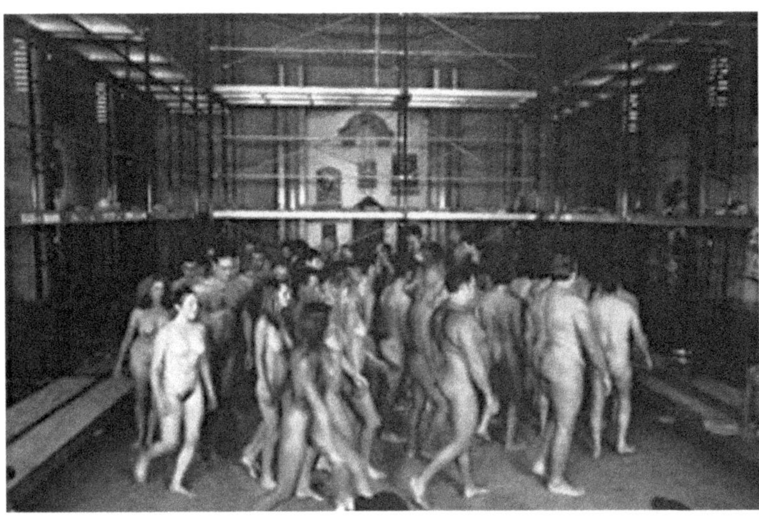

1.1 Zhang Huan, *Hard to Acclimatize*, 1999, performance at Seattle Asian Art Museum

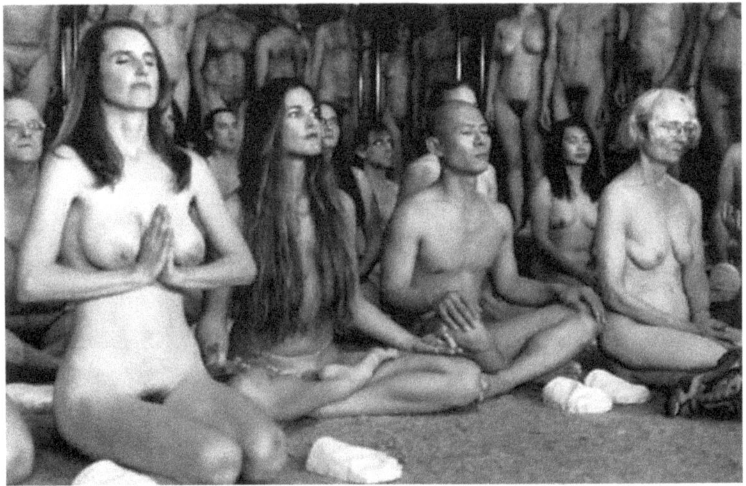

1.2 Zhang Huan, *Hard to Acclimatize*, 1999, performance at Seattle Asian Art Museum

who presented a series of body-art engagements on the subject of Chinese immigration in the late 1990s and early 2000s. Moving to live in the United States from Henan province, Zhang is a key figure of the post-1980s *shiyan meishujia* experimental artists and *xianchang yishu* live-art practices from China. In his 1989 essay, 'The Peripatetic Artist,' Jason Kuo had interviewed the artists *leaving* China for the United States during the country's conflicted political period because they could 'express diverse opinions about global exhibitions, about nationalism vs. internationalism and about their relationships to cultures other than their own.'[3] But Zhang was well known for staging collaborative performances (with other performers as well as local townspeople) mostly in the environs of Beijing.[4] And instead of focusing on difference, as demonstrated in his 1999 performance in Seattle, *Hard to Acclimatize* (see figures 1.1 and 1.2), Zhang continued to collaborate with artists and members of his new community in the United States while presenting his body art in group and solo shows around the world. *Hard to Acclimatize* explores the dynamics of how individuals 'acclimate' to the actions of the group at large, resulting in a dramatic expression about assimilation. The fifty-six performers, presenting an hour-long performance at the Seattle Asian Art Museum, consisted of academics, gallery owners, and Seattle residents who were invited to the event. Zhang theatricalizes the role of the *Pied Piper* by leading a group of nude performers through a series of physical movements such as running rapidly around in a circle and exercising methodically using Tai Chi motions. As each performer attempts to 'follow the leader' under the simplest rules of the childhood game, the challenge is to stay in step with the rest of the crowd. Viewers are led to feel the awkward effort made by the group as they attempt to synchronize their physical movements.

By conceptualizing the complex process of assimilating into a new social environment, Zhang's bodily-oriented expression creates an entirely different visual-sensory understanding of what constitutes a community. Performance artists adopt the bodily-oriented medium to connect with the audience in a somatic way, and in Zhang's expression of the immigrant subject, the issues of ethnicity and race become personal in the body to body connection with the audience. In his artist's statement, Zhang explains the objective of his 'staged actions' as aiming to 'explore migration and relocation, reinscripted meanings, and anxieties about shifting cultural boundaries.'[5] The *huayi* ethnic Chinese who lives outside of China is different from the *huaqiao* who is staying elsewhere temporarily. Zhang went on to emphasize the personal nature of the performance by adopting the new title, *My America*, for the series of works initiated by *Hard to Acclimatize*, including *My New York* for the 2002 Whitney Biennial. Zhang's exploration of different forms of 'acclimatization' are expressed through foregrounding the actual body in immigration as the subject of art, thereby staging an embodied human representative that supplants the abstracted figure of 'the immigrant' in American political discourse. Exacerbated in the age of Trump with his border wall and refusal of asylum seekers, immigration in the United States is generally reduced to the statistics for legislated quotas that signify refugee movements at any given moment in history. The very origin of the restrictive exclusion act in US legislation began in 1875 with Chinese immigration and the Page Law. The historical figure of the 'cheap laborer' is usually defined by the racial stereotype as differentiated from the figure of China's 'new wealth' associated with the moneyed-class of visa-holders. Zhang provides an aesthetic experience that upends the political dynamic by making a human connection with the viewer, an exchange that shows the potential of the medium of body art for expressing issues of immigration in the twenty-first century.

As exemplified by Chang and Zhang's works, the *performance* of Chineseness is related to issues of nationalism, migration, citizenship, boundaries, and embodiment; through an exploration of these determinants of identity, the engagements of global art today can be connected to the modern history of art and cultural representation. The potential for making these issues apparent is one that bodily-oriented art engenders, and the case studies of artists like Chang and Zhang in this book focus on the artistic medium that can reveal the difference among diverse Chinese identities, usually ascribed to mainland China. As established in the corpus of theory by Amelia Jones, performance and bodily-oriented art have expanded the vocabulary of contemporary art, and their integration with video art provides another key form of engagement through phenomenological encounters of an ontological 'self' mediated by film.[6] Artists adopted the embodied expression because of the significance of artistic identification by Chinese affiliation, but the emergence of post-1980s *Zhongguo xiandai yishujia* as the new contemporary art from China has brought to the fore questions regarding what should be considered as 'Chinese art.' The change after Deng Xiaoping's 1980s reforms was a paradigmatic shift in regard to both the Western views toward China's economic modernity and the emergence of a hybrid form of contemporary Chinese art. Under Deng's 'famous four-character policy *gaige kaifang*, a reform of the economic system and an opening up to the outside world' brought the import of Euro-American legacies through literature, materials and new exchanges.[7]

By the 1990s, the first generation of artists who graduated from the reopened universities and art schools that were closed during the Cultural Revolution (1966–76) had established a syncretic Chinese/Western form of contemporary art. Art theorist Zhu Qi explains that the 'forms of modern art, performance art, installation, video and conceptual photography, which emerged with the New Wave or Avant-garde Movement in 1985, are often referred to as pioneering or experimental art.'[8] But Zhu states clearly that in China, none of these 'pioneering' movements exist in the 'narrow sense of the terms as the Western world defines them. In fact, it can only be said that such forms of art in China are elite forms of art that derived their sense of modernism, post-modernism, postcolonialism from the particular experiences engendered with in those rising industrial countries in Asia.'[9] The rapid changes for art in China have unfolded over the decades since the 1990s – from a repressive regime for government-controled exhibitions to the state sanctioning of corporate-sponsored museums. By the end of the first decade of the twenty-first century, the 'elite forms' of China's art became a dominant factor in the emergence of the global art category, verifying the growth of contemporary artistic production outside of exclusively European and North American countries. But, as Zhu emphasizes, the pioneering movements in China were perceived as such by the Euro-American art institution. Moreover, Chinese American artists were never considered as part of the movements in China. In the aftermath, the question of artistic authenticity and what constitutes 'Chinese contemporary art' compels new approaches to addressing identification and artistic subjects – primarily the difference in identifying artists from Hong Kong, Taiwan, and diasporic Chinese artists from elsewhere – which is the question addressed by this book. In other words, an inquiry into 'Chineseness' is a *historical* and specific one that involves the contested meaning of the term, used both in the Orientalist distinctions of the past and, more recently, as a fluid, unstable, unfixable meaning of 'Chinese' in historical and contemporary discourses for the staging of art and culture.

A discursive history of Chineseness

The conceptualization of Chinese identity as related to artistic representation specifically can be clarified by reviewing the history of the word *Chineseness* in cultural analysis. The 1990s shift in China and in the greater global order provides the key historical periodization for marking the critical theoretical discourse in Chineseness. As defined by Meiling Cheng, Chineseness is an 'ambiguous, fluid and [a] potentially deterritorialized concept which may be employed by individual subjects – native, diasporic, sinophonic or affiliated by choice – as a multivalent identity marker.'[10] Cheng describes a diverging and variable form of identification that is particular to Chinese constituents and communities in the flux of changing political administrations and migrating populations in the twenty-first century. The term has been adopted in today's vocabulary and used in both scholarly and mainstream descriptions including the Discovery Channel's 2014 television series, *Chineseness: The Rise of Chinese Art.*[11] The use of the term by the television program was primarily to denote the production of Chinese artists who move across borders between China, Hong Kong, and Taiwan.

The general acceptance of this terminology in the contemporary zeitgeist has shifted from the earlier context. As late as 2005, many scholars considered Chineseness to be a contentious term and it was rarely used in discussions about art. In the aftermath of Edward Said's 1978 book, *Orientalism*, the recognition of the Orientalist imaginary led to the quest for authentic cultures that were not produced by the European imagination. When Rey Chow published her influential 1998 essay 'On Chineseness as a Theoretical Problem,' she argued that the very 'notion of "Chinese" is the result of an overdetermined series of historical factors, the most crucial of which is the lingering, pervasive hegemony of Western culture.'[12] Chow refers to the Orientalist debates predicated on the European representation of 'subject races' explained by Said as inclusive of 'Arab, Islamic, Indian, Chinese, or whatever' in the colonialist ideology reducible to the most simplified logic: 'There are Westerners, and there are Orientals.'[13] Asian Americans, in particular, considered Chineseness to represent the reductivist logic of Orientalism and as an appropriation of Chinese culture by the West. Based on Said's 1970s model, the primary interpretation of the word Chineseness was therefore associated with Chow's analysis of the 'systematic exclusivism of many hegemonic Western practices,' including the elitism of the fine arts. And, as reiterated by Zhu Qi, the 'elite forms' of China's experimental art in the 1980s and 1990s was not a concept of China's recognition but intrinsically Western in its orientation. Still, the change from the exclusivity of Western art to include China's art under the new global art category was considered as a movement away from the insular 'fine arts' during the same moment that Chow wrote about the effects of Said's binary for the hegemonic West and its others.

The specific use of Chineseness in the visual art discourse in the 1990s was negligible, due largely to the nexus of Orientalist concerns including those raised by Chow. In the United States, Orientalism's association with racial stereotypes was a form of objectification – as defined in 2016 by Mee Moua, Director of Asian Americans Advancing Justice, '"oriental" is derogatory because it objectifies Asian-Americans, as if we were rugs.'[14] In the United States, the objecthood of visual art in the modernist model for painting and sculpture caused a contradictory premise for Chineseness since all art is purportedly a manifestation of the artist's self – in the context of Orientalism and identity, what is the difference between a rug and an artistic object, especially in postmodernist and conceptual terms for readymades in contemporary art? The objectification of people and rugs becomes a cover, a mask for the larger problem in which Chinese artists are expected to represent Chinese identity for an entire populace through their art objects. The difference between objectification and subjectification was always problematic for artistic and cultural representation. As Hal Foster once disparaged, the function of the 'artist as ethnographer' pointed to anthropology and the *ethnographic* return to the 'real' subjects of identity and ethnicity.[15] But his overall attempt to separate the 'elite forms' of the twentieth-century avant-garde from those 'cultural forms' of the ethnographic category supports Chow's argument that the systematic exclusivism separating the hegemonic West and its others remains a theoretical problem for Chineseness.

The more expansive terminology of Chineseness, however, was effectively used in the study of film and world cinema as distinguished from art and art historical categories during the 1990s. Theorists such as Sheldon Hsiao-peng

Lu were using the term in their analysis of 'national cinema' and the complicated development of *nationhood* in film discourse, particularly the discussion of films produced in the Chinese diasporic states, across China, Hong Kong, and Taiwan. Hsiao-peng Lu illustrates Chineseness by referring to the actor Jackie Chan whose kung-fu hero stereotype ascribed to his films provides a 'subtle or not so subtle assertion of Chineseness. There is never a mistake about his Chinese identity.'[16] This implicit positioning for Chineseness seems ambivalent in its stance about the kung-fu stereotype and the ethnographic 'real' of Chinese identity in film. Jackie Chan's embodiment of the Chinese subject functions to fill a physical role in the comedy action film, but he is also a speaking subject for Chinese identification in the script-based cinematic form. The scholarship of film studies is usually ascribed to the literary discourse for this reason, which other film theorists, including Shu-mei Shih, have emphasized as their theoretical focus. Shih's discussion on 'Sinophonic articulation' best defines the significance of speech and language in the representation of film, although she includes the visual arts in her description of Sinophonic 'acts and practices of cultural production – naming, writing, making art.'[17] In her book, *Visuality and Identity*, Shih asserts the change to a more current definition of Chineseness that 'disrupts the symbolic totality that is Chinese and instead projects the possibility of a new symbolization beyond reified Chinese and Chineseness.'[18] Shih argues for a revision from inimical connotations of the Orientalist terminology in order to acknowledge the potential for re-interpreting Chinese subjects in film. Following Shih's example, *Staging Art and Chineseness* tracks the Chinese subject in video performances by artists like Chang and Zhang who are actively using *reinterpretation* as a practice – Chang's return to cinematic subjects, for instance, is an act of reinterpreting the gaze toward the Chinese subject in historical film.

In this way, the discourse of Chineseness can be attributed principally to film theory in the visual culture debate, especially since Chow presented her argument as a film theorist and literary critic who initially made waves with her book, *Primitive Passions: Visuality, Sexuality, Ethnography, and Contemporary Chinese Cinema*, in 1995. Among the book's different references to Chineseness, Chow denotes the growth of China's film industry in the 1990s by suggesting that the '"ethnicity" of contemporary Chinese cinema – "Chineseness" – is already the sign of a cross-cultural commodity fetishism.'[19] The consumption of films made in China by filmmakers such as Chen Kaige and Zhang Yimou played a major role in Chow's theory of the cultural hegemony of the West, as she pointed to the 'habitual obsession with "Chineseness"' as a kind of cultural essentialism that 'easily flips over and turns into a narcissistic, megalomanic affirmation of China,' fantasized by the West as 'somehow better – longer in existence, more intelligent, more scientific, more valuable, and ultimately beyond comparison.'[20]

But, as related to film, an entirely different and largely neglected debate in Chineseness can be reviewed by the intellectual formation of *interpellation* in a Marxist intellectual history, which involves Louis Althusser and the Tel Quel school (including Julia Kristeva, Philippe Sollers, Roland Barthes, and Marcelin Pleynet). The books by fellow Italian intellectual Maria-Antonietta Macciocchi – *Letters from Inside the Italian Communist Party to Louis Althusser* (1969) and *Daily Life in Revolutionary China* (1971) – provide a record of the influence of Maoist thought on Communist intellectuals in Europe (especially the French) during the 1960s. The utopic anti-capitalist dream and the fantasy of a proletariat revolution was thought to be realized by Mao's Cultural Revolution (1966–76). The end of the anti-capitalist dream was secured by the 1989 collapse of Communist orders, signaled by the Tiananmen Square massacre, the dissolution of the Berlin Wall, and the break-up of the Eastern Bloc. More recently, theorists have made connections between Althusser's reading of Mao's writings and his own development of the 1970 essay 'Ideology and Ideological State Apparatuses.' The relationship is significant for the art discourse in Chineseness, particularly in regard to the interpellations of film as mediations of identity in visual culture. Althusser's study of the 'imaginary relationship of individuals to their real conditions of existence' continues to be easily adapted by film theorists who use cinematic examples to illustrate those imaginary relationships – individuals are made into subjects of capitalist reproduction through *interpellation*, the coercion of the social unconscious in the various mechanisms that activate ideology through state apparatuses.[21]

It is the film mechanism of video, studied in this book, that links the interpellation of Chineseness to the Marxist and Maoist past of Althusser. Chow explains this mechanism in relation to viewing film in China by suggesting that audiences are 'interpellated not simply as watchers of film but as film itself. They "know" themselves not only as the subject, the audience, but as the object, the spectacle, the movie.'[22] These structuralist premises from Althusser's theory of interpellation would, of course, lead to his student Michel Foucault's development of 'The Subject and Power' (1982); but in this development, Althusser's study of Mao's thought, through French translations between 1960 and 1964, has come to be associated with the development of poststructuralist theory. Researchers such as Camille Robcis have argued convincingly that 'Althusser, Maoism, and Structuralism' are inextricably connected in intellectual history as a dialogically important intersection of influences.[23] She argues that, although Althusser rejected the distinction of 'structuralism' for his own work, his engagement with '"China" and his structuralist interpretation of Marx were both answers to the specific theoretical and political impasses confronting French Marxism in the 1960s.'[24] Rather than viewing the French obsession with China's Cultural Revolution as simply a narcissistic and Orientalist misreading of the Red Guard's violent repressions, the integration of Marxist thought can be assessed for its contribution to the poststructuralist methodology, one that still functions effectively for a decolonial critical analysis, especially for film theory and Chineseness. This analysis is extended in my study of video performances as media that is informed by film theory but is significantly different due to its conceptualist form of expression. My argument is that interpellation continues to be a useful and viable concept for addressing the subjects of art/philosophy production in the era of transnational capital.

The art/philosophy distinction is different from film/theater in a number of ways. Unlike the staging of movies in the cinema, the art exhibition is a necessary part of the consumption and exchange of the video installation. Here, the structures of the exhibition itself can be viewed by Chow's theoretical logic for Chineseness as they are often characterized by the 'grand tradition' concept of museum shows of '5000 years of Chinese art,' connoting something enduringly better and competitively more significant. Chow cites Etienne Balibar's conception of 'differentialist racism' to define the aggressive ethnocentrism that locks individual groups 'into a determination that is immutable and intangible in origin.'[25] Under this ethno-determination, neither philosophy nor art can be culturally integrated by shared affinities and influences – not unlike the discourse of Althusser, Maoism and structuralism, the separate intellectual traditions can validate longstanding nationalisms. The important shift into the *new* ethnocentric version is often exemplified by exhibitions of 'Chinese Contemporary Art' as a category that refers exclusively to the post-1980 generation of experimental artists from China. *Xiandai Zhongguo Yishu* is considered the country's most remarkable artistic production, which differs from expressions of Chinese artists from the United States, Taiwan, or Hong Kong, for instance. The expansive development of museums in Beijing and Shanghai in the twenty-first century further establishes a post-socialist global status for China's contemporary art. Private entrepreneurial parties, in collaboration with China's government, support an internationally auctionable and marketable *jinru yishu* (today's art). The ethnocentric distinction of a new global status for China's art is a profitable one for the competitive art market. Ultimately, China's 'new' cinema and contemporary art, reflecting the fulfillment of Deng Xiaoping's 'Capitalism with Chinese Characteristics,' confirms the mega-fantasy of Chow's prognosis.

As such, the questions that Chow posed in presenting Chineseness as a theoretical problem can function in the twenty-first century as a means to review, test, and update those issues of nationalism, boundaries, and embodiment, specifically in relation to capital and contemporary global art. Beyond the elite auction houses, what are the differences among Chinese ethnicity, Chinese nationalism, and Chinese culture in a globalized society? Unlike cinematic representations, the staging of the visual arts provides a platform for exploring these distinct concepts, firstly through the inscription of the artist as representative of a culture or nation, and secondly, through the categorization of exhibitions by culture or by nation. These are the two forms of representing Chineseness explored in this book. Chow's complex argument remains important to any analysis tracking the changes and contributions to a destabilized concept of Chinese culture and to the politics of a contemporary Western art turned global – today, neither Eurocentrism nor ethno-Chinese-centrism serves the twenty-first-century definition of 'Chinese culture.' Nonetheless, in both the Western stereotype and in the Han classification, Chinese people are often still unproblematically assumed to be of one ethnic unity under the signifier of China. Ethnic, racial, and nationalist identifications are always-already affixed to geographic origins, especially in relation to art and to its exhibition. The geographical provides a tangible expression for both the meaning of locations of exhibitions and the origins of the artist, constituting a particular cultural knowledge for understanding Chineseness.

My argument overall is that the rigid and categorical boundaries of nationalist identifications are changing in the era of globalization, which has enormous consequences for the institutions of art.[26] In the global discourse for art, theorists and historians are rapidly rethinking the outdated art historical methodologies that circumscribe artists to cultural and identity categories. As explained by Chow, academic scholarship often strives to attain a *'geopolitical realism*, to stabilize and fix [an] intellectual and theoretical content by way of a national, ethnic, or cultural location.'[27] The assumptions can be seen in the reproduction of the classifications of 'Western Art,' 'Asian American art' or 'Chinese art' according to nationalist affiliations. The limitations of national categories are problematized by the tension between the location from which the artwork originated and the ostensible 'nationality' of the artists. Of course, art history is fundamentally a Western academic category, but in the globalization of artistic traditions, media, and practices, what is the way forward for cultural history and analyses? The term Chineseness, in coherence with terms like creolization, can function to acknowledge the ambivalence and tensions that are connected to nation-statist identifications that were largely constructed during the nineteenth-century period of colonialism and imperialism. Édouard Glissant's explanation for the 'principles of creoleness' in the practice of poetry focuses on the mixing of diasporic traditions 'more or less innocently' toward 'negritudes ... Frenchness, of Latinness, all generalizing concepts.'[28] The shift in attention that began in the 1990s toward the study of transnational Chineseness was also acknowledgment of the lingering influence of Western artistic legacies that coexisted with the diversity of subjectivities among Chinese mainland and diasporic expressions of contemporary art. By questioning, analyzing, showcasing, and representing Chineseness, this book seeks to understand the creolizing shift through performative, conceptual, and video works, mostly video performances, that are advantageous for understanding transnational identities.

Interpellation beyond interpellation: media and performances in the twenty-first century

During the 1960s–1970s moment in French and Maoist Marxism, political theory was associated with both meanings of Chineseness as a term: the Orientalist fetishization of Revolution that objectifies the Chinese situation (often ascribed to Tel Quel), and the other multivalent, deterritorialized concept of a syncretic intellectual revolution. Through Althusser, Maoism's contribution to intellectual Marxism and the development of poststructuralist thought was a syncretic moment of French/Chinese theoreticization. But in the twenty-first century, the 'real conditions' in post-socialist China can be considered as evidence of the final conclusive end of the socialist experiment worldwide, or as Kwai-Cheung Lo argues, the 'failed interpellation' of the alternative to capitalism, which 'in the Althusserian sense, by no means succeeds in establishing a full and imaginary subject ... it is unlikely that China can still be seen as a communist state disseminating political ideology rather than an emerging nation competing for hegemony and for limited global resources.'[29] Lo characterizes the Chinese people as having unprecedented freedom through the advantages of an inchoate market economy while maintaining an unquestionable conviction to the Communist state. This imaginary relationship to the capitalist 'China Dream' in contradictory agreement with China's Communist ideology introduces an 'interpellation beyond interpellation,' which Lo defines as the condition common to the new urban class of millennials 'who appear to be far more interested in the culture of consumerism than in politics.'[30] Living the very bourgeois lifestyle that Mao once derided and demonized through anti-bourgeois, anti-rightist campaigns, Lu describes the current generation's obsession with video games, social media, and online society as one that allows them to 'live in the "beyond" or the imaginary transgression from the interpellation conferred upon them.'[31] In essence, interpellation through the computer screen has offered a radically different reality for the post-socialist generation.

Marking an entirely new era for the conception of identity, 'interpellation beyond interpellation' provides the current context for Chineseness and art/film theory. While Chineseness functions as a political critique and cultural representation in the analyses of cinematic narrativity established by Chow, Hsiao-peng Lu, and Shih, the current forms of representation in the digital era propose completely new and different questions. In the mediation of Chinese identity, artists and audiences are impacted by computer screens far more than they are by cinema and film. Moreover, photographic and videographic forms in the technological shift have become essential for *any* artistic practice, in the understanding that all artworks will end up on the computer/smartphone/tablet screens of social media. As a clear example, the artist Cao Fei had staged the scene of new media for the inaugural moment of *interpellation beyond interpellation* by creating digital online avatars situated in a virtual reality that viewers experienced through her Second Life project *RMB City* (begun in 2007 and ended in 2011). The fantasy world of Cao's Second Life exemplifies a digital 'living in the "beyond"' as her avatar China Tracy engages in relationships with other avatars in the utopia city replicating Beijing and named for the *renminbi* Chinese currency. The online identity engenders a kind of performativity that is 'live' and in real time, but is distinguished from Zhang Huan's live-art expression in *Hard to Acclimatize* and also from Patty Chang's video performance in *Configurations*. While Cao as the artist engages in a 'live' performance via her avatar 'China Tracy,' the screen mediation is second-removed from the video capture since the avatar bears no visual trace of the online handler.

To explain this further, Cao portrayed the irony of interpellation in the digital age when she staged her 2009 *RMB City Opera* at Teatro Astra in Turin (see plates 3 and 4). A multi-media, interactive, live-stream online event, Cao presented actor-dancers recreating the *Yang Ban Xi*, the model operatic ballets of China's Cultural Revolution and then staged their Second Life avatars enjoined in the same choreographed movements projected on the screen backdrop in the theater. In an even more provocative part of the performance, Cao included the avatars' handlers on the stage as they digitally 'performed' on their laptops the movements of their avatars, Nemeth and Masala, removing the Brechtian 'fourth wall' separating the audience from the actors on stage. The real and imaginary relationships were fully represented to show both the virtual and live-art action. In the first act, the love story between the protagonists is narrated and then, after a staged computer crash, the next act commences with the actors and their avatars appearing in Red Army uniforms. The scene of revolutionary opera becomes the interpellative subject in which actors and viewers are meant to engage politically in the anachronism of Jiang Qing's 1960s dance of 'class struggle,' her literal visualization of the communist *movement* in the coalitional sense of the Cultural Revolution.

From 1966 to 1970, Jiang's eight model plays (*Yang Ban Xi*) were the primary source of entertainment in China while many other bourgeois forms were prohibited by the Party. Jiang was an actress before she married Mao, and she had revised four previously established theatrical plays to enhance such themes as the upper-class oppression of the proletariat underclass. She then declared that these four model plays were to be re-staged verbatim for the cause of the Cultural Revolution. Always foregrounding the subject of women, she was inspired to integrate ballet into revolutionary opera, and to this end, she also adapted two well-known movies, *Red Detachment of Women* and *The White-Haired Girl*.[32] The latter 1972 movie adaptation is perhaps best known to audiences outside of the country. The story of Xi'er as the *White-Haired Girl* (*Baimao Nü*) is a sad one about a country girl who is taken away from her family by their wealthy landlord – a symbolic exchange that reflects the status of women as property as much as the oppressions of the landlord class. Xi'er manages to escape into the mountains where her hair turns white during her long exile.[33] When her fiancé Dachun becomes a Communist soldier and returns to find her in the mountains, Xi'er loses her ghostly white appearance and is restored to her family and to the new Communist society in general. The *White-Haired Girl* drew from commoner folktales and Chinese ghost stories to express the didactic politics of the Cultural Revolution. As researched by Guang Lu, for a period of seven years during the Cultural Revolution, 'eight hundred million people were fed a diet of only the eight model plays. From live stage performance to concerts ... to publications and movies, *Yang Ban Xi* was omnipresent.'[34] *RMB City Opera* renews revolutionary opera, performed through every medium at that time, on stage, in the movies and on the radio, and Cao Fei's expression of 'interpellation beyond interpellation' becomes apparent – her replay of Mao's utopia of the revolutionary past functions to acknowledge the capitalist transition into *RMB City's* dystopia of the present.

Cao Fei's interpellation of Chineseness acknowledges and clarifies the technological shift and the digital currents instantiated by the performances, videos, and digital screens of contemporary art that are entirely different from film and movies, even when cinema comprises the recognizable *subject* of the performance. As such, works like Cao's opera define the conceptual divergence from the narratives and languages of cinema while emphasizing the continuing political use of bodily-oriented performance. Against the notion that the 'screen-based' era includes *all* filmic forms of technological media, Cao's project exemplifies the way in which experiences of the visual arts are radically different from those of the cinema. As *RMB City Opera* illustrates, the representation of Chineseness through the multi-media practice includes the messaging of the digital medium itself as Cao stages the actual portrayal of members of a generation communicating through video games, social media and online communities. And yet, the replay of the *Yang Ban Xi* represents the commitment of this generation's continuing appeasement with the politics of the state, emptying out *Yang Ban Xi's* original social meaning that now has relevance only for the proletariat past. On the whole, video art/digital art's unstable, unfixed premises for time-based and 'live' performances (such as Cao's ballet) serve as a metaphor for the current conditions of Chineseness as an identity; meanwhile, the narrative script of the movie offers a cohesive representation that reflects a continuing commitment to the past.

Acknowledging the discursive legacy from film theory and Chineseness, the studies in this book explore the meaning of media by investigating video performances that are conceptual in practice but often focusing on cinematic subjects and movie history. In Chapter Two, for instance, Patty Chang's 2005 video installation, *Shangri-La*, is an exploration of the subjects from Frank Capra's 1937 movie *Lost Horizon*, based on James Hilton's novel. Chang provides a clear contrast between the subject created for the movie and its representation through the conceptual methodology of video art. The discourse of Chineseness initiated in film theory has branched out to conceptual forms of representation, expressing metaphorically the instability of the loss of the discrete subject of identity, as digital expressions provide different methods for masking the subject. As Claire Bishop points out, while most art today adopts new technology at some point of production and distribution, there has been little analysis conducted to address the ways in which technology has changed the viewing relationship.[35] Accordingly, this book's discussion of video and digital forms are integral to the performances and social relations of Chineseness, which I argue provide a way to continue the interpellation of interpellated subjects through their cultural performances.

Chineseness and the transnational present of the Capitalocene era

While Chineseness accounts for the instability of artistic origins, meaning, and subjectivity in the cultural context, the use of the term 'transnational' in this book accounts for the fluidity of intercultural objectives, actions, and concerns, particularly in feminist artistic practice. The multivalent forms of Chinese identity in art can be reviewed through the transnational perspective; as a concept that was explained by Aihwa Ong, transnationalism refers to 'the *trans*versal, the *trans*actional, the *trans*lational, and [especially] the *trans*gressive aspects of contemporary behavior and imagination that are incited, enabled, and regulated by the changing logics of states and capitalism.'[36] As opposed to conventional models of nationalism established since the nineteenth century, transnationalism relinquishes the fixed boundaries for geopolitical spaces that now consist of communities of migrating, mobile, nomadic border-crossing constituents in categories that have been reimagined for the globalized twenty-first century. Since the 1990s, Hsiao-peng Lu and Shih have also espoused the idea of a *transnational* Chineseness in order to change the nationalist categories for cinema (largely among Hong Kong, Taiwan, and China), and their model can support the break from the art historical routine for classifying Chinese contemporary art according to a 'nation.'

The most significant transnational approach to Chineseness explored by this book is the study of ecofeminist objectives that can be attributed to the work of Patty Chang, Cao Fei, Wu Mali, and Yuk King Tan. Ong's argument for 'interconnectedness and mobility across space' resonates for the twenty-first-century shift toward a transnational understanding of a wholistic *planetary* population affected by greenhouse gases and global warming.[37] The ecofeminist perspective acknowledges the way in which national identity is an implicitly patriarchal idea, and in the 'imperative to re-imagine the planet' as exhorted by Gayatri Chakravorty Spivak, the focus needs to change toward implicating all human activity (socially and economically) in the environmental crisis.[38] Through the use of performance videos, the four artists adopt a deconstructive methodology for addressing the impact of environmental crisis in relation to communities and Chinese identities interpellated by old and new patriarchal orders. For instance, Cao Fei's 2013 video project *Haze and Fog* represents a constituency of zombie characters who reside in the 'airpocalypse' of Beijing's air pollution, the term denoting the air quality scale overtaken for the first time in 2013. Discussed in Chapter Three, the environmental crisis in China, Hong Kong, and Taiwan is perceivable as a direct result of the rise of multi-national industry in the late development of global capitalism. But the zombie identity of Cao's *interpellation* is important to denote as an apocalyptic *planetary* subject, another example of 'interpellation beyond interpellation' as the polluted conditions in Beijing are not isolated within Chinese states but interconnected with the rest of the world. In assessing the impact of global warming, the borders of the planet represent the geographical territory affected beyond the borders of nations.

Wu Mali has been a major feminist force in Taiwan since the 1980s as an artist who has responded to the political exigencies in her country, prioritized by the lifting of Martial Law in 1987 and the effects of economic boom and bust on the lives of Chinese women. Her work in the twenty-first century has moved directly toward environmental concerns. Wu's *Plum Tree Creek* project begun in 2011 is a community clean-up initiative that she had developed into an environmental performance. After decades of industrial over-use of the creek during the era of the Taiwan Miracle (the name of the rapid postwar industrialization), wastewater contamination had ruined the waters where people once swam and bathed. Reiko Goto situates Wu's ecofeminist work in the context of the 'philosophical ecologies' of ecofeminism and a 'deep ecology' related to Daoism and Buddhism, defined by 'places where ancestors have been buried. Humans, non-humans, and place begin to connect through this simple but important act and belief through out the valley of Plum Tree Creek.'[39] The transnationalism of Wu's ideals can be viewed by her materialist advocacy of water, a longstanding feminist focus by artists such as Betsy Damon, Dominique Mazeaud, Helen Mayer Harrison and Newton Harrison, Shai Zakai, Ichi Ikeda, Susan Leibovitz Steinman, Suzanne Lacy, and Yutaka Kobayasi, to name just a few cited by Goto. However, Goto's citation of the Confucian ideals for ancestral respect are distinctly important for an *ecofeminist Chineseness* that aligns with the theory of the Capitalocene. This discourse is based on the rejection of the separation of humans from nature in the Anthropocene, explained by Donna Haraway as representative of only a certain class of 'fossil-fuel-burning humanity' that does not include the rest of the species-beings or indigenous humanity. Jason W. Moore argues that 'Species Man did not shape the conditions for the Third Carbon Age. The story of Species Man as the agent of the Anthropocene is an almost laughable rerun of the great phallic humanizing and modernizing Adventure.'[40] Rather, indigenous cultures and ecological life were both destroyed by the Anthropocene's Industrial Humanity, which had initiated the conquering of lands in the project of colonialist capitalism since the fifteenth century. Ever since, the idea of industrial progress was used to denigrate primitivism and nature. In Moore's thesis, the reintegration of humans and nature is also a recognition of indigenous forms of knowledge. The 'deep ecology' that Wu engages, for example, can be understood as an indigenous Daoist/Buddhist/Confucian tradition for honoring the river as part of the same system for honoring ancestors.

Wu explains how 'water is essential to life and it has the ability to cross borders, connecting and gathering people who are concerned about the land we live on, as well as issues of urban development and boundless expansion.'[41] The reconceptualization of the borders of the community, a culture, a nation, an ecology, an environment can be achieved through the material and place associated with water.

The subject of water is central to Patty Chang's multi-project exhibition *Wandering Lake* (2009–17), the fluid material connecting a number of performances completed in the vast regions of China (see figures 1.3, 1.4, 1.5). In 2011, Chang went to Uzbekistan and the Aral Sea, formerly one of the world's largest inland seas and flourishing fishing ports located in the township of Muynak. The Soviet and Russian irrigation projects throughout the years dramatically reduced the volume of water in the sea. At the time, Chang was pregnant with her son and her trip was made memorable from her morning sickness. When she returned to the Aral Sea in 2014, she was in the process of weaning him from breastfeeding. The culmination of her Uzbekistan performances was a ritual washing of a deserted fishing boat she found in the area in 2014, and her photographs for the installation titled *Letdown* (2017) chronicled the experience. But because she was restricted by the government from photographing outdoor infrastructure, Chang included in *Letdown* the images of pumped breast milk which she collected in different containers, symbolizing the drying up of the Aral Sea in direct association with the drying up of her bodily fluids. The photographs express 'a sympathetic loss of flow' that stood in for 'her inability to represent and are meditations on waste, excess, and dislocation both in unfamiliar landscapes and her own body.'[42]

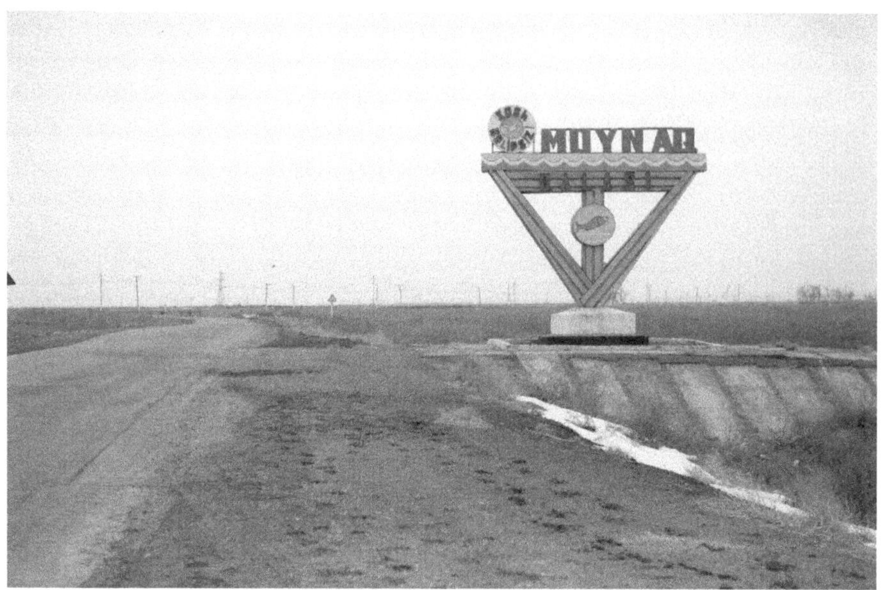

1.3 Patty Chang, *Letdown (Aral Sea)*, 2017, from the photograph series

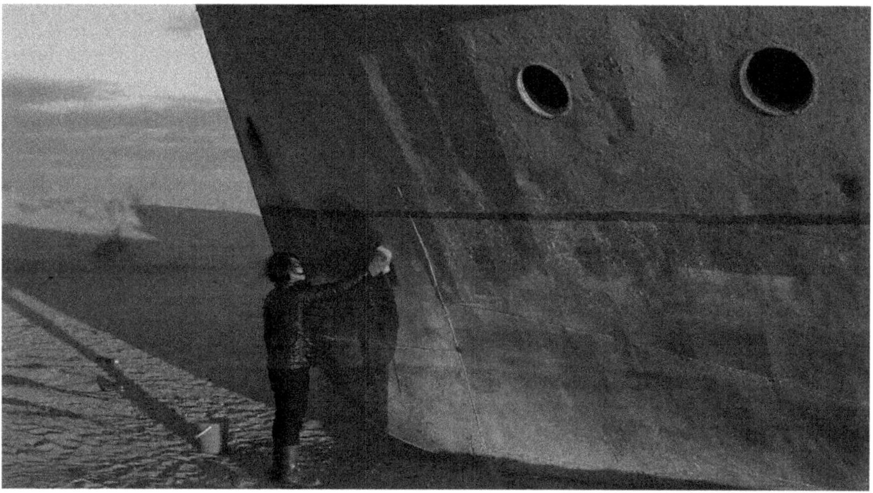

1.4 Patty Chang, *Invocation for a Wandering Lake, part II (Boat)*, 2016, video installation

The ritual performances of bodily fluids, breastmilk, and excretion manifest the deep ecology of human and geographical bodies of water. The maternal body is easily conceived as the body of nature in the indigenous conception of humans and nature. Through the subject of fluids, the deeply personal

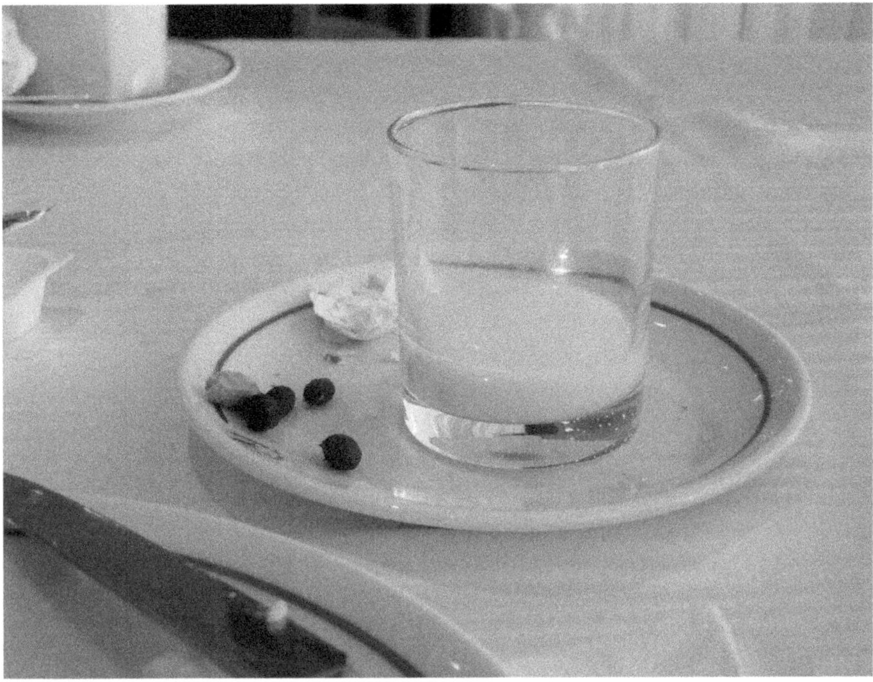

1.5 Patty Chang, *Letdown (Milk)*, 2017, from the photograph series

process of pregnancy and breastfeeding can also be viewed as a political act of ecofeminist advocacy.

Chang continued her performance of bodily rituals in 2015 when she embarked on her search for the aqueducts in the South-to-North Water Diversion from Danjiangkou Reservoir to Beijing. This performance ritual consisted of urinating to mark the route whenever she found the location of the aqueduct. Chang documented the journey in her 2017 *Configurations* video, describing the experience of arriving at the aqueduct's point of departure in Danjiangkou, which was demarcated at the edge of a parking lot with an inscribed pink stone:

> To the right was the edge of the reservoir and the opening of the dike. Below, the waters flowed toward Beijing very, very slowly. This was the beginning. Standing next to the stone, I unzipped my pants and pulled out my feminine urinary device to pee into an empty water bottle. (In case you don't know, a feminine urinary device cups over the vagina so that women can urinate standing up) ... When I was done, I capped the plastic water bottle, removed the fake dick, and zipped my pants.[43]

Chang collected the bottles and marked them according to the time and place where she located the aqueduct from Xianghua toward Denzhou. This act of urination may appear to be a 'marking of territory' or a 'pissing contest' in the spirit of Nam June Paik's 1963 *Fluxus Champion Contest*. But acts of territorialization are the very impetus behind patriarchal violence, and historically the reason why wars are declared and walls are erected (the Great Wall, for instance) to create or expand national and ethnic boundaries. Chang refutes the masculinist idea and asserts that hers was a ritualized concept in excreting bodily fluids. Viewing *Configurations* in the context of pumping breastmilk for her performance in *Letdown*, Chang's work visualizes Luce Irigaray's argument in her essay 'The "Mechanics" of Fluids' expressing the way in which the 'specular image by a sexualized feminine body' acknowledges 'the failure to recognize a specific economy of fluids' in the history of sexuality.[44] The abjection of female bodily fluids has long been a feminist point of resistance to the masculinist censure of reproductive processes, which Chang also acknowledges by referring to Julia Kristeva's *The Powers of Horror: An Essay on Abjection*. But overall, Chang's signifiers of morning sickness, breastmilk, and urination are conceptually inextricable from her quest for geographical bodies of water in the vast locations of China – the human inextricable from nature in the Capitalocene. Her work in this way illustrates Carolyn Merchant's description of the ecofeminist movement as 'the concept of reproduction construed in its broadest sense to include the continued biological and social reproduction of human life and the continuance of life on earth.'[45] The second-wave feminist adage, the 'personal is political,' has been updated to include the ecofeminist perspective toward reproductive processes in the transnational conception of geographical bodies that are mutually inclusive of biological bodies.

Taken all together, the ecofeminist works reviewed in this book contribute to a transnational approach to the arts in the construal of global identities that are ultimately constituted by the effects of global capitalism. When defined by the Anthropocene, the 'human' is the global identity that is implicated in the destruction of ecological life, and yet, the solution to environmental crisis is presumed to come from the mindset of petro-capitalist humanity and the excesses of its oil-dependent culture.[46] Instead, my argument is that the potential for solutions would have far greater success if developed from philosophical ecologies, indigenous knowledge, and the position in which humans are inseparable from *nature* as represented by the Capitalocene discourse. As expressed in the work of Wu Mali and Patty Chang, their ecofeminist ideals are compatible with the human-as-nature form of advocacy. Chang's performances involving maternal fluids, for instance, can be viewed as an act of essentializing the maternal body as a representation of the power of nature, a concept that was rejected by feminists for its association to primitivism. But, as shown in the Capitalocene debate, the norm of nationalism is based on denigrating the primitive (indigeneity and nature) in order to perpetuate petro-capitalist power. The key motivation for defining a transnationalist Chineseness in contemporary art is the ability to rewrite normative models of nationalism that are intrinsically patriarchal in their power structure – the unique way in which art objects represent cultures and nations today is still informed by the political economy of industrial capital and empire-building that hails from earlier forms of nation-statism. The view toward creating a new planetary model while maintaining cultural differences can be conceived through ecofeminist works, such as by Cao, Chang, Wu, and Tan, attributed to a Chineseness that breaks from nationalist conventions.

Chineseness, art history, and nationalism

One of the primary reasons why art history has remained the same (in the Euro-American context) is because of its association with an exhibitionary logic that classifies works of art according to national representation. The determination of categories according to a geopolitical place (nation, culture, region) as well as the fetishization of an 'authentic' culture is perpetuated by the art/exhibition structure that informs the political present of art and Chineseness. As such, the systematic exclusivism invoked by Chow of *both* Western contemporary art and Chinese contemporary art can coexist under the exhibitionary logic of artistic nationalisms. Moreover, the conflicting concept in which 'nationality' is not necessarily determined by *where* the work is created but by the origin of the artist her/himself is based on longstanding assumptions for art. While Zhang Huan is categorized by his origins from Henan province, and subsequently his work is considered as *Chinese art*, the idea that he represents the nation of China follows the paternalistic model for artistic birthright despite his use of the 'Western' conceptual medium of performance. Patty Chang, on the other hand, is simply included in the norm of Western art despite her engagements with Chineseness, since she was born in the United States. But, as exemplified by Chang and Zhang's embodied border-crossing expressions, and Cao's ability to cross virtual borders, the assumptions of ethnic unity are put into greater question as the disparate and multiple Chinese identities of the artists, attached to San Leandro, Xinjiang, Henan, and Beijing, as well as Taiwan and Hong Kong, problematize the fixed categories for Western or Chinese art. Cao's invention of a virtual online city can also be seen as an attempt to break from those fixed categories.

The birthright concept is a tradition of Western art history, going as far back as 1568 and Giorgio Vasari's writings, which established the importance of 'discovering the native city, the origin' of the artist in his documentation of 'the lives of the most eminent European painters, sculptors and architects.'[47] But the ascription of the artist to a culture was further complicated by the nineteenth-century hierarchy for progressive nations as articulated in Georg Hegel's *Philosophy of History* (1822). According to his model, the potential for nations in achieving a 'world spirit' was centered on the concept that 'freedom develops itself to a world.'[48] China did not meet Hegel's nineteenth-century criteria for the progressive ideal, whereby autonomy and self-governance was aligned to the new capitalist system, and thus, China was considered as an 'other' to this ideology of national classification. Historians such as John Emerich Edward Dalberg-Acton writing in 1862 explains more clearly Hegel's logic of progressive nationalism in his depiction of the cultural opposite, declaring that people 'emerging from barbarism … effete from the excesses … cannot possess the means of governing itself.'[49] Dalberg-Acton argued in his essay, 'Nationality,' that the nationalist authority of the British or Austrian Empire was the most important model for the entire progress of modern civilization. The modern management of Chinese subjects and art objects in the European order has ever since – stunningly, until very recently – been determined by historical polarities of the West and the East, or the West and the Non-West, as the most conventional discursive description for categorizing Chinese cultural production.

As part of what Chow articulated as the 'overdetermined series of historical factors,' the development of the binary model in art history that ascribes the work of art to either the West or the non-West bears the traces of the 'lingering, pervasive hegemony of Western culture.' The repetition of historical principles of 'systematic exclusivism' affected the consumption of the visual arts throughout the twentieth century, and this was done by securing and fixing the assumptions of difference between the arts of the West and the arts of the 'Oriental-East.' The impacts, effects, symptoms, and traces of this binary remain integral to the development of contemporary art in the discourse of Chineseness, but as examined in this book, it has changed rapidly in the decades since Chow published her essay in the 1990s. This binary has increasingly been challenged by global art theorists such as Hans Belting, who declares the end of colonialist methodology through the subjectivity of global contemporary art. Belting argues that global art and its 'new art worlds are opposing and replacing the colonial history of world art,' which means that the new global art status has elevated non-Western cultures to reach equal standing with the West.[50] He also views the global artfairs, the biennials, and triennials as evidence of the shift away from the Eurocentric exhibitionary order, which was played out in the theme of the 2008 Guangzhou Triennial, *Farewell to Postcolonialism*, asserting the end of the need to critique the Euro-American hegemony over the arts. As discussed in Chapter Five's study of the 'Archive of Chineseness – the Global Exposition and the Museum,' the declaration in Guangzhou came just six years after Okwui Enwezor broke new ground in the 2002 Documenta by using postcolonial critique to challenge the exposition's exclusive European roots as the first African director in its history. The relatively brief period in which cultural advocates such as Enwezor were finally able to present their case about the unequal structures of the art expositions suggests that postcolonial histories are still underrepresented, specifically when it comes to art institutions. One such history is the inclusion of Chinese states *for the first time* in the Venice Biennale – initially in the *Aperto* group shows, and then in national pavilions officially dedicated to Taiwan in 1995, Hong Kong in 2001, and mainland China in 2005 – emphasizing the need to understand the *systematic exclusivism* that took over a hundred years to address. The watershed moment for recognizing that need was during the 1980s and 1990s with the emergence of the *shiyan meishu* experimental art movement in China. Contributing to what was considered as the point of departure for 'global art,' the conception that the art biennials and triennials were new innovations appearing all over the world (also during the 1980s and 1990s) was paradoxical, given the fact that the artfairs originated as world expositions in the nineteenth century.

It is worth emphasizing that the fact no Chinese state was represented until the 1990s had less to do with any new contribution of artistic production by Chinese artists and more to do with the exposition's historical organizing principles.[51] In truth, Chinese artists have produced modern artworks since the Biennale began in 1895, and the inclusion of China in its roster of nations illustrates the much belated change to the fine arts category. It becomes important to track the historical factors associated with the organizing principles for the artfair, which include the geographical, philosophical, and intellectual determinations for Chineseness. In the classificatory order of the Venice Biennale, Chinese art, along with artistic production from most other non-European nations, was precluded from the fine arts category (with the exception of Japan). As the oldest exposition for contemporary art, the Biennale emulated the world's fair's model for the representation of nations, and as discussed in Chapter Four, the way in which cultural objects were managed and exhibited according to individual nations was influential to the development of the rubric of the 'fine arts.' The 1895 Venice Biennale was one of the first *artfairs* to map artistic nationalism according to the display of individual European nations. At the time, exhibitions of Chinese art were often presented in the anthropological displays of 'non-modern' cultures in the world's fairs, since China was categorized as a non-European, and thus non-modern 'Oriental' culture. The way in which art is mapped according to individual nations at these events in the twenty-first century tends to retrench the idea that art can symbolically stand in for a territory. Nonetheless, the global artfairs are considered as exemplary of the 'global art' scene, which suggests that the Eurocentric institution of art has been transformed.[52] As addressed in this book, the biennials and triennials continue to bear the traces of the nineteenth-century world expositions and world's fairs, since they could still create the visible example of cultural binaries and illustrate progressive differences. The identification of cultural objects according to a geographical place did not simply emerge from the exposition's method of categorization; rather it played an important role in the system for visualizing the nationalist ideal. This type of representation was the same as the classificatory order of the world's fairs, which was aligned with the nineteenth-century political economy established by Hegel's judgment of cultures in his 'geographical basis of history.'[53]

The opening up of Venice's artfair in the 1990s to include a greater number of countries was the conventional reason given for the sudden appearance of Chinese states at the Biennale. The impact of postcolonialist criticism in the 1990s was in contributing to this new growth of globalized art, explained by Rasheed Araeen as the expanding 'role of artists, particularly of African and Asian backgrounds' who had initiated the new 'postcolonial reality.'[54] The 1999 Venice Biennale director Harald Szeemann also acknowledged that 'every year additional countries demand a presence in Venice,' pointing to the 'problem of First and Third World, between the countries that have national pavilions in the Giardini and the ones that don't,' a tendency which Szeemann found both 'touching and frightening.'[55] A new perspective on the world was required in order to meet the challenges of more globalized exchanges, and the emergence of *Zhongguo Xiandai Yishu* contributed to this new concept of globalization, which referred exclusively to the post-1980 generation of experimental artists from China – as differentiated from expressions of Chinese artists from the United States, Taiwan or Hong Kong. Szeemann was one of the first curators to include China's artists in his 1999 Biennale's international group show, and the status of this 'new' emerging key player in the contemporary artworld brought attention to mainland artists rather than diasporic artists. In part, the attention can also be attributed to the pressing circumstances in which the post-Cultural Revolution artists were seen as avant-gardists negotiating the political repressions that culminated in the 1989 Tiananmen Square massacre. As curator Lu Peng explains, the major impact of the 1989 Tiananmen events was in causing many artists and critics to leave China for Western countries in order to obtain opportunities to exhibit, as well as the financial means to continue their work. An objective of those who stayed behind was to bring the 'art industry' *to* China, which led organizers such as Lu to develop the 1992 Guangzhou Biennial.[56]

Chineseness and the logic of cultural capitalism

China's art and commerce have developed rapidly during the same millennial decades in which globalization has surged in the burgeoning of multinational capital. Since the 1990s, China's contemporary art has contributed to the development of both cultural capital and monetary-capital, initiating the 'China Brand' as suggested by Meiling Cheng. By 2006, Sotheby's Auction House had hired Xiaoming Zhang to run its brand new contemporary Asian art department, establishing the rhetorical benchmark for headlines such as 'China Celebrates the Year of the Art Market' and 'An Art Market with Chinese Characteristics.'[57] The 147 contemporary works valued between six and eight million dollars at the first Sotheby's auction in 2006 legitimated their classification of 'Chinese art' as specifically a product of mainland China. The 'phenomenon' of art and economics in China can be understood as a confirmation of Chow's description of the ethnocentric paradox of a new capitalist brand and an old communist foe. In the aftermath, the 'China art market,' as coined by Sotheby's ostensibly for the market in contemporary Chinese art, compels a new category for both the art industry and the art institution.

As late as 2015, the mainstream media and marketing venues finally caught up with the fact that Chinese artistic production is diverse, and Chinese contemporary art cannot be solely attributed to artists from mainland China. Attention began to shift toward diasporic Chinese artists and the practices, subjects, and histories that are different from those of the experimental artists (*shiyan meishujia*) in China. In anticipation of Asia Art Week in New York and Art Basel in Hong Kong, Iain Robertson, Head of Art Business at Sotheby's, asserted that 'the content and form of contemporary art in China were inseparable from the global aesthetic because today a *Zeitgeist* was no longer the prerogative of one particular city, nation or culture, but instead was a universally shared condition that crossed national borders.'[58] This transition to a 'global aesthetic' of Chineseness has now become inextricable from the *Zeitgeist* of the 'China art market' as the mainstream artworld begins to follow the transnational shift. Thus, the new use of the term 'Chineseness' gains popularity in mainstream vocabulary which can be seen in the aforementioned Discovery Channel's 2014 television series on *Chineseness: The Rise of Chinese Art – Making New Waves in the World of Art*. Consisting of interviews with artists Yang Chihung and Li Chen from Taiwan, and Zhang Huan and Xu Bing from China, the show's definition of *Chineseness* implies diversity *within* Chinese culture by featuring artists from Taiwan and not just from mainland China.

But in promoting the four *Discovery Channel* shows, the old standard of the cultural 'East meeting the West' provided the key talking point, declared now as the perpetually 'new' relationship between China and the West. The prevailing logic that 'Western' signifies an exclusive artistic practice premised on Euro-American histories, philosophies, and media has become deeply problematic in the era of globalization.[59] For example, Zhang Huan developed his body-art practices that emanate from the 'Western' vocabulary of performance art when he was still living in China.[60] It is well understood that the post-1980s *Zhongguo Xiandai Yishu* generation of artists from China was influenced by Euro-American histories, philosophies, media, and practices when art historical literature was re-introduced in the country after the end of the prohibitions of the Cultural Revolution. According to Wu Hung, 'hundreds of theoretical works, from authors such as Heinrich Wölfflin to Jacques Derrida' were quickly made available to artists and students in the newly formed academies.[61] Wu adds that artists in the 1980s were 'particularly historiographically self-conscious: recognizing how much they had "fallen behind" art history and theory, they rushed to bring themselves to the current stage of contemporary art by reliving a century of Western art history in a few years.'[62] Yet, as this book will show, the 1980s–1990s generation of artists did not merely inherit or adopt these Western forms, but combined Western and Chinese traditions to develop a formative and crucially influential point of departure for successive generations of China's contemporary art.

Despite an increasing interest in Chineseness as an outcome of a greater acknowledgment of artists from locations outside of the Euro-American artworld, the scholarship of the Western institution of art history continues to be determined by conventions for nationalist and culturalist traditions. As Donald Preziosi recently asserted, the 'Western reinvention of "art" as a special kind or type of faux-secular thing' is actually the same 'old traditional art-historical analytic object of the artist-and/as-his-work (usually his, of course)'; and it is one that is recognizable under the 'aura and penumbra of which and by extension ostensifies while coproducing the tastes of its audiences.'[63] Indeed many of the works addressed in this book demonstrate a self-reflexive awareness and critical engagement with the historical and cultural institution and classification of 'non-Western art.'

Artists who use the subject of immigration in their works make apparent how the entrenched assumptions about immigration can coexist with their cultural subjectivities. Zhang's engagement through embodied maneuverings can be viewed by returning to *Hard to Acclimatize* (1999) and *My America* (2002). The siting of these performances in the specific locations of Seattle and New York reveals the way in which meaning is derived from the relationship between the 'subject' of Zhang as the emigrating artist from China and the geographical place of the community where his work is performed. In the aftermath of 9/11, New York became the symbol of solidarity for the United States, and subsequently Zhang's 2002 staging of *My America – My New York* (see plate 5) at the Whitney Museum of American of Art asserted the crucial significance of the immigrant subject within the context of the city. But integral to Zhang's subject is his celebrated status as one of the first *xianchang yishu* live-art performance artists to emerge in the formative period of China's post-1980s artists.[64] While dressed in the body armor made of raw meat to emulate an over-exaggerated muscle man, Zhang enlisted migrant workers from New York's Chinatown (who were actually fellow-townsmen from his native Henan village) to carry him onto the outdoor stage at the Whitney museum. As if to say that his meat costume transforms the status of the immigrant class to which he and his fellow Henan workers now belong, Zhang declared 'I, however, become Mr. Olympic Body Builder overnight' in his expression of the 'weak' carrying the strong.[65] The performance reflects the mythology of the heroic American ideal in the compatriotism in New York as the symbol of the United States as much as it conveys the realities of belonging to the immigrant class of Chinese Americans in Chinatown. In the most poignant manner, Zhang's expression of Chineseness underscores the disjunction of the myth of heroism by showing how the celebrated artist from China is no different from the Chinese American immigrant that he embodies. Overall, *My America* problematizes the categories for contemporary art by exposing the 'unclassifiable' bodies of the Henan/New York community and bringing focus to the embodied subject through the use of the 'Western' artistic practice of performance. The prevailing categories for this work fall short, whether described as Asian-American art, Contemporary Chinese Art – *Zhongguo Xiandai Yishu* – Western Art, or Eastern Art. The multivalent human subject that bodily-oriented artists have brought to light through their border-crossing acts provides a clear definition for a transnational Chineseness that has since transformed the old assumptions of artistic nationalism. Under this positive outlook, the writing of the history of the shift to global Chineseness constitutes the primary aim of *Staging Art and Chineseness* – a study of the vanishing present of embodied acts of nationalism and immigration, and their staging in exhibitions.

Notes

1 *Patty Chang: The Wandering Lake, 2009–2017*, 17 September 2017–18 February 2018, Queens Museum.

2 See 'China Diverts 10 Billion Cubic Meters of Water from South to North,' *China Daily* (4 October 2017) www.chinadaily.com.cn/china/2017-10/04/con tent_32830449.htm (accessed 7 January 2017).

3 Jason C. Kuo, 'The Peripatetic Artist: 14 Statements,' *Art in America* (July 1989), 133.

4 I am indebted to Zhang Huan and Hu Junjun for their response to questions and interviews that have informed this book. For reading on the work of Zhang, see Melissa Chiu, ed. *Zhang Huan: Altered States* (Milano: Asia Society and Charta, 2007).

5 Zhang Huan, *Hard to Acclimatize*, Seattle Asian Art Museum, Volunteer Park (Saturday 20 November 1999). Artist Statement.

6 See Amelia Jones and Adrian Heathfield, eds, *Perform, Repeat, Record: Live Art in History* (London: Intellect, 2012) and the bibliography of this volume for a comprehensive list of Jones's books on performance.

7 Ralph W. Huenemann, 'Economic Reforms, 1978–Present,' in Timothy Wright,

ed., *Oxford Bibliographies: Chinese Studies* (New York: Oxford University Press), introduction.

8 Zhu Qi, '1990s Conceptual Art and Artistic Conceptualization,' in Wu Hung, ed., *The First Guangzhou Triennial, Reinterpretation: A Decade of Experimental Art, 1990–2000* (Guangzhou: Guangdong Museum of Art, 2002), 20.

9 Ibid.

10 Meiling Cheng, *Beijing Xingwei: Contemporary Chinese Time-Based Art* (London: Seagull Books, 2013), 66.

11 See www.discoverychannel.com.tw/chineseness-english (accessed 19 December 2018).

12 Rey Chow, 'On Chineseness as a Theoretical Problem,' *boundary 2*, vol. 25, no. 3 (fall 1998), 3.

13 Edward Said, *Orientalism* (New York: Random House, 1979), 31, 36.

14 As quoted in Krithika Varagur, 'Obama Signs Bill Removing "Oriental" and "Negro" From Federal Laws,' *HuffPost* (23 May 2016), www.huffingtonpost.com/entry/oriental-negro-federal-law_us_574332d4e4b0613b512adf37 (accessed 15 January 2018).

15 Hal Foster, *The Return of the Real: The Avant-Garde at the End of the Century* (Cambridge: MIT Press, 1996), 208.

16 Sheldon Hsiao-peng Lu, *Transnational Chinese Cinemas* (Honolulu: University of Hawai'i Press, 1997), 17.

17 Shu-mei Shih, *Visuality and Identity: Sinophone Articulations Across the Pacific* (Berkeley: University of California Press, 2007), 35.

18 Ibid.

19 Rey Chow, *Primitive Passions: Visuality, Sexuality, Ethnography, and Contemporary Chinese Cinema* (New York: Columbia University Press, 1995), 59.

20 Chow, 'On Chineseness as a Theoretical Problem,' 6.

21 Louis Althusser, 'Ideology and Ideological State Apparatuses (Notes Towards an Investigation),' in *Lenin and Philosophy and Other Essays*, tr. Ben Brewster (New York and London: Monthly Review Press, 1971), 162.

22 Chow, *Primitive Passions*, 33.

23 Camille Robcis, '"China in Our Heads" Althusser, Maoism, and Structuralism,' *Social Text 110*, vol. 30, no. 1 (spring 2012), 54.

24 Ibid., 53.

25 Etienne Balibar, 'Is There a "Neo-Racism"?' in *Race, Nation, Class Ambiguous Identities* (New York: Verso, 1991), 21–2.

26 For a comprehensive study of the relinquishing of boundaries, see especially Nikos Papastergiadis, *Spatial Aesthetics: Art, Place, and the Everyday* (Amsterdam: Network Cultures Institute, 2010).

27 Chow, 'On Chineseness as a Theoretical Problem,' 6.

28 Édouard Glissant, *Poetics of Relation*, tr. Betsy Wing (Ann Arbor: University of Michigan Press, 1997), 90.

29 Kwai-Cheung Lo, 'Sinicizing Žižek? The Ideology of Inherent Self-Negation in Contemporary China,' *Positions: East Asia Cultures Critique*, vol. 19, no. 3 (winter 2011), 752.

30 Ibid., 753.

31 Ibid.

32 Guang Lu, *Modern Revolutionary Beijing Opera: Context, Contents, and Conflicts* (Kent, Ohio: Kent State University, 1997), 122.

33 See Meng Yue, 'On the Adaptations of *The White-Haired Girl (Baimao Nü),*' in Tang Xiaobing, ed., *Popular Arts and Ideology* (Hong Kong: Oxford University Press, 1993).

34 Lu, *Modern Revolutionary Beijing Opera,* 581.

35 Claire Bishop, 'Digital Divide,' *Artforum* (September 2012), 436.

36 Aihwa Ong, *Flexible Citizenship: The Cultural Logics of Transnationality* (Durham, NC: Duke University Press, 1999), 4. Emphases in original.

37 Emblematized by Kobena Mercer's volume titled *Exiles, Diasporas & Strangers* (London: Iniva, 2008).

38 Gayatri Chakravorty Spivak, *An Aesthetic Education in the Era of Gobalization* (Cambridge, MA: Harvard University Press, 2012), 335.

39 Reiko Goto, Margaret Shiu and Wu Mali, 'Ecofeminism: Art as Environment – A Cultural Action/WEAD,' *Bamboo Curtain Studio Newsletter* (3 December 2014).

40 Jason W. Moore, ed., *Anthropocene or Capitalocene? Nature, History, and the Crisis of Capitalism* (Oakland: PM Press, 2016), 51.

41 Ibid.

42 Patty Chang, *The Wandering Lake* (New York: Queens Museum and Dancing Foxes Press, 2017), 31; and from the exhibition materials for *Patty Chang: The Wandering Lake 2009–2017,* 18 February 2018 at the Queens Museum.

43 Chang, *The Wandering Lake,* 66.

44 Luce Irigaray, 'The "Mechanics" of Fluids,' *This Sex Which is Not One,* tr. Catherine Porter (Ithaca: Cornell University Press, 1985), 118, 114.

45 Carolyn Merchant, *Radical Ecology: The Search for a Livable World* (New York: Routledge, 1992), 209.

46 See Timothy Mitchell, *Carbon Democracy: Political Power in the Age of Oil* (London: Verso, 2011).

47 Giorgio Vasari, *Lives of the Most Eminent Painters, Sculptors and Architects, Volume 1, Cimabue to Agnolo Gaddi,* tr. Gaston Du C. De Vere (London: Macmillan and the Medici Society, 1912–14), xviii.

48 Hegel, *The Philosophy of History* (1822) (New York: Prometheus, 1991), 79. See also Ernest Renan, 'What is a Nation?' (1882) in Geoff Eley and Ronald Grigor Suny, eds, *Becoming National: A Reader* (New York and Oxford: Oxford University Press, 1996).

49 John Emerich Edward Dalberg-Acton, 'Nationality,' in *The History of Freedom and Other Essays* (London: Macmillan and Co., 1909). Reprinted in Vincent P. Pecora, ed., *Nations and Identities: Classic Readings* (Oxford: Blackwell, 2001), 154.

50 Hans Belting, Andrea Buddensieg, and Peter Wiebel, *The Global Contemporary and the Rise of New Art Worlds* (Cambridge, MA: MIT Press, 2013), 29.

51 In 1993, fourteen artists from *China's New Art* show and Taiwanese artist Lee Ming-sheng were invited by director Achille Bonito Oliva to participate in the 1993 international group show. See Achille Bonito Oliva, *La Biennale di Venezia: 45*

Esposizione Internationale d'Arte 1993 (Venice: Marsilio Editiori, 1993). Included in the section called 'Passagio a Oriente' (Passage to the Orient), the fourteen artists were Ding Yi, Wang Guangyi, Zhang Peili, Geng Jianyi, Xu Bing, Liu Wei, Fang Lijun, Yu Hong, Feng Mengbo, Li Shan, Yu Youhan, Wang Ziwei, Sun Liang, and Song Haidong. See also Meiqin Wang, *Confrontation and Complicity: Rethinking Official Art in Contemporary China* (New York: Binghamton, 2007).

52 See, for instance, Terry Smith, *Contemporary Art: World Currents* (Upper Saddle River, NJ: Pearson Education Publishers, 2016) and Belting, Buddensieg, and Weibel, *The Global Contemporary and the Rise of New Art Worlds*.

53 Hegel, *The Philosophy of History*, 79

54 Rasheed Araeen, 'What is Post-Apartheid South Africa and its Place in the World?' in Candice Breitz and Allan Bower, eds, *Africus: Johannesburg Biennale 20 February–30 April 1995: But is it Art?* (Johannesburg: Transitional Metropolitan Council, 1995), 366.

55 Robert Storr, 'Prince of Tides: Interview with 1999 Venice Biennale Visual Arts Director Harald Szeemann,' *Artforum*, vol. 37, no. 9 (1999), 160.

56 Lu Peng, *Passage to History: 20 Years of La Biennale di Venezia and Chinese Contemporary Art* (Venice: Biennale Arte, 2013), foreword.

57 See Carol Vogel, 'Sotheby's Bets on a Windfall for Today's Chinese Art,' *New York Times* (29 March 2006) and 'China Celebrates the Year of the Art Market,' *New York Times* (24 December 2006). Also, Jonathan Napack, 'An Art Market with Chinese Characteristics,' *Yishu: Journal of Chinese Contemporary Chinese Art* (March 2007).

58 Iain Robertson, 'Understanding the Chinese Art Market,' *Sotheby's* (12 February 2015).

59 Invoking Western art is problematic from the Euro-American perspective as well. As Amelia Jones warns, 'we cannot really generalize what "European traditions" are, even as the project of colonialism defined the non-Western by "what it is 'not.'"' Amelia Jones, *Seeing Differently: A History and Theory of Identification and the Visual Arts* (New York: Routledge, 2012), xviii.

60 See Cheng, *Beijing Xingwei*, chapter 3.

61 Wu Hung, Wang Huangsheng and Feng Boyi, *Reinterpretation: A Decade of Experimental Chinese Art, 1990–2000* (Guangzhou: Guandong Museum of Art, 2002), 13.

62 Ibid., 14.

63 Donald Preziosi, 'In the Light of the Fowler: Art, History, Museology, and …' in Jane Chin Davidson and Sandra Esslinger, eds, *Global and World Art in the Practice of the University Museum* (New York and London: Routledge, 2017), 39.

64 For example, *Hard to Acclimatize* was included in the 'Inside Out' exhibition that was first presented at San Francisco's Museum of Modern Art in 1999 and thereafter traveled across the United States.

65 Quoted in Xiaoping Lin, 'Globalism or Nationalism: Cai Guoqiang, Zhang Huan and Xu Bing in New York,' *Third Text*, vol. 18, no. 4 (2004), 290.

2

Patty Chang and the transnational cinematic subject of Chineseness

Chinese American artist Patty Chang is famous for her cringe-inducing live performance works such as *Alter Ergo* (presented in 1997 and re-staged in 1999 as *Candies*) (see figure 2.1), an endurance piece where she stood for hours at New York's Exit Art, her mouth held open with a dental apparatus and drooling because it was stuffed full of pink candies. In her 2001 performance *Eels*, the display of the artist in a button-downed shirt full of live eels squirming across her chest was both torturous and titillating – as critic Ken Johnson remarks about the experience, Chang's work calls 'attention to the viewer's own darker zones of fantasy and desire.'[1] Captured on video, these performances maintain the bodily-oriented objectives of the live art medium because they elicit the viewers' sense of their own skin, crawling with eels, or entice viewers with the pleasure of sweet candy, stifled by the pain of dental prosthetics. Both humorous and excruciating, these particular performances on film have no scripted dialogue and they are as different from the medium of cinema as any pure visual engagements can be. Correspondingly, the

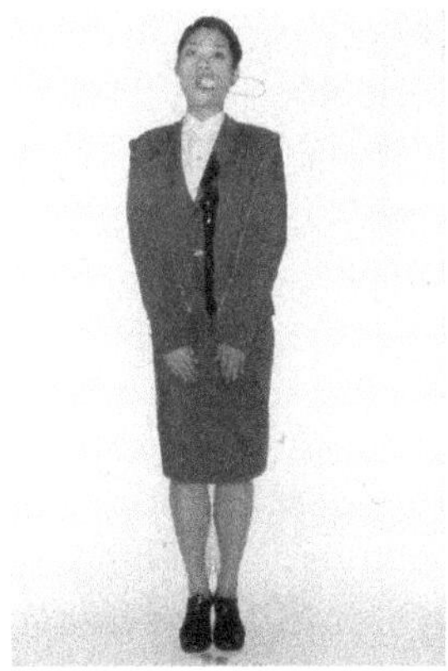

2.1 Patty Chang, *Alter Ergo*, 1997, performance at Terra Bomba, Exit Art / The First World, New York

conceptualism of the medium of video adds another dimension to the otherwise documentary premise of the recorded performance. The viewer looks for the metaphors, especially gendered ones, that pink candies signify, that eels symbolize, in the context of the artistic expression. This viewing position is a reminder that the video installation is a quasi-philosophical form with its legacy in theatrical conceptualism as well as ontological models of film and performance that have been informed by a diversity of critical theories, such as those articulated by Rey Chow and Shu-mei Shih, whose work addresses cinema and Chineseness, but also aligns with the feminist perspectives of Trinh T. Minh-ha and Teresa de Lauretis and the philosophical influences of Maurice Merleau-Ponty, Henri Bergson, and Jacques Rancière. Chang offers a unique form of engagement that requires an understanding of the vocabulary and practice of the medium itself.

A study of Chang's documented performances and conceptual videos sheds light on the important distinctions of the video-art medium that can be construed as extensions of her live performances and yet distinguished from the live-art expression. The photographic mediation through *performance video*, of course, must be included in the all-encompassing lens-based practice. However, the specificity of performance is not only ontological in scope since the video component also employs what Claire Bishop describes as an 'operational logic' and system of spectatorship that proves to be 'intimately connected to the technological revolution we are undergoing ... the digital is, on a deep level, the shaping condition – even the structuring paradox – that determines artistic decisions to work with certain formats and media.'[2] The screen-based format of the video installation form is structured in the logistics somewhere between Youtube digitalization and the movie experience, but technically the medium is really neither type, although Chang's *subjects* include early twentieth-century cinema. Accordingly, this chapter investigates the particular medium of performance video by looking closely at three projects by Chang – *Die Ware Liebe* (2009), *Minor* (2010), and *Shangri-La* (2005) – works that specifically reflect or engage in the subject of 1930s movies and film, providing a clear contrast of media to clarify the conceptual methodology of video art. But all three video expressions are also performance documents as Chang captures her travels to the outer regions of China as she participates in the peripatetic tradition of artists such as On Kawara, Marina Abramovic and Ulay, Janet Cardiff, and Hamish Fulton. The performance video encompasses a range of conceptual practices and feminist acts in the transnational context as Chang's movements *to* China as a Chinese American artist provide a preface to Chapter Three's examination of women artists from Hong Kong, Taiwan, and China.

Perhaps most importantly, Chang's works contribute to a particular cinematic context for Chineseness based on the film studies discourse that emerged in the late 1980s and early 1990s, one in which film theorists defined Chinese identity by studying the way in which movie characterizations constitute a social construction. The first video expression by Chang to be examined in this chapter is her 2010 installation titled *Minor*, documenting her mission to trace the 1920s–1930s expedition made by the Swedish explorer Sven Hedin to Lop Nor and the 'wandering lakes' in northern China. Hedin had published his research about his trip to the Silk Road in his 1938 book titled *The Wandering Lake: Into the Heart of Asia*, while his colleague Paul Lieberenz, who accompanied him, had made an early anthropology film titled *With Sven Hedin Across the Deserts of Asia* in 1928.[3] Through *Minor*, Chang engages in the historical subject of anthropology and the documentary film form in an entirely conceptual way. The second work explored is Chang's 2005 video project titled *Shangri-La*, named after the fictional paradise that James Hilton imagined for his 1933 novel *Lost Horizon* which Frank Capra made into a film of the same title in 1937. In 2001, the town of Zhongdian in the north of China near Tibet was renamed Shangri-La, transliterated to Xianggelila, when town officials won a national competition to remake the place into a tourist destination.[4] In Xianggelila, Chang filmed different and separate process-oriented performances whereupon she enlisted the help of local craftspeople to construct sculptural objects that reflect Shangri-La, both from the film *Lost Horizon* and from the invented place of Xianggelila itself. These include a mountain sculpture made of mirrors and a replica of an oxygen chamber for high altitudes.

The ultimate constructed illusion for her project, however, was the staging of a marriage with her artistic partner David Kelley. The conceptualization of getting married in *Shangri-La* raises several issues in regard to 'marrying into' nationality in the norm of obtaining citizenship based on the territorial borders of a nation. The ability to change citizenship by getting married in another country, as Gayatri Chakravorty Spivak explains, is to 'naturalize' and to adopt a nation as a symbol of the 'private conviction of special birth.'[5] The norm of citizenship is based on being born in one's homeland, and since Chang is a Chinese American citizen, the staging of a marriage performance in *Shangri-La* raises the issue of legislative laws throughout US history surrounding the nationalized rules of marriage, especially the first immigration law in 1875 prohibiting China's wives from emigrating to the United States. Heteronormative citizenship names and accounts for marriage as legislated and inextricable from citizenship, a norm that underlies the same-sex and miscegenation prohibitions in the history of legislated marriage discriminations.

The third and last discussion in this chapter focuses on the project *Die Ware Liebe (The Product Love)* (2009), the most extensive of Chang's three projects, since the work addresses the complex nature of the management of miscegenation in 1930s cinema. Chang's two-channel video presents another process-oriented work incorporating directors, actors, and locations in Los Angeles and in Hangzhou to show the transnational making of a film. For the staging of this cinematic project, the script is inspired by Walter Benjamin's 1928 essay, 'A Conversation with Anna May Wong. A Chinoiserie Out of the Old West,' published in the German magazine *Die Literarische Welt*. Chang uses Benjamin's essay as the text which she adapted for a movie featuring Benjamin and Wong as the title characters. Wong's legacy from 1920s and 1930s Hollywood cinema has represented her as the most famous Chinese American actress and yet the most fetishized in terms of her stereotyped roles playing slave girls, prostitutes, and fallen women. At a time when miscegenation laws were enforced in most countries, and when immigration laws prohibited women from China from obtaining citizenship, Wong's characters provided a titillating, law-breaking narrative for imagining illicit love in 1930s cinema.

Chang's contemporary review of historical cinema provides a conceptual comparison to the objects of *world cinema* representing Chinese language movies. In Shu-mei Shih's analysis, she discerns the transnational Chinese identity through the connection among movies made in China, Taiwan, and in the Chinese diaspora based on the oral/aural sinophonic Chinese language spoken in film.[6] Shih's study of sinophonic movies has brought attention to the scripts and narratives that offer first-person subjectivity while introducing settings and locations of Chinese culture. The diasporic form of the transnational subject in Chinese cinema was espoused overall by Sheldon Hsiao-peng Lu as the 'representation and questioning of 'China' and 'Chineseness' in filmic discourse itself, namely, the cross-examination of the national, cultural, political, ethnic, and gender identity.'[7] While these elements may indeed pertain to Chang's video art, this chapter seeks to clarify those distinctions engendered by the conceptual significations of video installations that are different from cinematic ones – even while her works acknowledge the diversity of a 'cinema' that is inclusive of mainstream movies, documentary shorts, and film in visual anthropology.

Chang's projects reveal the way in which performance video can represent the Chinese subject in complex ways that problematize Chineseness as the historical identity constructed by 1920s and 1930s cinema. Chang raises the spectre of the female stereotype by re-enacting performative rituals and disturbing the norms of the libidinal economy. The concept of love and marriage in heteronormative citizenship contributes to the biopolitical subject in all three works, *Minor, Shangri-La,* and *Die Ware Liebe,* and through their video installation form, the cinematic subject functions as a reflection of history but not in any conventional sense of dramatic narrative or replay of an anthropological docudrama. Moreover, Chang's explorations involving actors and events across continents and across history correspond to a particular 'trans' nationalism that Aihwa Ong once described as an 'interconnectedness and mobility across space,' a transnationality that 'alludes to the transversal, the transactional, the translational, and [especially] the transgressive aspects of contemporary behaviour and imagination that are incited, enabled, and regulated by the changing logics of states and capitalism.'[8] Not unlike the word *globalization*, the overuse of the word *transnationalism* has rendered it ineffective in terminology since it refers to multinational structures of capitalism more than anything else. But, as articulated by Inderpal Grewal and Caren Kaplan, the meaning of the word has served in various disciplinary contexts of transnational studies of sexuality. They look to the potential of a *trans*nationalism that 'can address the asymmetries of the globalization process' rather than suggest a seamless transition from Western Orientalism to diaspora.[9] Following their aims for rejecting globalization's totalizing assumptions, this chapter investigates the ways in which Chang's subjects problematize the normative circuits within the libidinal economies that continue to reverberate from the cinematic past.

Wandering lakes

The visual narrative of *Minor* evokes a visceral sense of travel as the viewer moves with the motion of Chang's hand-held camera while the artist looks out the window of the airplane flying above the Xinjiang autonomous region in the northwest of China. Embarking on this trip would mark the inception of an eight-year peripatetic quest for shifting bodies of water – from Uzbekistan to Newfoundland to Danjiangkou Reservoir in central China.[10] The 2017 exhibition, *Wandering Lake*, at the Queens Museum was the culmination of this quest. In *Minor*, Chang performs the role of explorer/anthropologist, and her videocam production emulates the documentary methods of visual anthropology but actually captures a conceptual endeavor. *Minor* can be viewed as taking after the model of Lieberenz's 1928 ethnographic film *Sven Hedin Across the Deserts of Asia* – a work that is now largely consumed as a Youtube expression. Beginning her trip in 2009 by 'bus from Korla to Ruoquiang, cities on the old route of the Silk Road,' Chang explains she 'wanted to try to find a way to the Wandering Lake and the ancient city of Loulan that was along its shore.'[11] The location of the Lop Nor lakes have been the object of fascination ever since the first century BCE when China's Grand Historian, Sima Qian wrote in the *Shiji* about the waters that 'flow eastward into the Salt Swamp (Lob Nor)' and the place nearby where the 'Loulan and the Gushi peoples live in fortified cities.'[12] Loulan was thought to be an ancient oasis along the Silk Road in central Asia.[13] Sven Hedin was the explorer credited with the theory that explained the disappearing lakes, since he surmised that the Tarim River flowing through the region changed course to the southeast during the fourth century, which resulted in their change of location. But his theory also foretold that the river could change course again bringing the lakes' return, which is why he called them the Wandering Lakes. In his book, Hedin describes his return to Lop Nor in 1934, to find the lake had actually wandered back, more than thirty years after he proposed his theory.

Hedin was considered a great explorer during his lifetime and was able to obtain appointments with leaders such as Chiang Kai-shek (a ruler of China at the time), who commissioned his expedition back to Lop Nor in 1933. But according to Chang, 'his definitive mapping of central Asia was used by subsequent explorers to loot treasures along the Silk Road.'[14] More importantly, his scientific ideals were ostensibly aligned with German nationalist conceptions about race. 'China is like a bowl that has become overfilled,' wrote Hedin, the 'yellow race is growing in number and strength. Meanwhile, the white race is weakening itself through constant wars between different nations of the same religion and culture.'[15] After World War II, his reputation was tarnished by his relationship with the Nazi elite and by his use of geography in the development of his own version of the final solution.

Minor would document Chang's search for the lakes, but the trip would actually memorialize a series of encounters such as a visit to the local museum where a Sven Hedin exhibit and an assortment of anthropological items were on display: 'combs, paper, stone mallets, lava, Tibetan tablets, wool cloths.'[16] However, the viewer then discovers with Chang the most astonishing exhibition amidst the ethnographic objects, which was the 'well-preserved and lifelike ... Beauty of Loulan,' one of eight mummies presented in the museum[17] (see figure 2.2). In relation to this discovery, the video narrates Chang befriending two young Xinjiang girls who become guests at her hotel where one, who is ethnically Uyghur, the beautiful Munira, 'pretended she was the Beauty from Loulan, laying on the hotel bed as if asleep while I filmed her' (see figure 2.3).[18] Through Chang's video lens, the juxtaposition of the living Beauty of Loulan emphasizes the loss of respect for the dead Beauty from Loulan as her skeletal remains on display next to the artefacts and the homage to Hedin suddenly appear entirely inappropriate. The televisual fantasy of the film medium transforms the qualities of the objects on the video in which the mummy can easily be viewed as an object of science fiction fantasy, even as Chang's video documentation engenders a sense of the real in the unfolding of the events.

The Beauty of Loulan represents a greater polemic in the politics of ethnicity in Xinjiang. The predominantly Muslim Uyghur population, speaking a Turkish-related language, inhabit a Soviet-bordering state that is ethnically closer to Central Asian culture than to East Asian Chineseness. The more than two hundred mummies discovered since the 1970s, the oldest dating to 2000

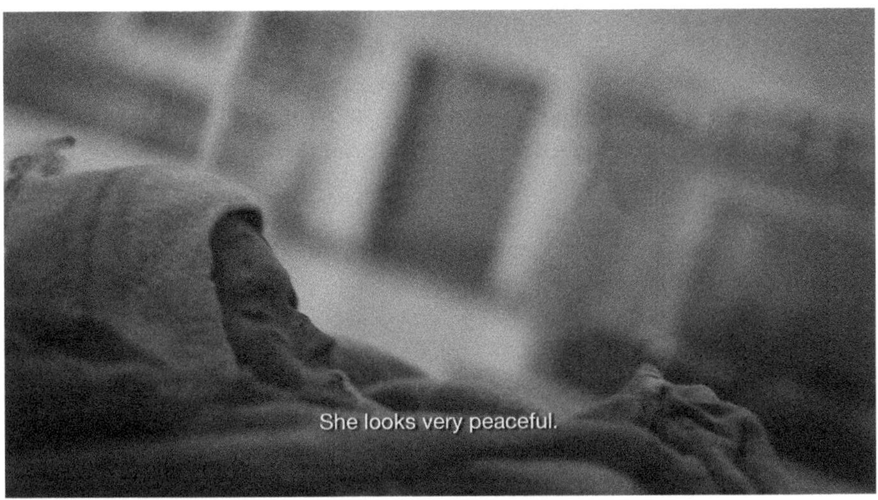

2.2 Patty Chang, *Minor*, 2010, video still, Beauty of Loulan, mummy displayed in municipal museum in Xinjiang

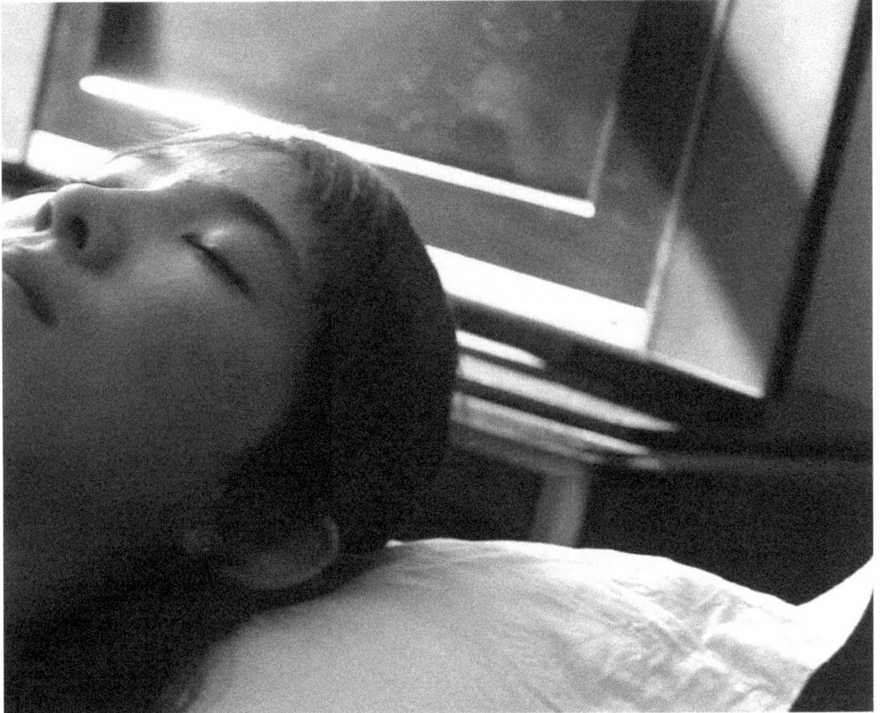

2.3 Patty Chang, *Minor*, 2010, video still, Munira from Ruoqiang

BCE, have been analysed by scientists and verified as mixed ancestry – mostly from Eastern Europe, Central Asia, and Siberia, but rarely from China.[19] Uyghur nationalists have adopted this research as proof that Xinjiang should not be considered as a territory of China at all, even as the province has been included within China's borders since the Qing dynasty took control in the eighteenth century.[20] The cause of the separatist movement was due to Russian influence in the twentieth century, which led to Xinjiang's independence as the East Turkestan Republic from 1944 to 1949. When Mao Zedong came into power in 1949, he obtained Russia's support to officially restore Xinjiang to China as an autonomous region. Under Chinese rule, the Muslim Uyghur constituency has long suffered oppression by the Chinese for their religious way of life, especially after the Han Chinese populace resettled in the region in order to develop the lucrative oil resources and petrochemical production. Currently, 40 per cent of the Xinjiang population are Han Chinese – in 1949, only 6 per cent were of Chinese descent.[21]

At the end of *Minor*, Chang asks Munira to think of a word to describe her Uyghur identity and she chooses *wolf* because 'the last Uyghur married a wolf, and that is where the Uyghur people came from.'[22] Chang also asked another new friend Wulina, a Han Chinese student living in the area to 'write one Chinese word that would describe the Chinese people,' to which she replied: 'a name from the Hundred Family Surnames.'[23] The classical *Baijiaxing* (960–1279AD) Song dynasty book of names is a Confucian text, and Wulina chooses the word *Wang*, since the Chinese character is a common surname that means 'emperor.' In one of the final scenes of *Minor*, Munira spells out the word *wolf* using scarves while Wulina writes the character for *Wang* using paper cups, both posted on chain link fencing that serves as makeshift trailers on the back of tractors (see figure 2.4). The question of normative citizenship in China has a long history that has more to do with the concept of a 'Han Chinese' identity than the borders of its territories. As Patricia Ebrey surmises, Chinese surnames are rooted in the spiritual past of such origin myths as *Shen Nong* and *Huang Di*, the Yellow Emperor, and they align with the concept of a common patrilineal ancestry, inextricably linked to a Confucian culturalism.[24] The Han ethnicity was a moral enclave ruled by the Confucian texts and since the period of the Han dynasty those on the outside were considered as 'barbarians.'

Always at the forefront of *Minor* is the historical and patriarchal text – from Sima Qian's grand history in the *Shiji* to Sven Hedin's mapping of territories – invoked through Chang's signifiers of culture: anthropological objects and Chinese names, and whether inscribed by scarves or paper cups, the visual signs of culture are woven into a reflection of Uyghur and Chinese identities. Chang's cinematic narrative conceptualizes the polemics of gender and ethnicity through the portrayals she draws from the embodied

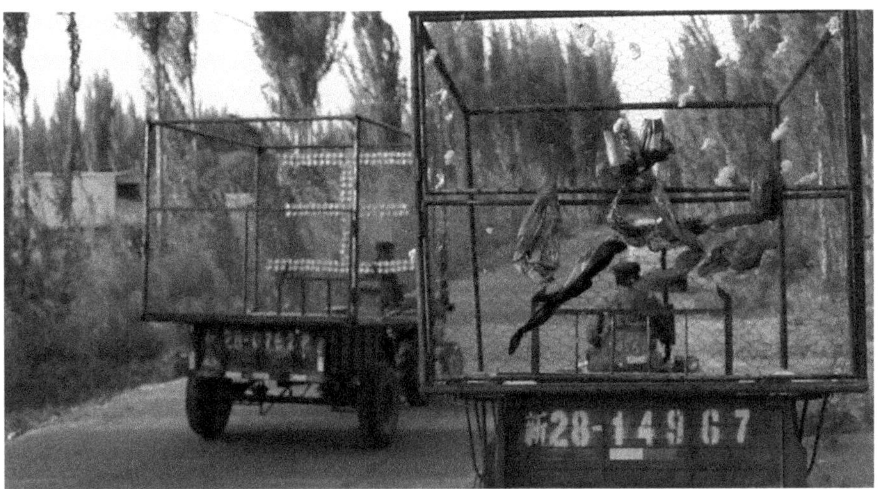

2.4 Patty Chang, *Minor*, 2010, video still, in Qiemo, chain-link trucks for harvesting cotton with the Uyghur character for *Wolf* made from scarves and the Chinese character for the name *Wang* made of paper cups

performances of her characters. However, her video's gaze refuses to take sides between the Chinese and the Uyghur, instead soliciting viewers' own moral questioning of their place in the locations, territories, and borders captured by the video. Chang uses the installation form in this way to create an embodied experience, completely autonomous and different from the conventions of movies, anthropological film, and documentary film as she brings the viewer along in the timeless search for the wandering lake.

Lost horizons

Chang has traveled to the geographical edges of China, from the northwest steppe of the Xinjiang autonomous region and now to the southwest Yunnan province and the Diqing Tibetan Autonomous Prefecture. Covering this north to south expanse of travel in China, the sense of the diverse terrain represents a country where Chinese identity is often contested and disavowed. At the same time, Chang offers images of 'trans'nationalist conceptions within Chinese culture itself, those which are far from the urban economic stereotypes of China's new capitalist society. Her 2005 project *Shangri-La* took her to an obscure county once called Gyalthang by the Tibetan farmers but officially named Zhongdian until 2002 when the local government won an endorsement from the Civil Administration of China to change its name to 'Shangrila,' or, in its Mandarin pinyin literation Xianggelila, based on Hilton's fictional creation of paradise for his 1933 novel.[25] During the late

1980s and early 1990s, China's government initiated 'ethnic tourism' by developing public campaigns to entice domestic and foreign visitors to the areas inhabited by *shaoshu minzu* or 'minority nationalities.'[26] Tibetan culture was already in high demand by tourists, and until the 1980s Tibet was one of the most difficult destinations for the outside world to reach.

Chang's trek to Xianggelila was on behalf of her video project emulating the location shoot that never happened for Capra's 1937 Hollywood production of *Lost Horizon*, which was filmed for the most part on a constructed movie set in Burbank. The story of the utopian 'lost world' where inhabitants are granted the gift of long life has been interpreted as a form of paradise, a peaceful, hidden refuge in the Shangri-La fantasy created for China's tourist destination. By 2002, the Heavenly Mountains and Waters Tourism Development Company and the Yunnan Ziyuan Company had become the corporate managers of Xianggelila tourism, and they promoted the 'last clean earth in the world' while setting up entrance fees for the one million visitors who visited the scenic areas in the county that year. One of the most important scenic vistas in the region is the Khawa Karpo (or Kawa Garbo), described as 'a massive mountain looming beyond the deep gorge, guarded by a range of ice-clad peaks sparkling in the autumn sun; this is one of the most powerful deities in cultural Tibet.'[27] In the spiritual tradition, the mountain itself is considered as a god, one of the special eight *neri* or 'abode mountains,' the holiest in Tibetan Buddhism.[28] Situated in the shadow of Karpo's lofty 22,000 feet terrain, the elevation of Xianggelila is 10,370 feet. Of course, the Tibetan monasteries are also main attractions, and new tourist pilgrims flock to the largest monasteries, the Songtseling and the Dhondrupling, which were both founded in the seventeenth century.[29] At one time, a trek to Diqing would have been considered as part of a spiritual Khawa Karpo pilgrimage.

Chang's *Shangri-La* is a performance of 'making things' as she documents on film her artistic process involving the people of Xianggelila, designers and craftsmen hired to help construct three material objects in particular: a ten-foot tall sculpture of Khawa Karpo made out of cut mirrors, an oxygen pod for treating altitude sickness, and a big cake sculpted with the images of both mountains and the oxygen pod (see plates 6, 7, and 8). Chang's project visualizes the concept of *construction*, demonstrated first by a state-sponsored place derived from the fictional origins of Hilton's Shangri-La and then by her artistic aim of showing the *act* of constructing objects. Chang saw the risks of her project being viewed as an ethnographic experiment, but she recognized how her performance 'rooted the mythical in something as everyday as construction' and was therefore able to show 'the work propping up the façade of any tourist destination. That interaction and process is a large part of the piece.'[30] She is, however, reproducing the movie images from Capra's historical fiction as much as she is recreating the new images being developed in Diqing's Xianggelila. Viewed through the reproduction of her video lens, Chang employs a structure of repetition that Deleuze once described as transformative: 'In every respect, repetition is a transgression … it denounces its nominal or general character in favour of a more profound and more artistic reality.'[31] The viewer sees through Chang's lens the conceptual effect of the profound redoubling of the Shangri-La fantasy as a never-ending fascination.

The 40-minute video begins the same way that Capra opens his movie, with a view from an airplane descending through the clouds over the awe-inspiring mountains. The scene continues into the next frames with Chang meeting a group of monks in the atrium of the Paradise Hotel in Xianggelila, and here the painted and sculptural backdrop of mountains functions as the flora and fauna scene for the real flowers, trees, and water in the spacious room. The mountains were a looming presence in Capra's film and they were thought to have derived from footage of the Himalayas taken from the 1934 documentary *Der Daemon der Berge*.[32] Next, the viewer gets to watch Chang's construction team build her ten-foot replica of Khawa Karpo, shaping the structure from wood and then overlaying with angled pieces of mirror. Chang describes her vision of mirrored facets imploding 'on themselves from reflecting their surroundings' because it was 'important that the mountain has motion,' and as shown in the video, the completed work is then placed 'on a vehicle to transport, to reflect its environment.'[33] In this scene the mirrored sculpture, exhibited on the back of a small pickup truck, drives by the big Xianggelila billboard with the mountain ranges behind it. As described by Chang, 'in the landscape, it becomes very small; with people surrounding it, it becomes human size.'[34] In essence, Chang performs the sculptural 'not-landscape, not-architecture' under the terms that Rosalind Krauss theorized for expressing 'a strict opposition between the built and the not-built, the cultural and the natural, between which the production of sculptural art appeared to be suspended.'[35] Discussing sculpture in the new conceptual field for art, Krauss cited Robert Morris's *Mirrored Boxes* (1965) as the enigmatic example, 'though visually continuous with grass and trees, they are not in fact part of the landscape.'[36] But here, at the very landscape of the sacred Tibetan mountains, Chang's creation of a moving hall of mirrors engenders a profound artistic reality since the construction of the constructed Shangri-La signifies an 'ontological absence' when faced with the real Khawa Karpo and the irreproducible work of nature.

The locals of Xianggelila believe in the origin story of a plane crash in the mountains during World War II as the way that the place came into being – a tale straight out of Hilton's book. The discovery of the lamasery in Hilton's Shangri-La was the outcome of the crash of a hijacked plane carrying white residents of Baskul escaping to Peshawar during the revolution against the British Raj in 1931 India. In the book, the plane was a special transport for high-altitude flights. Zhongdian's remote location and high elevation have only increased the belief that it is the true 'lost horizon' that people have searched for since Hilton wrote his fiction. Visitors are told to prepare for high-altitude sickness in Xianggelila, which adds to the unique experience, and there is a clinic in town where patients are treated by a spell in an oxygen pressure chamber that looks like a submarine/space ship. This 'ship' also functions as the signifier for the airplane crash in Shangri-La lore, and, as such, Chang builds a replica of the oxygen pod in the courtyard of a house where a relative of her guide Lhamu resides. But in adding to the imaginary objects from the fictions of Shangri-La, Chang also conveys the impact of a news story about a submarine full of soldiers that ran into an underwater mountain – they were led to their demise because it was not visible above water.[37] The viewer watches as Chang's hired team builds the pod, and once completed, the group of monks are hanging out in the pod, described by Chang as 'sometimes laughing, sometimes yawning, talking on their cellphones, singing songs, or telling jokes; moments of affection or nothing happening at all.'[38] Even here, in the company of the monks, the active construction of the mythical illusion can be perceived. As Chang notes, someone once told her 'that Shangri-La doesn't have any authentic Tibetan culture of its own. In the past, the government suppressed the culture, but now they are reinventing it themselves.'[39] This reminder of China's continuing oppression toward actual Tibetan constituents shows the political polemic of Xianggelila's touristic difference. Not unlike the conditions in Xinjiang, the fear of separatist independence has kept the Chinese state vigilant in its authoritarian repression of Tibet, as exemplified by the imprisonment of Tashi Wangchuk, an education advocate for Tibetan culture. Tashi was indicted in 2016 after contributing his views to the *New York Times* on the need to educate about and to protect Tibetan culture.[40] A reinvented Shangri-La culture of monks removes the separatist threat.

In Chang's exhibition catalogue for *Shangri-La*, a 1937 stock photo shows *Lost Horizon* actors Ronald Colman, Jane Wyatt, and director Frank Capra cutting into a cake decorated to look like the lamasery at Shangri-La. Much in the way that wrap parties for the completion of films end with cake and champagne, Chang orders the celebratory mountain and oxygen chamber cake from a local bakery. By making a painted sculpture with frosting and food dye, the bakers in Xianggelila are asked to create an image expressing 'how the oxygen pod crashes into the mountain' and the result is the frosted pod in a white peaked sugar vista.[41] As Chang performs this ritual from cinema, noting that 'my father brings the mountain cake for the workers to eat on their lunch break,' she reveals the significance of this moment for her own familial relationships.[42] The illusions and fantasies of Shangri-La are for consumption only, which the cake represents, but the Chinese rituals are maintained by relationships.

The ultimate illusion and fantasy that Chang constructed for *Shangri-La* was performed as a wedding ritual in which she made herself the constructed object by staging a marriage with her artistic partner David Kelley. The elaborate dressing up, full make-up treatment and bridal dressing, performed to produce a Taiwanese style of wedding photographs could symbolize the fiction in an ontological way (see plate 9). To make herself the object of focus is to emphasize the subject of Chang's identity as a Chinese woman, and in this case an immigrant subject since she is the 'outsider' Chinese artist who performs the wedding ritual in China, or rather, not simply *in* China but at the border of the separatist edge. If she were a 'true' citizen of China or a Tibetan ethnic subject, what would marriage to a white male from the United States signify? In actuality, she has simply masqueraded as a subject of China in place of her Chinese American, second generation Taiwanese self. Are these different variations of 'being Chinese' decided by blood, by territory, by borders, by appearances, by religious affiliation, by dialect, and so on?

In *Shangri-La*'s final constructed object of the 'bride,' Chang puts into question her own status as the gendered and raced subject of 'immigrant acts' or exclusion acts including miscegenation laws prohibiting racially mixed marriages in Chinese American history. Chang's act of getting married in Xianggelila, China's invented paradise, reflects the opposite of the historical convention that people living in China endeavor to fulfil their fantasies and find their opportunities in the United States. The first restrictive US law in 1875, the Page Law, prohibited Chinese women exclusively from emigrating to the United States from China. By theatricalizing the juridical act of marriage, Chang's performance problematizes the place of origin for 'wives' in this legislated history of heteronormative citizenship. As Kerry Abrams explains, the Page Law 'targeted female Chinese immigrants in an effort to protect traditional marriage and sexual norms,' and while places with large Chinese populations such as California 'could not exclude Chinese women for being "Chinese," it could exclude them by classifying them as outside the acceptable category of "wives".'[43] Abrams considers this legislation as a highly significant statute because it was the first of immigration laws to discriminate by method and by aims: 'Congress managed to exclude a group of people by defining them as outside the boundaries of legal marriage.'[44] Under the jurisdiction of territories and borders, the construction of 'the wife' is perhaps the greatest illusion Chang created on behalf of Shangri-La's heteronormative citizenship.

Die Ware Liebe

> The collective power that is common to these spectators is not the status of members of a collective body. Nor is it a peculiar kind of interactivity. It is the power to translate in their own way what they are looking at.[45]

The video installation by Patty Chang, *Die Ware Liebe: The Product (or Commodity) Love* expresses a 'trans'nationalist subject in historical and contemporary ways, beginning with its inspiration from Walter Benjamin's 1928 essay titled 'Gespräch mit Anne May Wong' (A Conversation with Anna May Wong, also subtitled, 'A Chinoiserie Out of the Old West').[46] Published in the important leftist review, *Die literarische Welt*, Benjamin wrote about his actual meeting with Anna May Wong who was the most famous Chinese American screen actor and yet the most type-cast in the Hollywood stereotype of slave girl, prostitute, and 'fallen woman' during the era of 'yellowface' cinema. In reality, Wong was a consummate transnationalist actor who traveled to Europe to work in films, to Berlin in particular, where she met Benjamin amidst the growing tensions of 1920s–1930s nationalism and fascism. Chang's contemporary project corresponds to Wong's movements of the past as she incorporates diverse actors and locations from Los Angeles to Hangzhou for her two-channel, 42-minute video installation exhibited at Mary Boone Gallery in New York in 2009.

The operative activity for Chang's *Die Ware Liebe* project is the *performance* of translation, which she explores through both videos of her installation (see plate 10). The very 'labor' of translation comprises the subject of *A Chinoiserie Out of the Old West*, as the first video engages viewers in the act of watching three different academic translators in Los Angeles interpret Benjamin's original German text (see figure 2.5). Benjamin had noted in 'The Task of the Translator' that 'translation is a form. To comprehend it as a form, one must go back to the original.'[47] Through the video medium, Chang takes on this challenge to conceptualize translation as a visual form, and the ability to see 'how' a translator reads and rereads the text is enlightening, since translation is subjective, never seamless, and often clumsy. Benjamin's Chinoiserie essay is performed for Chang's viewers in this way, and the translators in the video are interspersed with images of transnational locations such as the Benjamin archive in Berlin and the film studio in Hangzhou. She reminds the viewer that transnationalism was always a part of the past, while pointing to the current state of globalization in which cultural relationships are based on comprehension of visual languages beyond the production of the text. In modernity, the audience was always 'global' and meaning always contingent on the ability to comprehend both textual and visual languages.

For the second video titled *Die Ware Liebe*, Chang creates a sexual fantasy, an imaginary love scene, based on the very excerpts that were translated by the linguists in her first video. Among them were Benjamin's writings about Wong through his Orientalizing language: 'her hair flowing loose like a dragon romping in water' a cascade that 'cuts into her face and makes it most heart-shaped of all.'[48] The love scene is between Benjamin and Wong, and this provocative interlude is incited by Chang's casting of Chinese actors Hu

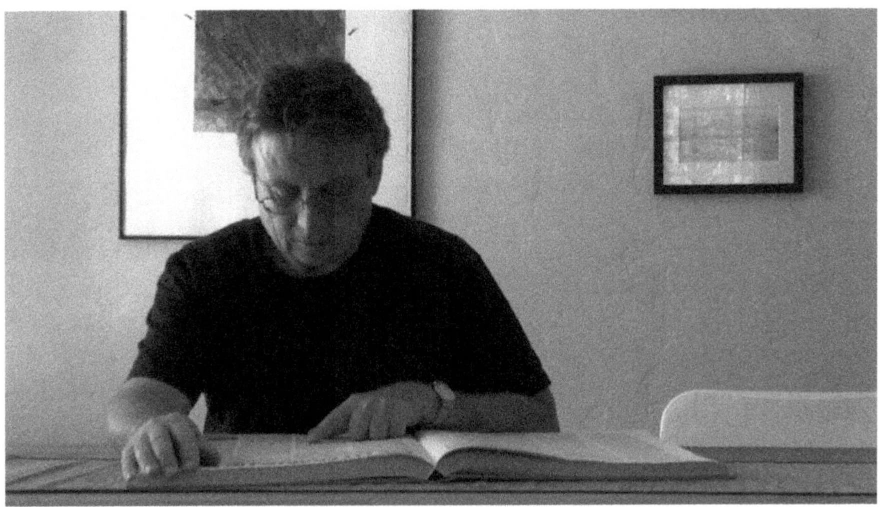

2.5 Patty Chang, *A Chinoiserie Out of the Old West*, 2009, video still

Huaizhong and Yi Ping to play the respective parts. Subtitled and delivered in Mandarin Chinese, Chang is, in essence, reversing the logic of sexual desire from 1930s cinema – the Asian female is still circumscribed to her exotica role; but the casting of Benjamin in the Chinese body breaks from the dynamic of the historical fantasy. The depiction of illicit desire between white male and Asian female characters was a titillating formula for mainstream movies in the 1930s because miscegenation laws made these relationships dangerous. Interracial marriage was prohibited in the United States until 1967 and legislation in fascist Germany in the 1930s was, of course, based on racial purity. In this way, cinematic history is rewritten by Chang, and the cinematic text functions metaphorically in her expressive play of political contexts for trans-nationalism.

Overall, Chang's theatrical role-playing and use of the cinematic medium pays homage to the theories of both Bertolt Brecht and Walter Benjamin. As explored in this chapter, the two Marxist thinkers established important political concepts for performance and film during the 1930s, which appear as inspiration for Chang's return to their historical subjects. Following the principles of Epic Theatre, the viewer watches the entire production of *Die Ware Liebe* from behind the stage in documentary style with the film crew blocking the scene at the studio in Hangzhou and the director Gu Bo providing the commentary.[49] The concept of 'live theatre,' however, is merely an illusion, since the actors are performing for the video – the mechanical distinction that Benjamin established for the medium of film was the assertion that the 'audience's identification with the actor is really an identification with the camera.'[50] The film actor is transformed by the camera's technology whereas the stage actor contends with 'aura,' or some cult remembrance of his persona from the past.[51] Reviving this distinction, Chang's cult remembrance of Benjamin is explicitly for film rather than for stage, particularly since she created his 'character-role' from a text that he had written. In this way, Chang puts to the test Benjamin's advocacy for radicalizing 'the functional relationship between stage and audience, text and production, producer and actor. Epic theatre, [Brecht] declared, must not develop actions but represent conditions.'[52] The question, then, is whether the performative expression is still able to reflect the dialectics of moral life and the ethics of class conditions that both Brecht and Benjamin had championed through their work, even if political Marxism is no longer viable and capitalism is wholly accepted in its overt multinational form.

The answer can be presumed by the fact that both critical theorists appear to have retained their relevance for contemporary thought. As Rey Chow asserts 'Walter Benjamin's work on Bertolt Brecht is exemplary of the conceptual innovations that continue to bear an impact on theoretical and artistic thinking in the twenty-first century.'[53] Chow's book on *transmedial* thinking was a critique of the problem in the current media age in which 'reflexivity becomes porn,' describing the viewing experience by which artistic practices 'become synonymous with the violence of medial exhibitionism.'[54] Concurring with others such as Jacques Rancière, Chow's reprisal of Brecht and his 'gay science, in all the pleasure of learning and testing' provided a renewed sense of coalitional purpose in artistic practice and theory.[55] This comes at a moment when art discourse is thought to be suffering 'intellectual fatigue' according to Nikos Papastergiadis and lacking in critical seriousness in its complicity with corporate entities for art.[56] The processes of globalization brought a new urgency to Brecht's deconstruction of power in the return to relationships between observers and performers in the age of performance. On the other hand, analysis of contemporary art has become intensely complex, which Papastergiadis attributes to 'the massive expansion of people and practices that are now considered as being part of the global artworld.'[57] The complexity of discourse emerges from the need to comprehend globalized cultural histories, traditions, and hierarchies that are played out in the new heterogeneous playing field for art. A 'Chinese Walter Benjamin' can therefore exemplify Rancière's conception of the 'new stage of equality, where different kinds of performances would be translated into one another,' the very act of translation – including the reading of performing bodies as a kind of text – underwrites the ideal that an 'emancipated community is in fact a community of storytellers and translators.'[58] A change in cultural centrism in the context of trans-nationality allows for an innovative freeing of expression.

Chang returns to historical relationships among 'stage and audience, text and production, producer and actor' in order to develop the Chinese subject that emerges from the texts of Benjamin and Brecht. Given the fact that *Die Ware Liebe* was the working title of Brecht's 1943 play *The Good Woman of Szechuan*, Chang's re-use of the title underscores the complexities of role-playing as represented by gender and Chinese identification.[59] Brecht's *Verfremdungseffekt* in theory and practice was developed from his own role as spectator of the 'Alienation Effects in Chinese Acting,' also the title of his 1935 essay. His translation of Chinese theatre was inspired from viewing a cross-dressing performance by the great Chinese opera star Mei Lanfang, who carried on the tradition of male actors groomed to play female roles. The translation of the operation of theatre is an interpretative act, and likewise, in viewing Chang's version of *Die Ware Liebe*, the spectator watches the production team in China in the act of interpreting the Chinese American subject of Anna May Wong.

Chang translates the fantasy from the history of the gendered Chinese subject for review in the contemporary transnational context for culture. In globalization, the internal diversity of Chinese culture is newly recognized, such that this context is engendered by 'Chineseness' as a complicated example of a heterogeneous Chinese identity, as articulated by the disparate historical and political dimensions that the term encompasses. Chang addresses this internal diversity through her conception of translation as a visual form. *Die Ware Liebe* shows how the *Chinoiserie* subject in Benjamin's essay can be viewed as the philosopher's translation of Wong's exotica fantasy stage-persona rather than assumed to be a naive Orientalist reading – especially since Chang implicates the fictitious character of Benjamin himself in her new narrative. As such, Chineseness affirms Rancière's fluid form of translation as 'the blurring of the opposition between those who look and those who act, between those who are individuals and those who are members of a collective.'[60] That is not to say that Orientalism had no 'real' consequences (especially as an impact on stereotypes), but that fantasy cannot be ignored and dismissed in the controversial distinction of Chineseness.

Ultimately, Chang's project can be conceived as a kind of defamiliarization through the staging of Chineseness, which functions on a political level to reveal the gendered history of nationalism that extends from the cinematic past. The citizen-subject that emerges from transnational circuits and libidinal economies was one that served an underlying mythology of nationhood expressed by cinematic narratives. In immigration history, the fictional role was no small thing as it contributed to the formation of the citizen-subject in modern nationalism. The eroticized Asian female character in American film arose during the period when the immigration of women from China to the United States was severely restricted and miscegenation laws were firmly established. Cinema therefore reinforced nationalist narratives through the telling of moral tales, narrated in film fantasies of illicit affairs between white male protagonists and Asian female seducers in stories that ultimately ended with the punishment and death of the Asian woman. The film archive of Anna May Wong provides a clear understanding of nationalist ideologies portrayed as fantasy.

Benjamin's writing about Wong in his essay 'Gespräch mit Anne May Wong' is unrecognizable from the intellectual discourse of the great literary critic, using descriptions such as her name 'like the specks in a bowl of tea that unfold into blossoms replete with moon and devoid of scent.'[61] Benjamin wrote his 'conversation' in a style that reflects his casual meeting with the movie star in the company of several others.[62] While most of the essay celebrates Wong and her achievements in film, there are odd moments, such as when Benjamin asks if movies are made in China, 'are there any Chinese directors?' Wong replies, 'yes, of course movies are made in China.' But Wong was hardly one to ask since she was a third-generation, Los Angeles born actor, who at the age of nineteen performed with Douglas Fairbanks Junior in *The Thief of Bagdad* (1924) (see figure 2.6). Often called the 'most beautiful Oriental actress in Hollywood,' her public appeal was established by her scantily clad, servile character as a Mongolian slave in the film. In order for her to accept the provocative role, the studio had to obtain her father's legal permission. The slave girl character, 'dressed in the skimpiest of bandeau tops and very tight briefs' as described by Celine Shimizu, was considered

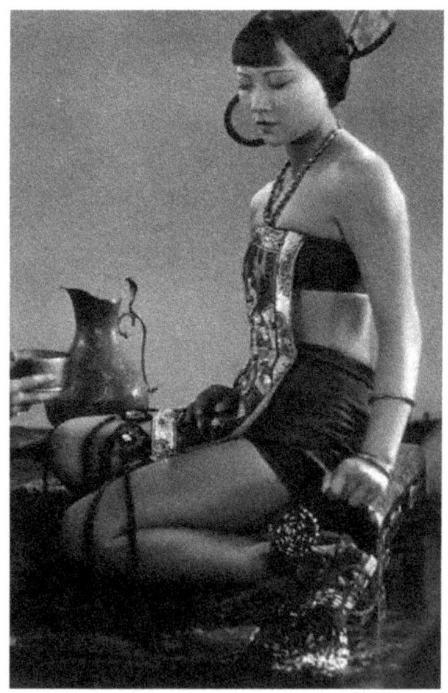

2.6 Anna May Wong in *The Thief of Bagdad*, 1924 (Fairbanks / United Artists)

as the perverse 'hypersexual' counterpart to the white princess character, a vision 'enshrouded in whiteness' in this Arabian Nights fantasy.[63] Films such as *The Thief of Bagdad* comprise the documentary record of the sexually passive-aggressive stereotype for Asian woman. Wong was also the first to play the sinister, duplicitous 'dragon lady' (the counterpart to the evil Fu Manchu) in *Daughter of the Dragon* (1931), a role that coexisted with the submissive, subjugated Chinese slave-girl character.

By 1928, Wong was a hot film commodity, and she had accepted an invitation to go to Berlin to work with the German producer and director Richard Eichberg on a series of movies, which fatefully brought the opportunity to meet with Benjamin. Eichberg was a pioneer of the international film industry. In his essay, Benjamin had commented on Wong's encounter with the Hollywood author Karl Vollmoeller who later convinced Eichberg to cast Wong in the movie *Song* (1928) because he had written the script with her in mind.[64] His movie *The Flame of Love* (1930) featuring Wong was shot in three different languages. During these early years of the talkies, Wong had to learn German and French for each version. *Piccadilly* (1929) was Wong's last silent film, which she made for the British public. Benjamin frequently went to the movies, and when he wrote about Frank Capra's *You Can't Take it With You* (1938), he made an example of the 'film industry's complicity with fascism, 'even over there' (that is, in the United States).'[65] But Benjamin's inference of an Orientalist gaze toward Anna May Wong appears oddly contradictory as he describes Wong in his essay, dressed in a 'dark blue suit, a light blue blouse, a yellow tie over that,' but then he remarks inexplicably 'one would like to know a Chinese verse to describe this.'[66] Benjamin appears to be expressing a desire for some vague Oriental perspective; but then he states forthrightly that Wong has 'always dressed this way, for she was in fact not born in China but in Chinatown in Los Angeles.'[67] For the spectator of 1930s film, gender and race were cinematic costumes, in which Orientalism functions as an exchange, the substitute of an illusion of a community, even as the sexualized identity of Asian women in film affected the real statutes for Chinese American citizenship.

In contrast, Brecht's 1940s version of *Die Ware Liebe*, the play *The Good Woman of Szechuan*, can be perceived as a 'live' disruption of the cinematic sexual illusion of Asian women in film. (This 'live' staging of bodies continues to underwrite performance theory, one that is largely attributed to him.) The key element in Brecht is the Marxist materialism of the body, which is central to the moral tale featuring the protagonist Shen Teh as the prostitute who is bestowed fortune from the gods because she proved to be a 'good person' – her willingness to give shelter to the gods (disguised as humans) represents the concept of 'good' in exchange for the character's 'bad' status as prostitute (the very status of the exotica Asian female stereotype in 1930s film). Brecht explained his vision for the Shen Teh role and the stage-setting for the play: 'the girl must be a big powerful person. The city must be a big, dusty uninhabitable place ... some attention must be paid to countering the risk of chinoiserie. The vision is of a Chinese city's outskirts with cement works and so on.'[68] Countering the Orientalist commodification of Chinese women and the place of China in film, the city of Szechuan stands in for the ubiquitous modern metropolis where 'man is exploited by man.'[69]

John Willett explains that the play pays homage to the Chinese parable form, since Brecht was inspired by the fourteenth-century scripts of Li Hsing-tao. With the money she is given, Shen Teh is able to go into business and stop selling herself as a prostitute to make a living. But the 'good woman' is unable to make ends meet because her neighbours learned of her windfall and constantly took advantage of her generosity. In the critical scene of the play, Shen Teh changes her costume in front of the audience to become another character, her cousin Shui Ta, who is able to conduct business shrewdly without being manipulated by the leeching neighbours because he is male. A prime example of defamiliarization, Brecht is referring, on the one hand, to the gendered relations of power in a 'society where women's role was to be sold, but salesmen had to be men,' and on the other, he is translating Chinese opera and its form of cross-dressing.[70] Alisa Solomon asserts that Shen Teh is 'a familiar (and derogatory) image of women ... the familiar cannot be rendered strange without first being established *as familiar*. By means of the *Verfremdungseffekt* – the central mechanism of which is the Shui Ta disguise.'[71] The cross-dressing act – live and in real-time – is meant to let the audience see and feel the way in which material conditions are a result of the costume of gender whereby the sexual expectation is also assumed.

Brecht had long ago addressed what Judith Butler articulates as the concern 'to rethink performativity as cultural ritual, as the reiteration of cultural norms, as the habitus of the body in which structural and social dimensions of meaning are not finally separable.'[72] Shen Teh literally embodies the idea that 'love' is an economic transaction particular to 'woman' and the female gender. Chang astutely adopted Brecht's working title *Die Ware Liebe* for *The Good Woman of Szechuan*, which emphasizes the Marxist exchange of 'love.' The German phrase translates into either 'Love for Sale' or 'The Commodity, Love,' and *Ware Liebe* 'product love' is also a pun on *wahre liebe* 'true love.' Reflecting his poetic use of irony, the wordplay expresses Brecht's primary objective, which is to expose the value of human life in commodity culture. Most importantly, Shen Teh is a Chinese character in name only, whose role was ostensibly written for the actress Elisabeth Bergner specifically and acted by any nationality wherever the play was presented (including Eitaro Ozawa's 1960 version in the Haiyuza Theatre in Japan).[73] Anna May Wong had also considered playing the part after she had acted in *The Caucasian Chalk Circle*, the 1924 version of Li

Hsing-tao's play *The Chalk Circle* rescripted by the German poet Klabund.[74] If the costume of gender and sex determines material conditions, Chang's casting of the Chinese subject appears to be a continuation of the translation of Chineseness that was part of the transnational history of *The Good Woman of Szechuan*. She questions, however, what happens today when the white actor cross-dresses in the costume of the Chinese body.

From the start of the viewing experience of Chang's first of the two-channel videos, *A Chinoiserie Out of the Old West*, the translators are clearly struggling to discern what Benjamin meant in his essay as we watch their attempts to read the phrases first in German and then in English (see figure 2.5). The word 'touch,' in particular, claims the focus of their translations. From the spoken performance to the eventual action on film, 'touch' becomes the textual-verbal-visual punctum of the movement on the screen, interpreted by translators, directors, and actors. Chang explains that the 'variations in their translations expand and make visible the slippage between language, culture and context' as she clarifies the connection between *A Chinoiserie* and *Die Ware Liebe* by noting that the same work of translation is being conducted by the film crew producing the 'love scene in China, with the Chinese director interpreting the characters of Benjamin and Wong.'[75] In the second video, the viewer is behind the scenes as we watch the staging of the love scene, the actors are in their chairs being made up to look like photographs of Wong and Benjamin (see figure 2.7). We are then included in the directing and shooting of the make-believe love-tryst between Wong and Benjamin.

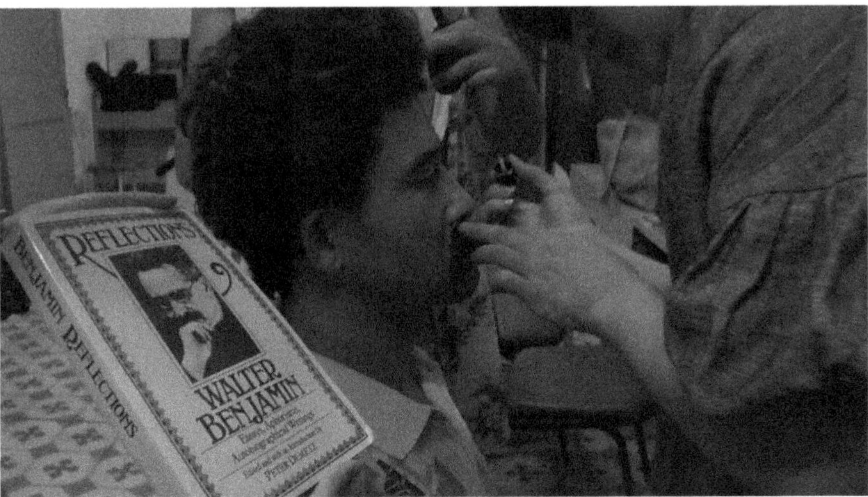

2.7 Patty Chang, *The Product Love (Die Ware Liebe)*, 2009, still from video installation, Hu Huaizhong being made up to look like Walter Benjamin

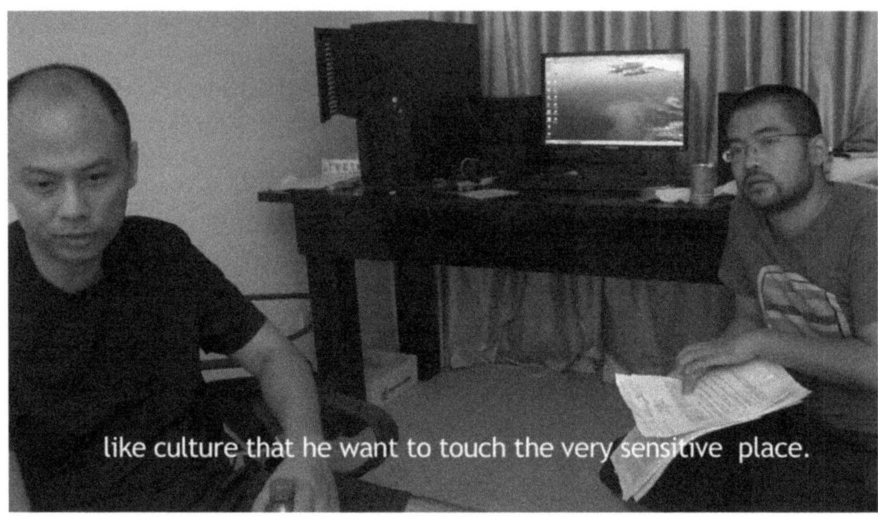

2.8 Patty Chang, *The Product Love (Die Ware Liebe)*, 2009, still from video installation, producer Jin Yu and director Gu Bo

Producer Jin Yu and director Gu Bo interpreted the sex scene in nationalistic terms. They directed the Benjamin character to 'treat the body of May Wong like he would treat or touch eastern culture. To find the *G point or G spot of culture* (see figure 2.8).'[76] The actors go through the motions of lovemaking, which the audience views through the lens of the director, staging every move in the pretense of the sexual act. Instead of eliciting sexual excitement, the characters appear to be out of their comfort zone as much as the translators were in translating Benjamin's text. The viewers are also made to feel awkward watching the staged sex act 'in the making' as we are compeled to recognize the fantasy but not to believe that it is real. And yet, the very function of pornography is to awaken desire in the body of the viewer. Chang's overt stage-directing of the video's pornographic set-up emphasizes Benjamin's description of the process of the actor who experiences a 'vague sense of discomfort he feels inexplicable emptiness: his body loses its corporeality, it evaporates, it is deprived of reality, life, voice, and the noises caused by his moving about.'[77] Benjamin refers to the 'live' context of the stage actor as compared to the difference in the film actor's 'mechanical contrivance.' The condition of Wong's exotica objectification shares affinity with what Benjamin describes as the film actor's ontological *exile* – 'not only from the stage but also from himself.'[78] As described by Chang, the 'bodies of the actors are uncomfortable, laboring manifestations of the ambivalence in the act of translation that could be a characteristic of the transnational.'[79] 'Trans'nationalism is therefore defined as a performance of translation in the reading of bodies as in the text. Comprehension is dependent on the meanings and significations of the cultural contexts that pertain to language. The awkward bodies become a metaphor for the difficulty in comprehending language due also to the mistranslations of the body from the historical cinematic text. Wong's 'role' during the 1920s and 1930s was prescribed by her Asian exotica character, functioning to titillate for the pleasure of the white male viewer. The thwarting of desire under Chang's manipulation through video is a 'trans' method of subverting the historical narrative, challenging the 'moral' conventions for miscegenation in history. In the reality of immigration, the impact of the mistranslation of the Chinese female body was confirmed by the legislation of American exclusion acts, specifically against Chinese women during the greater part of the twentieth century.

Sex as nation in the cinema – heteronormative citizenship

As mentioned earlier, among the majority of Anna May Wong's roles in American and European films, her cinematic character always served as the exotic and unobtainable object of desire who titillates and seduces the viewer with the dangerous potential for miscegenation. During the period when Chinese women were denied entry to Europe, as well as the United States, racial and sexual mixing was so improper that Wong's first onscreen kiss with a white male actor in Eichberg's *The Flame of Love* (1930) was a major topic of controversy in Britain.[80] The film was also titled *The Road to Dishonor*, and according to Anthony Chan, the newspapers 'raged for days' over the kiss: 'Since miscegenation was frowned upon in the British empire, especially in the colonies where the superiority of the white race was always proclaimed, the embrace and kiss between an Englishman and an Asian woman were sacrilegious even in a film set in Russia. The penalty for such a transgression could only result in the death of the woman.'[81] But Chang's focus is not so much on Wong's character as it was on re-translating the body of Benjamin as she casts him in what would have been the miscegenation scene. The real German-Jewish body of Benjamin paired with Wong's Chinese body would have been completely unacceptable on the cinematic screen in their 1930s moment. The rewriting of the film fantasy through the Chinese body of Hu Huaizhong causes a rupture to the historical film template of illicit desire between white male and Asian female characters.

Inevitably, interracial titillation resulted in the death of Wong's character, which was the storyline in almost all of her films. For instance, the character Hai-tang in *Flame of Love* is a member of a dance troupe traveling through imperial Russia, and in all three transnational versions of the same film, titled in English *The Flame of Love*, in German *Der Weg zur Schande*, and in French

L'amour maitre des choses, she falls in love with a Russian officer, whose rival the Grand Duke, eventually tries to seduce her. In the end, Hai-tang takes the fall for her brother (her father in the French version) and commits suicide rather than let him face the firing squad for coming to her defense.[82] Through this formulaic narrative, the forthcoming liaison was always resolved by the death of Wong's character. In many other roles such as Lotus Flower in *The Toll of the Sea* (1922) and Song in *Wasted Love* (1928), Wong's onscreen death would exhibit the penalty for illicit bi-racial affairs.

The degree of censure for narratives of illicit desire differed among viewers in European nations. The German review of the British version of *Flame of Love* for *Film-Kurier* acknowledges Eichberg's grasp of the prudish, censorious 'English mentality: eroticism without sex appeal, exoticism without miscegenation; instead, tender melodies are played on the piano in a homely setting. Hai-Tang's lover is her brotherly friend, he watches her dancing, alluringly undresses, but apart from that – nothing happens between them. This is truly English.'[83] Chan argues that in British cinema, the colonialist logic for an 'empire full of yellow, brown, and black people' was based on the 'exalted notion of its own [white] racial superiority' – if whites cohabitated with the colonized, the relations of power would shift and 'a consensual romantic liaison would imply equality.'[84] On the other hand, German critics in the 1920s were calling for realism in film and Chan suggests the motivation was for 'genuine physical interaction between yellow women and white men to be played in human ways.' Chan argues that the German contempt for modesty in English film was produced from a focus on 'emasculated love relationships' in British cinema that revealed 'more of their own arrogance than an understanding of the British.'[85]

Laws that were enforced in the United States prohibiting interracial marriage were the same kind of prohibitions eventually enacted in nationalist Germany. The state-legislated marriage provisions that applied to Chinese Americans proliferated in the early part of the twentieth century, and according to legal scholar Gabriel Chin, they 'more than doubled between 1910 and 1950.'[86] The prohibition began, however, in the nineteenth century when Chinese male laborers arrived to work in the United States. The notion that the 'amalgamation' of the Chinese 'with our people … would be the lowest, most vile and degraded of our race' was a legislative theme for politicians, as noted by a delegate of the 1878 California constitutional convention.[87] The 1882 Chinese Exclusion Act is considered the first national immigration law, and the preceding 1875 Page Law (named after the California congressman Horace F. Page) instantiated the provision banning immigration of female Chinese prostitutes. However, the law was widely understood to be a ban against single Chinese women in the effort to discourage the 'Yellow Peril' of unwanted Chinese settlements in the United States. The intention was to hire cheap male laborers, who would return to China instead of immigrating to the United States, which was the basic rule for all US immigrants of the labor class.[88] The Page Law was essentially a propagandist campaign that informed the stereotype of Chinese women, who were considered as passive but immoral concubines. The titillating miscegenation subject in film would enhance this campaign against the immigration of Chinese women.

Rancière explains that 'the citizen who acts as a member of the collective' demonstrates how the 'essence of theatre is the essence of the community,' since theatre is built upon long-held notions of the 'Platonic assignment of bodies to their proper – that is, to their "communal" – place.'[89] In the context of nationality, citizenship is a theatrical simulation of a birthright determined by the heterosexual kinship order, one in which, to be alien is to be outside of the nationalist norm. The logic of nationalism is distinguished by the understanding that citizenship originates from being born in one's homeland, and as Gayatri Chakravorty Spivak suggests, to 'naturalize' is to adopt a nation by proving a 'private conviction of special birth.'[90] To accomplish the 'special birth' of citizenship, the immigrant to the United States must perform in the communal theatre of the naturalization ceremony, through which the host nation officially 'adopts' the immigrant. Spivak argues that the very definition of nationalism is predicated on reproductive heteronormativity.[91] She goes on to explain that citizenship is premised on the belief in an abstracted maternity, in which, to 'legalize a simulacrum of displaced birth … becomes an actual birthright for the next generation.'[92] The granting of naturalization papers is a replication of the birth certificate, representing the legal documentation of the namesake's new 'nationality' for generations to come. And under the 'norm' of nationalism, marriage within ethnic nationality on behalf of clan purity has been the historical ideal for most cultures – Claude Levi Strauss developed his structuralist theory through those kinship rules. The period of exclusion acts in US immigration (1910 to 1950) was one in which Wong's portrayals in film serves as a record of the cinematic consequence of going outside of exogamous marriage. In this way, cinema becomes an archive of the 'moral' parameters of heteronormative desire.[93]

Alienation effect and the mistranslation of gendering

The mainstream narratives of film are informed by the politics of citizenship because both are contingent on the acceptance of a fantasy. In Chang's re-translation of the cinematic text, the two Asian bodies representing the Benjamin and Wong characters are no longer a threat to the original immigration marriage laws. The historical norm of legislated desire was kept intact, but it is within this imaginary context that the meaning of Chang's video is representative of the historical drama in association with long-held illusions required for citizenship in the theatre of immigration. During Brecht's moment of Marxist criticism, he saw great potential in an expositive 'live' theatre, which can examine all the events of life: 'Everything must be seen from the social standpoint … a new theatre will find the alienation effect necessary for the criticism of society and for historical reporting on changes already accomplished.'[94] Brecht contributed an important methodology for translating social positions and relations of power according to the roles that people play in capitalist society. Related to contemporary performance art, Amelia Jones explains how 'body art does not strive toward a utopian redemption but, rather, places the body/self within the realm of the aesthetic *as a political domain*,' which shares affinity with Brecht's objectives for theatre.[95]

As effective as Brecht's *Verfremdungseffekt* has historically been in performance practice, it is important to discuss the argument made by theorist Wu Zuguang, who asserts that the alienation effect derives from a *mistranslation* of the motivations of Chinese theatre. Wu argues that 'Stanislavsky believed in the "fourth wall," Brecht wanted to demolish it, while for Mei Lanfang such a wall didn't exist, since the Chinese theatre has always been so highly conventionalized.'[96] Considered as the innovator of Peking Opera, Lanfang is perhaps the most famous transnational actor of the 1920s and 1930s – known around the world, he received honorary degrees from Pomona College and the University of Southern California for his work.[97] But against the idea that his was a new contribution to Chinese opera, Lanfang was descended from four generations of male actors using the female name 'Mei' as their stage name, having first cross-dressed for the stage at the age of eleven.[98] The point was to create a 'realism' around the change of genders, unlike the costume change in *The Good Woman of Szechuan*. Brecht believes that the Chinese actor 'makes it clear that he knows he is being looked at.'[99] To him, the transparency of the actor's relationship to his character was the distinguishing element of Chinese opera, a tradition in which the actor is always the spectator of his own performance. But for the Chinese viewer of Peking Opera, Wu suggests the goal and expectation were nearly the opposite of Brecht's alienation. The artform had long relied on a traditional system of codes and gestures to express the meaning of the play, and viewers were encouraged to fall under the spell of the drama and buy into the illusion of title *dan* female characters who were exclusively played by male actors (see figures 2.9 and 2.10). Similar to the training of the Italian castrato, the opportunity for boy-actors was premised on the aesthetic protocol of precluding females from the art form.

The disjunction in Brecht's political use of his alienation effect was in advocating its ability to 'underline the historical nature of a given social condition'; meanwhile, the very historical conditions in China were overlooked in terms of the politics that perpetuated the taboo against female actors on the public stage.[100] Chinese opera denied female actors the right to play their

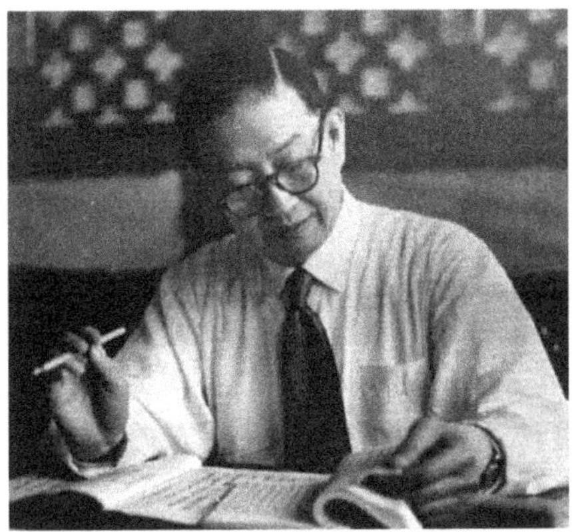

2.9 Mei Lanfang, 1950s photograph

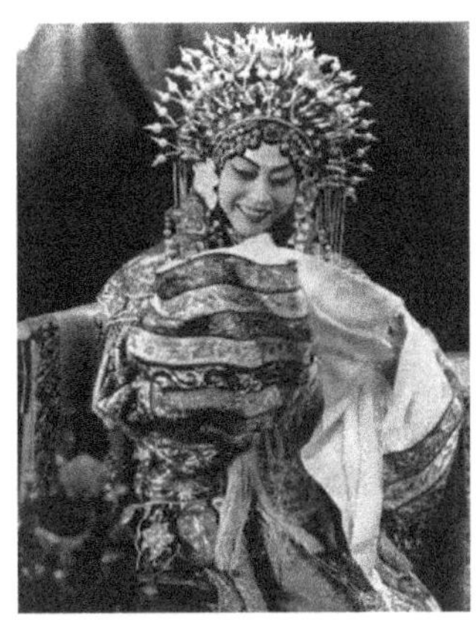

2.10 Mei Lanfang as Yang Yuhuan in *Drunken Beauty*, 1950s, Peking Opera

own female roles, in the same way that 'yellowface' denied Chinese actors the opportunity to play Chinese roles in film. China in the 1930s was in the middle of the radical movement called *xin nuxing* (new woman), in which women's roles in opera were finally being played by female actors. Carol Martin sums up the 'trans'nationalist differences:

> For feminist theatre in the US, cross-gender casting has been a major means of exposing the conventions of gender. For the Chinese *xin nuxing* movement, cross-gender casting was the major means of excluding women from the stage. Women playing women was the radical new means of putting the physical signs of the actor and the performer's body in historical context.[101]

The asymmetries of theoretical Brecht are nothing more than its development in the 'globalized framework of encounter and exchange' under Inderpal Grewal and Caren Kaplan's argument that today's power relations 'are connected to inequalities that result from earlier forms of globalization.'[102] Acts of mis-interpretation, such as Brecht's use of gender roles, contribute nonetheless to the current model of a fluid nationality. The 'trans' for theorizing transnational studies of sexuality takes into account the circulation of identities no differently than the flow of goods and people in global capitalism.

In her rewriting of the 1930s *Chinoiserie* filmscript, Chang questions the fluidity of cult manifestations that are always bound to the fantasy of nationality. As a spectator of Anna May Wong, Benjamin obviously plays with the spectacle of Oriental desire. He had explained clearly the way in which 'film responds to the shrivelling of the aura with an artificial build-up of the 'personality' outside the studio. The cult of the movie star, fostered by the money of the film industry, preserves not the unique aura of the person but the 'spell of the personality,' the phony spell of a commodity.'[103] Here, the title *Die Ware Liebe*, 'the commodity love,' serves as an ironic example, and Anna May Wong appears as the object of Benjamin's fake aura. Wong's Hollywood persona and her true 'self' were generally indistinguishable from the industry's creation of the exotic female Asian stereotype. But Chang's film turns the focus onto the object of Benjamin himself, as he is the title character in her version of *Die Ware Liebe*. Whether the viewer could even find plausible the sexual fantasy of Wong and Benjamin becomes a 'testing' of the cult value of the film actor: could the viewer actually fall under the spell of the Chinese actor in the role of the Benjamin 'character-type'? In the case of audiences in New York and Berlin, where Chang first presented *Die Ware Liebe*, and in the few times that I've presented this work for an academic audience, the Benjamin character has often caused a nervous reaction – usually, the audience cannot 'believe' in his persona in the sex scene, since the pornographic context can be viewed as a slight to the philosopher king. Benjamin is lionized as the author of the holy grail of the 'work of art in the age of mechanical reproduction.' Chang also noted that when she first exhibited the video installation at the Mary Boone gallery, her work was criticized for being too 'didactic.' Amidst the denial of the libidinal economy of intellectual practices, the alienation effect functions to acknowledge one's own desire in the act of interpretation. It is precisely the erotic narrative in Chang's conceptual defamiliarization that is meant to imagine something entirely different in contrast to the intellectual aura of the great literary critic who changed the contemporary understanding of mechanical reproduction. Through Chang's cinematic imaginary, the bodily intertwining of the eminent film theorist and the ultimate film fetish functions as an embodied metaphor for the trans-libidinal co-mingling of separate histories, philosophies, and *nationalities*. Thus, in viewing the historical object of Benjamin, *Die Ware Liebe* raises the very condition from which his writing about Wong is 'translated,' the condition of desire based on the different priorities within cult intellectual interests.

Alienation effect of yellowface and nationalism

As this study of *Die Ware Liebe* has sought to bring to light, the cinematic apparatus has had profound effects throughout history, since the audience identifies with the camera, as Benjamin theorized, not the 'real' person/actor of the film. In the 1930s, 'yellowface' characterizations by white actors would enable the audience to accept the narrative portraits of the Chinese. By casting Benjamin in Hu's cinematic Chinese body, Chang reverses the order in which white actors were cast in Chinese roles such as Luise Rainer and Paul Muni in the leading parts for Pearl S. Buck's *The Good Earth* (1931). Anna May Wong understood clearly that the good roles depicting Chinese characters were reserved for *white* actors. Much like Brechtian distanciation, the viewers of yellowface do not fully 'believe' that Rainer and Muni are actually Chinese, but they can safely fall in love along with the characters who are, in truth, white people. As exemplified by Anna May Wong, the eroticized female character in the Chinese body follows a different viewing convention. Chan describes the logic of the narrative as 'the European American male writers' fantasy of Asian women lusting after European American men.'[104] The very crux of Orientalism in the yellowface form of power is through the appropriation of the Chinese body and its subjugation through invented narrative.

Films were also being made in Shanghai during the 1930s, and women actors such as Hu Die and Ruan Lingyu were the cinematic counterparts to Anna May Wong. At the time, the Guomingdang nationalist party was the ruling party of China during the period before the civil war with the Communist party and at the onset of Japanese military aggression in 1932.[105] During the same year, Josef von Sternberg's *Shanghai Express* had just opened and Paramount brought the film to Shanghai. Wong was cast in perhaps her most famous role, along with Marlene Dietrich and Warner Oland, in the film whereby she played the prostitute Hui Fei, another of her type-cast immoral women, in a story set in the realpolitics of Shanghai. China's last dynasty had fallen and Japan had taken over Manchuria; meanwhile, the stage was being set for the political scene of Chinese Communism. *Shanghai Express*'s sophisticated plot involved opportunistic men and women, out to experience adventurous desire in the cosmopolitanism of modern Shanghai. The train becomes a liminal 'trans'nationalist space to contain the characters in the setting of a journey.

In 1936, Wong had traveled to China to see if she could move back to her ancestral home, since her father and most of her family had moved back to Guangdong province.[106] During her visit to Shanghai, she met with her friend Mei Lanfang from the Peking Opera and visited the national film board in Nanking.[107] By then, *Shanghai Express* had been banned by the Guomindang because its subjects of licentious behaviours and prostitution were an embarrassment to China. Paramount disregarded the ban and ignored the censors' demands in Shanghai. Chan recounts the way in which Wong, while attending a banquet hosted by the Guomindang, received the brunt of the criticisms for her portrayal of prostitutes and dubious women in American films.[108] The idea that Anna May Wong was no different than the character she portrayed brought reprimands from the Chinese officials, and later from the newspapers and magazines circulating in China. She was thought to have represented China in a shameful way. On the other hand, Warner Oland, who was well known in China for his yellowface portrayal of Charlie Chan, was lauded as a great actor because it was so obvious that he was not the character he represented. In *Shanghai Express*, his character Henry Chang was a warlord who raped Hui Fei

(Wong's character). She was, of course, killed off in the end, this time apparently for her illicit lesbian desire toward the Marlene Dietrich character.

In China, the mistranslated cinematic persona placed the Chinese American female body into the convenient submissive role for representing patriarchal nationalist power. Spivak asserts that for a descriptive heteronormativity, 'woman is the most primitive instrument of nationalism.'[109] Amidst the different histories of feminist resistances, Chang raises the spectre of Wong in a way that confounds the master narratives of film by focusing on the linguistic punctum, the 'touch,' in order to show that cinematic nationalism was always a visual process for evoking the sensual. As an additional film loop in the installation, titled *Laotze Missing* (2009), Chang includes a 3-minute clip of the 1928 silent film *Schmutziges Geld* (1928, also called *Show Life*) (see figure 2.11). In one act of the movie, Wong plays the role of the target for a knife thrower. As each frame flickers on the screen, the viewer eventually sees Wong's bodily outline showing that she is not there when the knife thrower misses and hits the spot where her body would have been. In this one scene, Wong glances knowingly at the viewer to suggest that this time, she had escaped the inevitability of her cinematic death.

Cinematic performances, embodiments, and transnational video

As explored in this chapter, Chang's return to the films of the early twentieth century are conceived as re-interpretations of Sven Hedin and Paul Lieberenz's

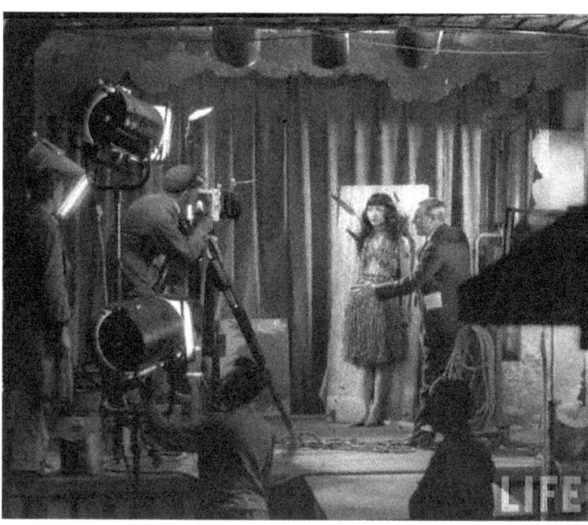

2.11 Anna May Wong, *Schmutziges Geld* (*Dirty Money*, also called *Show Life* in the UK), 1928, Richard Eichberg, Berlin

visual anthropology, of James Hilton and Frank Capra's Shangri-La movie utopia, and of Walter Benjamin's Asian exoticism based on Anna May Wong's film persona. The 'trans'nationalism of Chang's vision is transformative and transgressive, breaking from the stereotypes and exoticas prescribed for a Chineseness that was depicted by Hedin's occupying gaze, by Capra's mystic Orientalism, and by Eichberg's miscegenation scene. Chang's actions, live and in person, as the Chinese American traveling in Xinjiang, in Zhongdian, in Beijing and Shanghai performs the mondialization of Chineseness as the embodied acknowledgment of the global present. Through the video installation form, Chang is able to re-envision the filmic past of both Euro and ethno-centered fantasies of Chineseness to show how they continue to haunt the current geographical consciousness. Through the capacity of video, attributed largely to both the conceptual and documentary distinctions of the art form, Chang's work is completely different from the cinematic norm of made-up characters and narratives. The visual remembrances of historical actors located in fictional places had somehow become the 'real' cultural territories, as evidenced by Xianggelila's realization of Shangri-La. Chang's focus on Hedin as the actor of history who 'discovered' the Lop Nor reveals the way in which film's documentary record-keeping is inextricable from the cinematic fantasy of a place. And perhaps most significantly, Chang's construction of *Die Ware Liebe*'s transnational stage-sets rewrites the entire narrative for the libidinal economy of Chineseness by envisioning a Chinese body for Walter Benjamin. Such an act appears entirely irreverent for the Benjaminian subject of philosophy, an almost sacred realm inhabited by the author of 'The Work of Art in the Age of Mechanical Reproduction.' But ultimately, Chang's use of 'bodily knowledge' for her cinematic fantasies – as she assumes the roles of the explorer of Loulan, the bride of *Shangri-La*, and the producer of *Die Ware Liebe* – is expressed through a feminist staging of her own body as both the subject and object of the film's gaze. She elicits what Pierre Bourdieu describes as the 'imprescriptible right to truth-telling that every creator claims by definition for herself, especially when the object is none other than herself, in her singularity as an irreplaceable being.'[110] The ontological assertions of the border-crossing artist empower Chang's performances through the irreplaceable beingness of both her authorial perspective and her embodied 'self' in video. In this way, Chang rewrites the historical narrative and the 'real' of her embodied acts as they collide with the purported 'real' of the documentary record to create something entirely new and powerful through her video performances.

Notes

1 Ken Johnson, 'Art in Review,' *New York Times* (23 November 2001), E.37.
2 Claire Bishop, 'Digital Divide,' *Artforum* (September 2012), 436.

3 Sven Hedin, *The Wandering Lake: Into the Heart of Asia* (London: Tauris, 2009); Paul Lieberenz and Rudolf Biebrach, directors, *Mit Sven Hedin durch Asiens Wüsten (With Sven Hedin Across the Deserts of Asia)* (Sweden: Svensk Filmindustri (SF), 1928).

4 See Åshild Kolås, *Tourism and Tibetan Culture in Transition: A Place Called Shangrila* (New York and London: Routledge, 2007).

5 Gayatri Chakravorty Spivak, 'Nationalism and the Imagination,' *Lectora*, vol. 15 (2009), 80.

6 Shu-mei Shih, *Visuality and Identity: Sinophone Articulations Across the Pacific* (Berkeley: University of California Press, 2007).

7 Sheldon Hsiao-peng Lu, *Transnational Chinese Cinemas* (Honolulu: University of Hawai'I Press, 1997), 3.

8 Aihwa Ong, *Flexible Citizenship: The Cultural Logics of Transnationality* (Durham, NC: Duke University Press, 1999), 4.

9 Inderpal Grewal and Caren Kaplan, 'Global Identities: Theorizing Transnational Studies of Sexuality,' *GLQ: A Journal of Lesbian and Gay Studies*, vol. 7, no. 4 (2001), 664.

10 See exhibition guide, *Patty Chang: The Wandering Lake, 2009–2017.*

11 Patty Chang, *The Wandering Lake* (New York: Queens Museum and Dancing Foxes Press, 2017), 46.

12 Sima Qian, *Records of the Grand Historian: Han Dynasty II*, tr. Burton Watson (New York: Columbia University Press, 1993), 233. See also, Dunfu Wu, ed. (吴敦夫f), *Footprints of Foreign Explorers on the Silk Road* (丝绸之路上的外国探险家的足迹英) (Beijing: China Intercontinental Press, 2007).

13 See Jianping Zhang, Houyuan Lu, Naiqin Wu, Xiaoguang Qin, and Luo Wang, 'Palaeoenvironment and Agriculture of Ancient Loulan and Milan on the Silk Road,' *The Holocene*, vol. 23, no. 2 (2012).

14 Chang, *The Wandering Lake*, 38

15 Hedin as quoted in Sarah K. Danielsson, *The Explorer's Roadmap to National-Socialism: Sven Hedin, Geography and the Path to Genocide* (London: Routledge, 2016), 116.

16 Chang, *The Wandering Lake*, 48.

17 Ibid.

18 Ibid.

19 Chunxiang Li, Hongjie Li, Yinqiu Cui, Chengzhi Xie, Dawei Cai, Wenying Li, Victor H. Mair, Zhi Xu, Quanchao Zhang, Idelisi Abuduresule, Li Jin, Hong Zhu, and Hui Zhou, 'Evidence that a West-East Admixed Population Lived in the Tarim Basin as Early as the Early Bronze Age,' *BMC Biology*, vol. 8, no. 15 (February 2010), doi:10.1186/1741-7007-8-15.

20 See Edward Wong, 'The Dead Tell a Tale China Doesn't Care to Listen To,' *New York Times* (18 November 2008), A6. See also Wang Binghua, *Xinjiang gu shi: gu dai Xinjiang ju min ji qi wen hua, The Ancient Corpses of Xinjiang: The Peoples of Ancient Xinjiang and their Culture* (新疆人民出版社, Wulumuqi-shi: Xinjiang ren min chu ban she, 2001).

21 See Eleanor Ross, 'What's the History behind China's Current Obsession with

Xinjiang?' *Newsweek* (10 March 2017), www.newsweek.com/protest-xinjiang-china-muslim-central-asia-terrorism-559161 (accessed 15 August 2017).
22 Chang, *The Wandering Lake*, 51.
23 Ibid.
24 Patricia Ebrey, 'Surnames and Han Chinese Identity,' in Melissa Brown, ed., *Negotiating Ethnicities in China and Taiwan* (Berkeley: University of California Press, 1996).
25 Kolås, *Tourism and Tibetan Culture in Transition*, 1.
26 Ibid.
27 Emily T. Yeh and Christopher R. Coggins, *Mapping Shangrila: Contested Landscapes in the Sino-Tibetan Borderlands* (Seattle: University of Washington Press, 2014), 3.
28 Ibid., 4.
29 Kolås, *Tourism and Tibetan Culture in Transition*, 38.
30 Russell Ferguson, 'Paradise on Earth,' in *Patty Chang, Shangri-La* (Los Angeles: Hammer Museum, 2005), 18.
31 Gilles Deleuze, *Difference and Repetition*, tr. Paul Patton (London and New York: Continuum, 1994), 3.
32 See *Lost Horizon* (1937), notes, Turner Classic Movies, www.tcm.com/tcmdb/title/3770/Lost-Horizon/notes.html (accessed 3 January 2018).
33 Patty Chang, 'Notes from Shangri-La,' in Ferguson, ed., *Patty Chang, Shangri-La*, 44.
34 Ibid.
35 Rosalind Krauss, 'Sculpture in the Expanded Field,' *October*, vol. 8 (spring 1979), 37.
36 Ibid., 36.
37 Chang, 'Notes from Shangri-La,' 44.
38 Ibid., 37.
39 Ibid., 35.
40 See Edward Wong, 'Rights Groups Ask China to Free Tibetan Education Advocate,' *New York Times* (18 January 2017), www.nytimes.com/2017/01/18/world/asia/china-tibetan-education-advocate.html?_r=0 (accessed 3 January 2018).
41 Chang, 'Notes from Shangri-La,' 42.
42 Ibid.
43 Kerry Abrams, 'Polygamy, Prostitution, and the Federalization of Immigration Law,' *Columbia Law Review*, vol. 105, no. 3 (April 2005), 643.
44 Ibid., 641.
45 Jacques Rancière, 'The Emancipated Spectator,' *Artforum* (March 2007), 278.
46 Walter Benjamin, 'Gespräch mit Anne May Wong,' *Die literarische Welt*, no. 27 (July 1928).
47 Walter Benjamin, 'The Task of the Translator,' in Marcus Bullock and Michael W. Jennings, eds, *Selected Writings, Volume 1, 1913–1926* (Cambridge, MA: Harvard University Press, 1996), 254.
48 As quoted in Graham Russell Gao Hodges, *Anna May Wong: From Laundryman's*

Daughter to Hollywood Legend (New York: Palgrave Macmillan, 2004), 77–8.

49 I am indebted to Patty Chang and the Margaret Herrick Library in Los Angeles for the primary resources.

50 Walter Benjamin, 'The Work of Art in the Age of Mechanical Reproduction,' in *Illuminations* (London: Pimlico, 1999), 222.

51 Ibid.

52 Walter Benjamin, *Understanding Brecht*, tr. Anna Bostock (London: Verso, 1998), 99.

53 Rey Chow, *Entanglements, or Transmedial Thinking about Capture* (Durham, NC: Duke University Press, 2012), 2.

54 Ibid., 28.

55 From Bertolt Brecht, *Diaries 1920–1922*, reprinted in Jacques Rancière, *The Politics of Literature* (Cambridge: Polity, 2011), 99.

56 Nikos Papastergiadis, 'A Breathing Space for Aesthetics and Politics: An Introduction to Jacques Rancière,' *Theory, Culture & Society*, vol. 3, no. 7/8 (2014), 5.

57 Ibid., 6.

58 Jacques Rancière, 'The Emancipated Spectator,' 280

59 See Alisa Solomon, *Re-Dressing the Canon: Essays on Theater and Gender* (London: Routledge, 1997), 74.

60 Ibid.

61 Hodges, *Anna May Wong*, 77.

62 See Shirley Jennifer Lim, '"Speaking German Like Nobody's Business": Anna May Wong, Walter Benjamin, and the Possibilities of Asian American Cosmopolitanism,' *Journal of Transnational American Studies*, vol. 4, no. 3 (2012), 3. Lim suggests the passage reveals Benjamin's desire for reconciling identity: 'An eloquent man of letters, Benjamin is stymied by the paradox of Wong's cosmopolitan Western modernity and racialized Chinese body. Although he invokes the national to describe the racial, he wants to merge her Chinese and Western identities. In fact, the subtitle of this essay, "A Chinoiserie from the Old West," indicates his fascination with her complicated and contradictory star image' (p. 7).

63 Celine Parreñas Shimizu, *The Hypersexuality of Race: Performing Asian/American Women on Screen and Scene* (Durham, NC: Duke University Press, 2007), 67.

64 Lim, '"Speaking German Like Nobody's Business,"' 6.

65 Howard Eiland and Michael W. Jennings, *Walter Benjamin: A Critical Life* (Cambridge, MA: Belknap Press, Harvard University Press, 2014), 640.

66 Quoted in Lim, '"Speaking German Like Nobody's Business,"' 5.

67 Ibid.

68 Bertolt Brecht, *The Good Person of Szechwan*, tr. John Willett (London: Bloomsbury, 1985), v.

69 Ibid., vi.

70 Ibid., v.

71 Solomon, *Re-Dressing the Canon*, 79. Emphasis in original.

72 Judith Butler, Ernesto Laclau, and Slavoj Žižek, *Contingency, Hegemony, Universality: Contemporary Dialogues on the Left* (London and New York: Verso, 2000), 29.

73 See Tatsuji Iwabuchi, 'Brecht Reception in Japan, The Perspective of Theatrical Practice,' in Antony Tatlow and Tak-Wai Wong, eds, *Brecht and East Asian Theatre* (Hong Kong: Hong Kong University Press, 1982), 115.

74 Brecht, *The Good Person of Szechwan*, vi.

75 As noted by Chang to the author.

76 Transcribed from the *Die Ware Liebe* video.

77 Ibid., 223. Benjamin cites Luigi Pirandello, *Si Gira*, quoted by Leon Pierre-Quint, 'Signification du cinema,' *L'Art cinematographique*, 14–15.

78 Ibid.

79 As noted by Chang to the author.

80 Anthony B. Chan, *Perpetually Cool: The Many Lives of Anna May Wong (1905–1961)* (Lanham: Scarecrow Press, 2007), 50–1.

81 Ibid., 51.

82 Ibid.

83 Ibid., 52.

84 Ibid., 53.

85 Ibid.

86 Gabriel Chin, 'Preserving Racial Identity: Population Patterns and the Application of Anti-Miscegenation Statutes to Asian Americans, 1910–1950,' *Journal of Asian Law* (May 2002), 1.

87 Ibid., 2.

88 George Anthony Peffer, 'Forbidden Families: Emigration Experiences of Chinese Women Under the Page Law, 1875–1882,' *Journal of American Ethnic History*, vol. 6, no. 1 (fall 1986) and Ben Railton, *The Chinese Exclusion Act* (New York: Palgrave Macmillan, 2013), 25.

89 Rancière, 'The Emancipated Spectator,' 278.

90 Spivak, 'Nationalism and the Imagination,' 75, 80.

91 Ibid.

92 Ibid.

93 See Jane Chin Davidson, 'Displacements of the Desiring Machine,' *Interventions: International Journal of Postcolonial Studies*, vol. 14, no. 3 (2012), 381. The nineteenth-century manifestations of 'race' and queer in the historically 'white' entertainment sphere illustrated an 'abnormal' sexuality to the public that potentially 'freed the viewer from the pressing rigours of judging normal sexuality as well as normal "race" during the period when biopower became the force of the normalizing state.'

94 Bertolt Brecht, 'On Chinese Acting,' *The Tulane Drama Review*, vol. 6, no. 1 (September 1961), 136.

95 Amelia Jones, *Body Art/Performing the Subject* (Minneapolis: University of Minnesota Press, 1998), 13.

96 Wu Zuguang, Huang Zuolin, and Mei Shaowu, *Peking Opera and Mei Lanfang* (Beijing: New World Press, 1981), 19. See also, Chou Hui-ling, 'Striking Their

Own Poses: The History of Cross-Dressing on the Chinese Stage,' *TDR (1988–)*, vol. 41, no. 2 (summer 1997).

97 Zuguang, Zuolin and Shaowu, *Peking Opera and Mei Lanfang*, 52. Wu Zuguang suggests that he was both a successor and a pioneer of Chinese opera.

98 Ibid., 8, 30.

99 Brecht, 'On Chinese Acting,' 130.

100 Ibid., 136.

101 Carol Martin, 'Brecht, Feminism, and Chinese Theatre,' *TDR (1988–)*, vol. 43, no. 4 (winter 1999), 83.

102 Inderpal Grewal and Caren Kaplan, 'Global Identities: Theorizing Transnational Studies of Sexuality,' *GLQ: A Journal of Lesbian and Gay Studies*, vol. 7, no. 4 (2001), 663.

103 Benjamin, 'The Work of Art in the Age of Mechanical Reproduction,' 224.

104 Chan, *Perpetually Cool*, 169.

105 Hodges, *Anna May Wong*, 144.

106 Ibid., 150.

107 Ibid., 148.

108 Chan, *Perpetually Cool*, 117.

109 Spivak, 'Nationalism and the Imagination,' 75.

110 Pierre Bourdieu, *Pascalian Meditations* (Cambridge: Polity Press, 2000), 128.

3

Environment, labor, and video: (eco)feminist interpellations of Chineseness in the work of Yuk King Tan, Cao Fei, and Wu Mali

Yuk King Tan's video *Limits of Visibility* (2012) transports the viewer to the bay of Hong Kong and the cargo area where a tonnage of paper (the perpetual waste, even in the digital age) is compacted into modular cubes, stacked and waiting to be craned onto long barges. Tan asserts that the 'material is prepared to become another kind of vast colony [see plate 11]. Sent to less developed countries [to be] further broken down and salvaged, the waste material is a literal paper trail about the scale, power and wastage of economic development and trade.'[1] The need to understand the most basic human responsibility in the global cycle of mass consumption provokes a rudimentary return to the foundation of historical Marx. Jean-Luc Nancy explains this position with simplicity: 'Human life becomes dependent upon products when it is thought of as production, and away from the unproductive, or a life in tune with the cosmos, with existence.'[2] Refuse, garbage, becomes the unproductive end in the cycle of reproduction, unless there is recycling, and then it becomes another industry that often supports the present-day gleaners of bottles, cans, and cardboard and the precarious labor of the poorest in society. Tan's 8-minute, single-channeled video, documenting the workday processes at the Chai Wan recycling depot, implicates the viewer in the overwhelming enormity of what humans throw away. The advantage of this form of representation is the way in which conceptual video effectively interpellates viewers, causing them to identify as fellow human wasters, and to reflect upon what it might mean to live 'a life in tune with the cosmos.' The seventh-century Buddhist monk Fazang once compared the principles of the cosmos to the physical form that material takes in a lesson on dharma that he prepared for Empress Wu.[3] To make his point, he used the example of the statue of a golden lion to show how neither the lion nor the gold it was made from could exist outside of each other since human consciousness was the essential component for creating the physical manifestation. The teaching continues to be important for thinking about the laws of nature and material forms, especially in the context of the *value* of things in material life in the advent of the Anthropocene era – or, more precisely, the era of the Capitolocene, distinguished by an understanding that not all humans are part of the industrial humanity of the Anthropocene.

This chapter explores the use of the video-graphic form by focusing on the work of three women artists – Yuk King Tan, Cao Fei, and Wu Mali – whose focus on environmental and labor issues in the last decade or so have contributed to a dialectical materialism for the current conditions of global capitalism. The cycle of economic boom characterized by the 'made in China' trope in the twenty-first century, emerging successively after the 'made in Taiwan' label of the twentieth-century, has accelerated the conditions of environmental crisis. Situated in the circuit of multi-national trade, moving rapidly since the 1990s, Tan, Cao, and Wu's subjects expose the ways in which environmental concerns are explicitly connected to the unabated growth of market economies in Hong Kong, China, and Taiwan. And by extension, they acknowledge how the exponential growth in industry has brought about an expansion of insecure forms of precarious labor, and perhaps more importantly, how labor in global capitalism has affected a gendered class of society. For example, Yuk King Tan's earlier 2008 video titled *Scavenger* focuses on the elderly class of women whose everyday life is to move cardboard on pushcarts across the city to the recycling plant. The fact that Hong Kong was hailed the world's most competitive economy in 2017 while air quality standards have remained legislatively the same for the past twenty-seven years reveals the persistence of the government's industrial priorities.[4] Cao Fei's 2013 video project titled *Haze and Fog* addresses the problem directly by locating her zombie characters in the apocalyptic environment of Beijing. 'Airpocalypse' has become the city's signature problem as air pollution toppled the US EPA scale at 755 in January 2013, well beyond the 500 maximum on the scale.[5] In 2017, the new efforts to clean up air pollution in China were hindered when anticipated seasonal winds did not arrive due to affected weather patterns caused by climate change and rising global temperatures.

The industrial competition over the worst smog in all three Chinese states is often measured by 'Red Alerts;' the warning was announced in January 2017 to constituents of greater Taipei.[6] Since 2006, Taiwanese artist Wu Mali has devoted her energies to performative, live, ecofeminist engagements through organizing 'community based eco-art' projects in Taiwan, such as cleaning up the dirty Plum Tree Creek. Wu is well known for her feminist video installations, such as the *Stories of Women from Hsin-Chuang* (1997) documenting the experiences of laborers in the textile factories, as an expression of which she 'wove their stories into a piece of cloth and fixed it to a wall,' creating a space integrated with the film projection.[7] The use of the video expression differs from cinematic film, and under the most optimistic terms, the installation as a form, according to Boris Groys, 'allows the artist to … take public responsibility, to begin to act in the name of a certain community or even of society as a whole.'[8] Through tracking her work from video to performance, the shift from Wu's subject of the community of women during Taiwan's economic boom to the subject of the community cleaning up the polluted aftermath is reviewed in this chapter. Wu established a legacy of feminist art representing an activism that began in the 1970s–1980s, with women's labor as an artistic endeavour, and continues with the interconnected feminist movement in environmental advocacy.

Most importantly, Tan, Cao, and Wu's representations of Hong Kong, China, and Taiwan provide a historical and philosophical context for the interpellated subject of Chineseness. As a political identity that developed with globalization, Chineseness is based on a variable, changing concept that coincided with the critical period of rapid economic change in China during the late 1980s and early 1990s. As discussed in Chapter One, the earlier meaning of the term denoted Orientalist representations of Chinese culture. But the conception of Chineseness as an expansive diasporic and creolized identity can be traced to the interpellated subject in the discourse of film studies. Just twenty years after China's Cultural Revolution, when Rey Chow acknowledged the impact of Wu Wenguang's retrospective film titled *1966 Wo de hongwebing shidai* (*1966: My Time in the Red Guards*), she argued that the 1990s viewer's response to the 'spectacle in collectivity in 1966 constituted the ethnic and nationalistic self-consciousness of "being Chinese" once again ... a proud, rather than shockingly shameful, experience.'[9] Discussed in her book, *Primitive Passions*, Chow had used Althusser's Marxist terminology to explain the contemporary context for viewers in China who were 'interpellated not simply as watchers of film but as film itself. They 'know' themselves not only as the subject, the audience, but as the object, the spectacle, the movie.'[10] This sort of cinematic subject is most often theorized as the analytical example for identity in the discourse of Chineseness.

As discussed in Chapter One, film engages in a linguistic, literary practice that has been a useful form of representation for an empowered subjectivity that distinguishes from Orientalist models of stereotyped Chinese identity.[11] But, as this chapter aims to emphasize and explore, cinema is different from the media of contemporary visual art practice, also from film installations and other moving photographic and digital forms, precisely because contemporary artists can express something as poignant and urgent as ecofeminist activism through the video form. While Chow's definition for the interpellation of film may still pertain to twenty-first-century video installations and online digital engagements, the specular expanse of conceptual and performative expressions has now transformed the viewer's relationship with artistic subjects in embodied ways. The portrayal of subjects in Cao Fei's 2013 film titled *Haze and Fog* (see figure 3.1), for instance, would enable viewers to fully 'know' themselves in the everyday life of the new, clean luxury environs of the

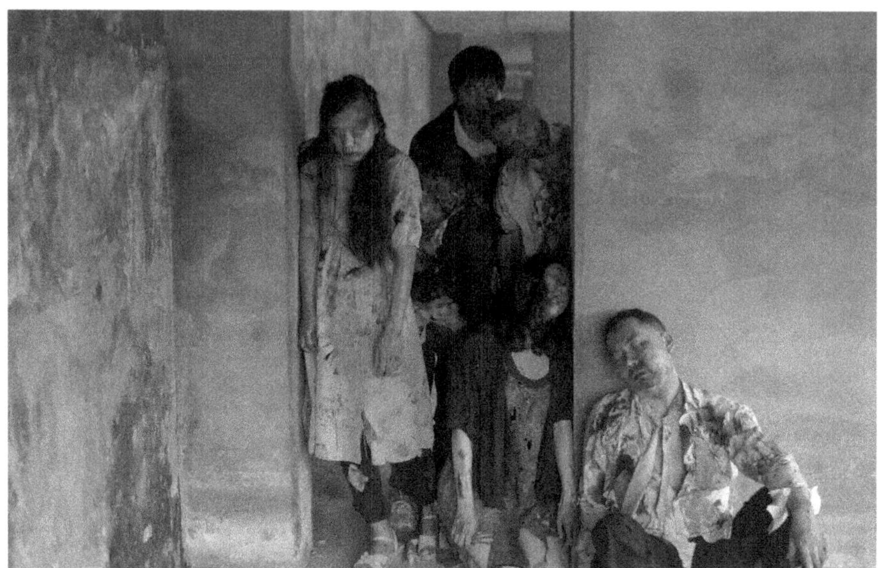

3.1 Cao Fei, *Haze and Fog*, 2013, still from 47-minute film

metropolitan estates through Cao's video capture of the rapid socio-economic transformation of China. Cao suggests that the settings for *Haze and Fog* were actually located in her own neighborhood in Beijing. But unlike Wu Wenguang's 1992 documentary, the characters in Cao's 40-minute single-channel video are zombies living in the 'airpocalypse' of haze and fog because the egalitarian element of pollution creates an entirely new class of society. The zombie represents the class of the 'dead' in the wake of global warming, having an impact on all living beings in the currency of dialectical material-ism. In a nod to Wu's documentary work, Cao actually casts him in the role of an old man struggling with his walker in *Haze and Fog*, acknowledging video art's ability to create a documentary record of people in the vanishing present of China as much as it can create a fantasy of characters and narratives.[12] The moment captured for Cao's imaginary society nonetheless depicts the new social-status system associated with the environmental conditions of Beijing.

Conceptual video's destabilized 'real' and unreal open-ended meanings, non-linear narratives, and unfixed modes of exchange correspond to the post-structuralist critiques of the subject that Althusser was considered to have initiated through the revelation of his 'apparatuses.' Mao's influence on Althusser has changed the understanding of its diverse and global contexts, and while Chow's use of his interpellations continues to be significant for film theory, the use of analyses by Michel Foucault and Judith Butler have chal-lenged the discrete wholeness of the subject even further.[13] But Cao's use of digital online media in her virtual conceptualism is even more distinct from the interpellation of cinema, in which works like her Second Life site, *RMB City* (2007–11) is where the apparatuses of the real world and the cyber world converge. In her depiction of utopia, Cao invokes the state-run institutions of her imagined community, emblematized by the city's name RMB (*renminbi*) City, which represents China's monetary system. The rapid transition to Deng Xiaoping's ideal 'to get rich is glorious' (*zhifu guangrong*) dramatically changed the cultural context in which the American Dream became the model for China's utopia of global capitalism. Films such as *Beijing Ni Zao* (*Good Morning, Beijing*) 1991, and *Nan Zhongguo* (*Southern China*) 1994, by the filmmaker Zhang Nuanxin, began to address the contradictions of capitalism in the 'China Dream,' while theorists such as Liu Kang acknowledged the irony of the artists' *renewed* challenge to capitalist modernity, suggesting that the 'historical connection between the 1960s' Cultural Revolution and the 1980s' Cultural Reflection should be kept in mind.'[14] Mao had transformed the ideals for the visual arts in his 1942 *Talks in Yanan*, and until the 1980s, his revolutionary form was circumscribed to the socialist realist model for expressing those 'real conditions of existence.'[15] The artistic movements begun with Mao were marxist movements against the inequalities of moneyed-class societies, which are paradoxically in agreement with the kind of critiques that Cao Fei and Zhang Nuanxin have expressed more recently.

Meanwhile, China's Cultural Revolution was the revolutionary model for the French Communist Party during the 1960s and 1970s, at a time when China was considered as the 'projection screen' for the group of Maoist intellectuals that included Maria-Antonietta Macciocchi, Julia Kristeva and other Tel Quel thinkers, not to mention Althusser's students Jacques Rancière and Alain Badiou.[16] The anti-bourgeois and anti-rightist campaigns in China would become the model for French intellectuals, which I argue had left an impact on the future of political philosophy in globalization. Feminists like Kristeva were enamored of Mao's empowerment of women, even as the Confucian system connecting gender to kinship and the state perpetually underlies the definition of 'woman.' For instance, the familial term *funü* came to represent the equality of woman as worker while the sexual term *nuxing* became the signifier of the hetero 'feminine' subject attached to bourgeois commodification.[17] Of course, the Chinese revolution that ended in 1976 was ultimately a repression of culture in China, against the marxist ideals of the Western left. But Althusser's interest in Mao's thought coincided with the formation of his structural Marxism and ideological state apparatuses during the period when he was defining ideology as the '"representation" of the imaginary relationship of individuals to their real conditions of existence.'[18] The coherence and compatibility of Mao and Althusser's political philosophy has been neglected in writing about the history of the formation of interpellation (due largely to the post-1989 taboo of the Communist subject). As such, I argue that the double meaning of ideological 'representation' – in dialectical materialism and in the film *installation* form – resonates even more in the era of global capitalism. If indeed subjects are made by the social structures and economic conditions of material life, the artistic use of the film installation form is often strategically focused on understanding the same structures and conditions through video interpellation.

Badiou and Rancière have revived the political study of the material-ist suppositions for the twenty-first century, acknowledging the transna-tional currents in marxist philosophies that constitute the foundation for Chineseness as a post-Cultural Revolution identity.[19] Their work aligns with the ideals of the artists in this chapter, who also exemplify the continuation of the use of Althusser's interpellative methodology for portraying subjects that emerge from capitalist globalization. By looking at Wu Mali's 1990s labor and environmental expressions and Cao's in the subsequent decades, the artists show the generational divide that marks the cycle in which 'offshore Taiwan' became 'outsource China' in the development of factories for multinational corporations. The use of filmic media and artistic conceptualism by artists like Cao, Tan, and Wu continue to question and challenge those conditions of existence in China, Hong Kong, and Taiwan but in an entirely new way. Their gendered resistances to the patriarchal norm of capital follow in the footsteps but ultimately innovate from the outdated marxist revolutionary model for both labor and art. Cao's digital invention of *RMB City* as a virtual location reflects the 'unreal' of imaginary relationships in the fantasy of 'China' that is both *conceptual* and revolutionary. Tan tracks the materialist philosophy that can be construed as sharing affinity with the consciousness of the femi-nist authority of the past – through Empress Wu, whose Buddhist approach distinguishes the metaphysical ideal for materialist conditions. And Wu Mali embodies the relentless advocacy for justice in respect of gendered divisions of labor that becomes all the more significant in the era of the Capitolocene. By reviewing the work of three artists in relation to this particular concept and history of Chineseness, the metaphor of *reproduction* and modes of existence can be connected through the legacy of transnational marxist resistances – even as the Marxist project was declared a fatality in 1989.[20]

Scavenger labor and the Buddhist matriarch

Yuk King Tan's 2008 video *Scavenger* (see plate 12) focuses on the figure of the matriarch in contemporary Hong Kong by documenting a day in the life of Lam Po Po (Grandma Lam), whose work routine for the last ten years was to transport enormous stacks of cardboard by pushcart across the busy downtown streets to the Sheung Wan weighing station. Once delivered, she receives her cash payment. On this particular day, however, the cardboard stack is laser cut to replicate the life-sized lion statues guarding the iconic HSBC building designed by Norman Foster for the Hong Kong Shanghai Banking Corporation. The viewer follows the video journey with the elderly Lam crossing paths with the bank lions, at one moment, standing side by side. The visual compare-and-contrast continues with the coincidental pushcart meeting alongside another elderly 'scavenger' grandmother, whose disorderly pile of cardboard trash constitutes a deconstruction of Lam's artistic lion sculpture. The conceptualist ability to re-view readymade objects, trash, has transformed the interpretative exchange, as Tan's video engages much more than the signifiers of straight documentary film. As trash becomes an object of importance in the global economy of climate change and environmental protection, conceptual eco-art raises new questions about material value.[21] At the same time, the documentary real is heightened by the viewer's sense of the performative trek alongside Lam's trolley, which is a laborious navigation against traffic and over curbs, jostling claustrophobically through the crowded streets. The terse timing of Tan's video places the viewer in an experience much like watching a reality video from Youtube instead of engaging in the viewing structures of the cinema or the conventions of the video installation. Youtube's digital real is a different kind of documentation, infusing an extemporaneous 'being there,' and Tan's use of this model of viewing brings attention to a number of important historical precedents as well as contemporary considerations.

Scavenger can be construed as the present-day *Ragpicker* under the political history of modern art and class relations that Manet established in 1870 (and for the record, the painting subject always colonially segregated from the history of the Chinese subject). By focusing on the subject of a subaltern woman in the city of Hong Kong, Tan's video correlates to Manet's monumentalizing of the subject from Marx's lowest class order: 'the *chiffonnier* salvages rags from the garbage for sale to paper manufacturers. Ragpickers … were the emblems of the modern city and those it had left behind.'[22] Tan's subject is far more complex as the elderly female *Scavenger* reverses the power relations; instead of being left behind, she is given the radical task of disposing, in essence, destroying one of the iconic emblems of British and Chinese colonial power in the city of Hong Kong. Symbolizing 'growth and prosperity,' the two lion sculptures serve as the symbol of HSBC branding for the largest bank in Europe – the cast bronze statues were made in the mid-1930s, copied from the original 1923 sculptures designed by Henry Poole in England for the opening of the Shanghai branch.[23] Replicas of the lions decorate HSBC branches all over the world. But the two in front of the Hong Kong headquarters have become true emblems of the history of the Hong Kong and Shanghai Banking Corporation, described by the *South China Morning Post* as 'closely aligned with the evolution of Hong Kong' itself.[24] The Scotsman, Thomas Sutherland, founded the original bank in 1865, after obtaining enormous capital wealth from working at the Peninsular and Oriental Steam Navigation Company (P&O) in Hong Kong. The British shipping company moved maritime freight consisting largely of opium from India to China. The lions are conceivably the symbol of HSBC's capitalist occupation of Hong Kong (after its 1841 ceding in the first Opium War), a reminder of the way in which British imperialism was founded on drug-pedaling leverage, considered now as simply the historical period of 'trade between Europe, India and China.'[25]

Accordingly, the symbol of Tan's paper lion shares affinity with Mao Zedong's rhetorical use of the term *zhilaohu*, 'paper tiger,' to illustrate the empty governance at the time of US imperialism: 'in appearance it is very powerful but in reality it is nothing to be afraid of, it is a paper tiger ... made of paper, unable to withstand the wind and the rain.'[26] Presented in his 1956 speech, Mao's aim was to state his position on imperialism, citing the need to unite with the indigenous Indians in the United States, since 'the history of class society for thousands of years has proved this point: the strong must give way to the weak' – the very signifier embodied by ragpickers and scavengers.[27] Money and wealth was the driving force behind imperialism, and it is important to note that by 1955, HSBC headquarters were moved to Hong Kong from Shanghai after Mao took power and changed banking to a socialist system of finance. The irony of Mao's rhetorical depiction, however, would come later in the aftermath of the 4 June 1989 Tiananmen Square massacre. The British Foreign Secretary Geoffrey Howe was derided as a 'Paper Lion' when his three-day visit to Hong Kong failed to placate the anxieties of the local Chinese, who were angry when he refused to offer concrete assistance for asylum seekers, denouncing 'the shame of the Thatcher government' for denying a system of UK residency for Hong Kong British subjects. Reporter Emily Lau with the *Far Eastern Economic Review* concluded that the 'political reality for Britain is that the people of Hong Kong are of a different race, a different culture' as a reminder of the colonialist past – meanwhile the UK *Mail* compared the British government's attitude to their former 'appeasement of Nazi Germany in the 1930s' as no different toward the 'murderous regime' in China.[28] In the history of imperialism, the weak are always the 'different race, different culture.' This characterization is, of course, a standard one for colonialism in order that the British could remain in control of the capital enterprise, the reason for being in Hong Kong in the first place. By 1993, the primary HSBC headquarters were moved to London in anticipation of Hong Kong's return to China in 1997, and that is where it remains to this day.

The political history of the paper lion informs the meaning of Tan's *Scavenger* as the matriarch Lam Po Po literally moves the symbolic past into the realm of the material present. Here, it is the Buddhist symbolism of the *Golden Lion* that counters the money-branding of the HSBC symbol while acknowledging the gendered relations of power in philosophical history. The famous *Jin shizi zhang*, Treatise of the Golden Lion, was the monk Fazang's seventh-century teaching created for the enlightenment of his patron Empress Wu Zetian. As retold by Jinhua Chen, the monk Fazang was once trying to explain to the Empress the 'teaching on the interpenetration, interdependence between all the dharmas [cosmic laws or principles] of any space and time,' but the 'teaching was so abstruse that it confounded a brain even as brilliant as Empress Wu's. Recognizing this, Fazang resorted to a golden lion in the palace as a metaphor.'[29] As interpreted by Wing-Tsit Chan, the statue provided a material example for *dharma* in which the very concept of the lion made out of gold 'exists because of our feelings, arising from vast imagination,' and while the craftsman produces from the real material of gold, what humans believe about the value of the substance is also 'not nonexistent.'[30] Gold exists because of its material form, and the concept of the lion illustrates how dharma is produced from causes and effects: 'the moment when we see the lion come into existence, it is only gold that comes into existence.'[31] The Buddhist logic reveals how manifestations of the material world are subject to consciousness in which 'emptiness has no character of its own; it shows itself by means of matter.'[32]

The Golden Lion resonates as a teaching today to remember the laws of the cosmos, particularly as the China Dream has become the new model for the material ideal. The value of things to be consumed requires a serious reconsideration in view of the mountains of waste depicted in Tan's *Limits of Visibility* – her compacted modular cubes of recycling appear ominous when considering the daily transport of the mountain of refuse. In the Buddhist context, the emptiness of gold is no different from the fullness of garbage, especially when viewed in the context of Lam Po Po's daily life. Together, Tan's *Scavenger* and *Limits of Visibility* reflect a questioning of the manifestations of the material world in regard to a consciousness of the value of garbage in the scope of the matriarchal imagination attributed to Empress Wu. But presented in the video installation form and staged at the 2P Contemporary Art Gallery in Hong Kong, the work addresses the Hong Kong viewer as a reflection of their local place. The material existence of garbage, however, is a product of every neighborhood, every regional center, requiring the viewer to see material existence differently, according to the laws of the cosmos. Moreover, Hong Kong's port is one of the busiest in the world, and the tens of thousands of containers ships, many of which are old diesel transporters, are still permitted to burn highly sulphuric fuels as they approach the dock. These transporters contribute to the air pollution that has become the most detrimental cause of health problems in the region.[33] Unfortunately, the drive to live a life of consumption remains undeterred by the health risks of simply breathing in Hong Kong.

Dialectical images: haze, fog, cars, banks, museums

Through their artistic subjects, Cao Fei and Wu Mali represent the opposite ends of the cycle, at the height of China's economic boom and at the end of Taiwan's. If China today occupies the central position of the 'Asiatic threat' in the global outsource economy, that position was once held by Taiwan. What connects the two nations today is the environmental pollution that has resulted from industrial expansion. As introduced earlier, Cao's 2013 film titled *Haze and Fog* is a depiction of the *airpocalypse* of Beijing, the foreboding smog of 2011–12 that kept people indoors and dependent on air quality reports. Cao created a doomsday scenario that was influenced by the American television show *The Walking Dead* by channeling the anxiety of Beijingers into a character portrayal of the ordinary urban dweller turned flesh-eating zombie in the apocalypse of pollution. Shooting the film in the environs of her Beijing neighborhood, Cao explains how the work was inspired by her 'observations and imaginations' of the city's diverse-classed society where 'migrants and social elite share the same space … people from all levels of society, including the middle class, the laborers, the security force, and the sex workers; all we can see in the film. We see all different kinds of lifestyles on this one street, where people from all walks of life make up our image of a modern community.'[34] The actors in *Haze and Fog*, however, are not focused on scripted lines or dialogue, as Cao bypasses the 'sinophonic' relationships that Shu-mei Shih attributes to a cinematic Chineseness. In contrast, the tango music soundtrack functions as the backdrop for the interactions of Cao's community – life is a dance, a tango, in the film's summertime setting until the haze turns everyone into the 'living dead.' The egalitarian pose of the film points to a society that will all come to the same inevitable end from an environmental apocalypse, which does not discriminate, and by the same logic, the zombies, like the dead, are no longer part of a human system that privileges race, gender, or sexuality.

Haze and Fog contributes to the dialectical dialogue on the structures of social life in relation to commodity production and the capitalist exchange, which continues to be the premise for artistic strategies centered on human priorities. But Cao has also entered the discourse of the new materialism of the Anthropocene – when climate change and greenhouse gases take precedence over all other issues affecting the planet. The posthuman position has authorized a 'new materialism' according to Stacy Alaimo, in which the scale of the impact of human activity on the planet requires a shift in thinking that 'the world exists as a background for the human subject.'[35] The Marxist legacy of class relations was always centered on the human subject, and the new perspective toward the materialism of the earth and nature has changed those priorities.

Cao's implicit critique of the new capitalist world of Beijing is centered on the human cost of what actually causes the fog, the startling industrial growth by which 14,000 companies in China violated pollution regulations in 2017.[36] But much of the cause of the visible haze in Beijing is from the 5.7 million motorized vehicles, which are known to produce 30 per cent of the city's 'hazardous breathable particles' and over 80 per cent of the carbon monoxide in the air.[37] In 2017, Beijing banned vehicles that did not meet emission standards from entering the city. At the same time, the number of cars sold in China in 2016 was estimated to be 28 million, with 952 different brands of cars manufactured. The global partners in China's auto industry include BMW, and they alone manufacture 450,000 cars a year at the Dadong and Tiexi in Shenyang province.[38] It should be noted that the Tiexi plant was built as a sustainable 'green' production site, not just for building low emission cars but as a factory run by an 'energy source tunnel' to centralize electricity, water and heating. Moreover, the BMW plant has been named an 'industrial tourism' destination and was the first and only example of a manufacturing plant recognized in 2017 as a National AAAA Tourist Attraction by the Chinese state.

The object of the *car* is central to Cao's artistic strategy, one that can be compared to Wu Mali's, since they have both designed and produced *art cars* during different moments in the temporally situated high and low periods of industrial manufacturing. Wu Mali's 1991 *Prosperity Car* (see plate 13) illustrates the engine of prosperity in Taiwan, which was launched in the 1960s, embodying what curator Yang Wen-I describes as 'the money worship of the Taiwanese spurred on by the economic miracle.'[39] The inoperable *Prosperity Car* is a box on wheels, constructed from wood panels, cloth and gold paper and decorated with a lucky red bow. Yang explains that the 'popular and profane image of the car becomes ironically "sanctified" through the application of gold' in the ritual of gift-giving that entices prosperity blessings from the gods.[40] Cao's 2017 design #18 for BMW's Art Car Series (see plate 14) appears to be in direct opposition to Wu's artistic intentions since it was created as a promotional tool for the 'newest member of BMW's global production network.' Wu's artistic ideals in the 1990s were radically different from Cao's critical methods, posing important questions about the difference between feminist forms of artistic resistance in the 1990s and what could be considered as the post-socialist critiques by women artists in the second decade of the twenty-first century.

One way to compare the artistic distinctions and meanings of Wu and Cao's cars is to review the staging of the artcars in the institutional context of the museum. Presented at Yellow River Art Centre in Taichung, Taiwan,

Wu's 1993 'car show,' titled *When Mini Van Meets Super Mali*, showcased other inoperable cars including three different models called the Proletarian Car, the silver Mercedes-shaped car, and the Pink News (Sex Scandal) car inspired by 'propaganda vehicles,' selling their ideologies in Taiwan. Wu explains that she wanted to find a way to 'escape from a stereotypical art collection system, which always saw the route of art museum-gallery-collector.'[41] She noted that art galleries have become 'so beautiful, even far too beautiful, whereas more and more car shows have come to be like art galleries for me. If a car show could be like an art gallery, it would be natural to make an art gallery like a car show. Perhaps only some viewers sensed the mockery within the work.'[42] Wu was acknowledging how the status of the art object was becoming indiscernible from the status of cars in the moneyed world of galleries, museums and collectors. In the 1990s, the mockery of a Proletarian Car would have been apparent to the viewer. When Cao Fei unveiled her BMW car at the world premiere in Beijing's Minsheng Art Museum, she not only confirmed Wu's criticism but provided a self-referential example of the *status of the artist* contributing to the status of the car and the museum. Her futuristic design was hailed as a 'sleek non-reflective all black rendition of the M6 GT3 race car that seems straight out of one of Cao's animations or virtual reality.'[43] Cao's artcar was the very fulfillment of Wu's critique in 1993.

The successful artist today has become a celebrity commodity, a product of the global circuit of exhibitionary venues, artfairs, biennials, and triennials. The moneyed institutions of art have grown into another global industry, and in China they are noticeable for their capitalist transformation in conjunction with the state. For instance, the Minsheng Art Museums in Shanghai and Beijing (inaugurated in 2010 and 2015, respectively) were founded and funded by the China Minsheng Banking Corporation, one of China's largest banks. The support of museums by financial institutions is nothing new; but in the 'museumification' of China, corporate funders became collaborators in the governmental plan to 'build 100 museums a year,' a stark contrast to the most idealistic of the Socialist conceptions in the Maoist past to 'let a 100 flowers bloom.'[44] In 2014, Shanghai boasted over ten contemporary art museums, whereas ten years prior, the count was just two prominent museums, the Shanghai Museum housing Chinese antiquities and the Shanghai Art Museum representing modern and contemporary art.[45] In the ten years of entrepreneurial growth, the new museums were largely free from restrictions and they functioned as spaces for rent. Philip Tinari has suggested that the Shanghai Himalayas Museum was 'built to increase the value of Zhikang's real-estate project. The developer did indeed sell shortly after it was built to a Hong Kong company for a significant profit.'[46] The new erection of museums contributes overall to the development of the art center and megacity scheme, one in which China plans to create metropolises comparable to New York, Paris, or London.

The purpose of the proliferation of museums emerging in China since 2010 was to confirm the idea that the country is a bonafide cultural and economic power in the global economy. While this phenomenon of museumification in China is discussed as a 'museum boom' in academic circles, the institutions of the exhibitionary complex have long functioned as a cultural/economical showcase in the global competition.[47] As discussed in Chapters Five, the shift to the museum era began with Lu Peng's entrepreneurial efforts to bring the 'art industry' to China, which entailed organizing and presenting the first Guangzhou Biennial in 1992. The global expositions, artfairs, biennials, and triennials are now symbolic writ large of the globalization of the arts, even as their organizing principles bear traces of the colonial world's fairs. As explored in Chapter Four, Chineseness in the context of globalization is not a new discussion, since cultures and nations were originally depicted and categorized at the nineteenth-century world's fairs. The fairs were once described by Walter Benjamin as similar to the Paris arcades because they are both 'preceded by national exhibitions of industry.' Benjamin characterizes the arcades as the shopping center model for the image of capitalist power, always dependent on the façade of the 'new' but actually something that already exists in the landscape of capital. In the same way, the new global art exhibitions remain timeless in their representation of the status of economic power in global capitalism.[48] The new museums and the biennials in China therefore visualize a type of 'dialectics at a standstill' under Benjamin's explanation for the 'relation of what-has-been to the now [as] dialectical ... not progression but image' that suddenly appears.[49]

Cao's ready complicity with BMW and the Minsheng Museum represents the twenty-first-century difference from Wu's previous artistic ideals for resisting the status symbol of the car. However, Cao is the first Chinese artist chosen in the history of designing artcars for BMW, and she joins the shortlist of three women, including Jenny Holzer and Esther Mahlangu, who were commissioned since the tradition began in 1975.[50] As a non-driver without a driver's license, Cao's design caused her to be heralded nonetheless as a woman who is conquering 'the domain of the car after its consummation by computers, stripping the car bare of its testosterone-driven cultural significance (as stereotypically coded).'[51] Indeed, this characterization illustrates the implicit biases of gender, the continuing signifiers of the masculinist realm of commodity culture, and the implications of the economic competition among cars, artists, and museums overall. Cao's work seems to imply that the image of the BMW car has entered into the realm of pure advertising, since the emptying out of the real has long passed in the realm of representation. Giorgio Agamben acknowledges the current difference since resistance to the 'banal' images of advertising is the same as resisting pornography, like resisting nothing at all.[52] Nonetheless, the context for the banal advertisement is one in which the BMW factory is now heralded as the first recreational tourist site by the Chinese state (in the form of the tourist bureau) and no longer differentiated as a place of labor and manufacturing. While the simulacral sign of the car and the actual car itself have become one and the same in the economy of images, the state apparatuses for work/labor and leisure/recreation have solidified their interchangeable positions. The transformation of Mao's state-supported labor against the bourgeois cycle of the culture industry has been all but completed.

Liu Kang has tracked the intellectual development of the culture industry in Chinese marxism in association with the Frankfurt School, which historical parallels, he believes, 'are often forgotten under the geopolitical and biopolitical dichotomies of East and West and of totalitarianism, communism, liberal democracy, and so forth.'[53] Liu suggests that the contributions of Chinese Marxism to capitalist resistances have not been duly recognized. The revolutionary politics of China's Marxist legacy have gradually become abandoned as China's social order embraces the very capitalist modernity that Maoism sought to reject. But like most marxist historians of China, Liu associates the marxist intellectual movement to the May Fourth (1919) Movement and thinkers such as Liang Qichao, Cai Yuanpei, and LuXun. The parallel to the Frankfurt School was through aesthetics and consciousness in China's literary movement, which continued into the era of Communist rule, led by Qu Qiubai who was a participant of the May Fourth Movement. In regard to the influence of the Frankfurt School after the Cultural Revolution, Liu argues that the introduction of translations of critical theory into Chinese in the 1980s had profound influence, instantiating several decades of humanist advocacy as Chinese intellectuals used it to denounce and transform the violence of the 1960s and 1970s. By the 1990s, China had started to change into a market-driven, consumer society, and Liu has since denounced and rejected the new misappropriation of Adorno's critique of the culture industry. He cites President Hu Jintao's 2007 Report exhorting the CCP 17th Congress to 'vigorously develop the cultural industry, launch major projects ... speed up development of cultural industry bases and clusters of cultural industries with regional features, nurture key enterprises and strategic investors, create a thriving cultural market and enhance the industry's international competitiveness.'[54] Under this state-driven mandate, the BMW tourist site and the Minsheng Museums are the same kind of enterprises in Hu's industrial approach to *culture*. Liu believes that the arts and humanities in China has all but lost its intellectual relevance in the space of ten or so years, as a media-dominated consumer culture quickly took the central focus for academics in the country. By all appearances, Cao Fei's artcar would seem to align with this moneyed view of culture, especially in comparison with Wu Mali's *Prosperity Car*. But as Cao's other works explored later in this chapter will show, her strategy for artmaking is highly complex and is one that reflects the paradoxical critiques of an entirely new generation of artists.

Factory labor – Chinese women

In the work of Wu Mali and Cao Fei, the shared affinities of the effects of industrialization in Taiwan and China are gendered ones; and, as expressed through their interpellated subjects of Chineseness, the political upheavals and the Confucian kinship tradition still haunt the relations of labor. Wu has been a major figure of feminist art in Taiwan, instantiated by her first public exhibition in 1985 of the installation *Time Space*, an entire room filled with crumpled newspaper. Interpreted as a critique of the news media, the expression is reflexive of the volatile period before 1987, the year that martial law in Taiwan was lifted. Wu represents the activism of artists who 'saw a huge gap between the art being produced and the ground-shifting social movements in Taiwan that were criticizing the government and the international political order.'[55] As shown by *Infinity Car*, Wu's social critique was also directed at the art institution, implicating both the culture of commodity and the status-making museum. She has continued her socially activist expression but, since 2006, her focus has shifted to environmental issues. A close look at her body of work reveals an artist whose current performative engagements, cleaning up the pollution in her home environs of Taipei, began with the use of video installations in the 1990s to explore the gendered relations of Taiwan's rapid industrial expansion. The history of the work of one artist can show the development of a feminist activism that begins with labor and continues with environmental advocacy. Wu explains that 'Taiwan in the 1970s was dominated by strong nativist sentiment. It was caused by the despair people experienced in the industrialization process, when traditional values were quickly vanishing.'[56] The artist's film and mixed media installations, titled *Epitaph* and *Stories of Women from Hsin-Chuang*, both dating to 1997, are seminal works that acknowledge this despair as Wu recovers the existence of women in political and labor history. Extraordinarily, one of the stories told in the 1990s by Wu on behalf of women in the once booming textile factory town of Hsin-Chuang was recounted almost verbatim by Cao Fei when she was discussing her 2007 video work *Whose Utopia?*, a documentary/fantasy video installation capturing the workaday life of laborers in the Osram lighting factory in Foshan (the area of Guangdong where factories sprung up early in China's new industry). In the logic of capitalist reproduction in China, industrialization is repeating the cycle that Taiwan has already completed.

Beginning with her most recent environmental work, Wu's projects are interactive, as they involve viewers in performative projects that would implicate them in what's happening to the place where they live. *By the River, On the River, Of the River* (2006) was a four-day boat trip led by the artist to the Danshui River. Wu collaborated with the city of Taipei and the local community colleges when she invited viewers to engage by boat, exploring one of the four smaller tributaries each day of the project. Enlisting the expertise of Chen Chien-Yi from the Taiwan Land Ethics Association, her goal was to contextualize the Danshui as the historical gateway to northern Taiwan, which flows into the South China Sea, an ancient passage that could be compared to the 'tour abroad to see the origin of ancient civilizations.'[57] Not unlike many art explorations that are ecological in nature, *By the River* was a visual and embodied adventure that incorporated the viewer's experience in the advocacy event. Similarly, Wu's exhibition at the 2008 Taipei Biennial titled *Taipei Tomorrow as a Lake Again* constituted a movable kitchen garden with arranged beds of vegetables and herbs on the terrace of the Taipei Fine Arts Museum. Viewers were invited to pick from the harvest while learning about global climate change and the fact that 'as the sea level rises, many parts of Taiwan could become underwater.'[58] Wu appears to be developing different models for educational performances, finding ways to involve viewers in a problem that has drastic effects for the current generation. By 2011, Wu had started her long-term project *Trekking the Plum-Tree-Stream*, focusing on cleaning up one tributary of the Danshui River. Upon learning about the original plum tree plantation that the river was named after, Wu also found out that the rich agricultural area filled with rice fields, local produce, was developed during the Japanese occupation of Taiwan from 1895 to 1945. But in the decades after Chiang Kai Shek's forces moved into Taiwan in 1949, in the aftermath of the defeat of his Nationalist Party to Mao's Communist forces, industrial activities and commercial development presided over the enormous environmental changes in the region. Wastewater contamination from residential and industrial pollution transformed the Plum Tree creek, and the stream where people once swam and bathed became filthy, dire, and hopeless. No longer strictly an artistic endeavor, Wu organized the governmental agencies and residential community to help clean the creek and restore its natural biodiversity. Most of her efforts at Plum Creek entail innovative communication and education strategies with the Taipei community at large, with the aim of changing 'how a person treats a river and the environment.'[59]

In an interview, Wu was asked how she arrived at her 'latest focus on environmental issues' after working on a range of advocacies and subjects, including 'critiquing the media, the condition of Asia, political criticism, feminism, art institutional critique.'[60] Her reply explains her experience which led her to become an ecofeminist:

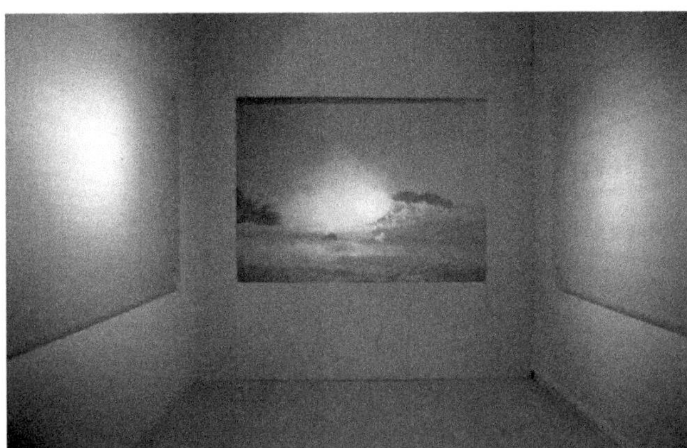

3.2 Wu Mali, *Epitaph*, 1997, video installation.

when a person faces their surroundings, it is a land issue as well as an institutional issue. When I returned [to Taiwan] from Germany, I encountered
a society robustly pursuing changes. Taiwan had backed out of the United
Nations in 1971, the United States severed their diplomatic relations with us in
1968, and '87 was the lift of martial law. Seeing these historic moments became
vital to my growing experience.[61]

The culmination of this experience was expressed in her video installation
presented in the groundbreaking 1998 *Inside Out: New Chinese Art* exhibition
of Chinese contemporary art. *Epitaph* (see figure 3.2) is a symbolic and medi-
tative work commemorating the massacre of thousands of Taiwanese citizens
who were killed by Chiang Kai Shek's Nationalist troops on 28 February
1947.[62] (The Kuomintang had been given control of Taiwan following the
surrender of Japan in 1945.) In the White Terror aftermath, the Taiwanese
endured forty years of martial law in which tens of thousands of people were
executed between 1949 and 1992 for suspected anti-government activities.[63]
Wu asserts that while male victims of the tragedy have been acknowledged,
rehabilitated, and commemorated as martyrs, the accounts of female victims
continue to be neglected, which *Epitaph* sought to address. The video screen
in the center of the installation projected the scene of the ocean and pound-
ing waves, while placed adjacent on the two sides of the video screen are large
glass panels etched with excerpted text from Juan Mei-shu's 1992 book *Sound
of Weeping in a Dim Corner*, a remembrance of the victims of the 28 February
White Terror.[64] Art historian Elsa Hsiang-chun Chen describes the visual
encounter: 'text is presented in an abstract manner to create an imaginary
historical distance, and the painful experiences of the women victims and
survivors are heard, experienced' but the expression was never a 'reenact-

ment of violence.'[65] *Epitaph* was a gender-specific engagement, and during the 1990s, Wu's feminist challenge to the male-dominated sphere of both art and politics in Taiwan was through creating sights and spaces specifically for women.

Wu's cinematic 'enclosures' contributed to a particular feminist model in the 1980s and 1990s for the theory and practice of film installation. She shares ideals that are mutual with Trinh T. Minh-ha's conception of a film form that could provide an alternative to perpetuating the 'master-centered text' whereby film offers another kind of historicizing text – Trinh explains that by 'putting representation under scrutiny, textual theory/practice has more likely helped to upset rooted ideologies by bringing the mechanics of their inner workings to the fore.'[66] The patriarchal text has long been under the scrutiny of Wu's critical analysis, and in works such as *Library*, discussed in Chapter Five, the annihilation of books such as Confucius's *Five Classics* was literally and visually orchestrated to show the destruction of the patriarchal canon as Wu shredded the actual books and put them in individual cases that emulated books. The use of both text and film in *Epitaph* in the invented space of the installation allows for the creation of what Chen describes as 'feminine subjectivity that can interchangeably take either men or women as its primary self.'[67] The installation form could foster this kind of experience for the viewer.

The same use of the video installation method was exemplified in the *Stories of Women from Hsin-Chuang* (1997) (see plate 15). For this project, Wu was not simply narrating the stories by female workers who had left their farming villages after finishing elementary school to work in textile factories. Instead, her *Stories* are layered montages of image, sound, text, and frames in the deconstructionist ideal that Minh-ha had also adopted with great success in the late 1980s. Always aware of the need to 'decolonize' the social and human sciences, Minh-ha's work (such as *Surname Viet Given Name Nam*, 1989) manipulated the 'real' of the documentary and the fantasy of film through her textualist and cinematic installations, especially as a critique of the Western authority of anthropology. Her aim was 'thereby to challenge representation itself even while emphasizing the reality of the experience of film as well as the important role that reality plays in the lives of the spectators.'[68] Wu adopted this same strategy for creating filmic experiences.

When Wu was invited to present an exhibition in the town of Hsinchuang on the outskirts of Taipei, she saw the opportunity to make the very spectators of her work the subjects of her film and textile installation. She wove into cloth the repeated machine-sewn images that expressed the stories of women who worked day and night at the textile factories during the prime of their youth to send money home, often to support their brothers who were completing their university educations. In the proper Confucian role for women of a certain class, these sisters were not encouraged to further their education and were expected to fund their brothers' education instead. Amidst the sound of spoken text and sewing machines looped on the video, and the written text embroidered onto the cloth, the narratives unfolded to reveal factory marriages and divorces in the flow of time, during which the industries moved offshore in the 1990s at the end of Taiwan's economic boom. It was also during the 1990s that China saw exponential growth in the development of factories for multinational industries which reproduced and inevitably replaced the rural-to-urban migrant labor of Taiwan. The current statistics for the percentage of women aged fifteen and over in China's labor force is 68 per cent, more than the numbers in many other developed nations.[69]

When Cao Fei spent six months in the German-run Osram light bulb factory in 2005–6 in order to film *Whose Utopia?*, she was not too far from where she was born in Guangzhou, the city northwest of Hong Kong in a region that opened up to Western investors earlier than in the north of China. *Whose Utopia?* (2007) features laborers at the company in Foshan who became ballerinas and break dancers as they 'perform their utopia' in the factory workspace. Differing from Wu's retelling of stories, Cao visualizes a hard-to-get glimpse of actual factory life in *Whose Utopia?*, reflecting the 'real' of the video's capture of nothing but the sound and movement of machinery in the first four minutes of the film. When the workers finally appear, they are staged as objects in the assembly line, and the unfolding of the sequence of workers dancing, amidst laboring workers who ignore them in their concentration over their tasks, expresses the fantasy and the 'real' of everyday life in the factory. Cao notes that the place where the company is located was once her hometown, but is now 'referred to as 'the world's factory.' I watched it change completely. But change is so normal in China.'[70] Some things don't change, however, in the repetitive cycle of labor and gender; Cao conveys how she 'met a lot of women workers who send money home to support their brothers, because in traditional families boys are considered to be more important, and so the girl's work will support their education. Stories like this are very common.'[71] The sisters from Hsin-Chuang, Taiwan in the 1970s could very well be the sisters in Foshan, China in 2005.

It is important to note that Cao's performers are the actual workers of the Osram factory and not simply actors of cinema, showing how the medium of film installation has moved a great distance from what Jacques Rancière describes as Postmodern cinema's 'documentary fiction' which he argues was invented in the age of the 'Maoist theatricalization of Marxism,' adapting the 'fragments of the intermingled history of the cinema.'[72] Harkening back to those fragments, however, Cao's interpellated subjects of film are precisely the sort of subjects representing Althusser's Maoist ideal, especially since her father Cao Chong'en is a famous 'official' sculptor in China who is known for his political statues created in the socialist realist tradition.

Digital interpellation

Taking into account the specific Marxist relations here, the current political identity of Chineseness is inextricably linked to the way in which Althusser's interpellated subject was influenced by his reading of Mao's writings, especially his theories of contradiction. Rey Chow's use of his interpellation in film reveals the continuing connection by which Althusser's poststructuralist ontology has now replaced his original Marxist methodology in the analysis of art, literature, and film. Film theorist Kwai-Cheung Lo explains how film can force 'an individual to dramatically become a subject while simultaneously conferring on him a recognizable identity,' a subjectivication he credits to traditional Althusserian interpellation.[73] Elsewhere, however, Lo updated his argument by implementing his concept of 'interpellation beyond interpellation' (discussed in Chapter One), which is 'the opportunity to negate or call its identity into question, allowing it to imagine a transgression that is a necessary part of interpellation.'[74] While this problematizing of identity is usually the very point of video performances, Lo is pointing here to the new generation of transgressive bloggers and video gamers in China who, 'as major beneficiaries of the economic success of the last three decades,' are reluctant to 'foment democratic reform, allegedly beyond the materiality of political ideology.[75] While bloggers and gamers appear to be interpellated by digital life, they have moved away from Althusser's ideal for a 'whole' subject of identity, unattached to materialist life. The interconnections among the historical subjectivication in the Marxist project and the present-day fragmentation of identity that Chineseness represents remain important, if only to recognize Mao's continuing influence on the transnational development of both intellectual history and global contemporary art. The hallmark of the poststructuralist subject is the rejection of a cohesive or whole identity, one that is susceptible to simplistic notions of Chineseness.

For example, during the seminal decade of the 1980s, intellectuals in China, such as Li Zehou, were renewing collegial relationships in Europe and the United States by engaging in cultural studies outside of China, contributing to a moment known as 'high cultural fever.'[76] Li was a philosopher who reinterpreted Kant, Confucius, and Marx during this critical moment when a new idealism for individualism was the impetus for 'high subjectivity and humanism' exemplifying the spirit behind the 1989 Tiananmen square demonstrations.[77] While most believe that this ideal has now been replaced with the capitalist impetus for the China Dream, artists like Cao Fei have benefitted from the 1980s' humanist spirit in the legacy of China's contemporary art.

At the same time, she adopts the blogging, gaming techno aesthetic in filmic and digital works that could be described as depicting the 'interpellation of the interpellated.' In her 2004 video installation titled *Father* (shown at the Moscow Biennale in 2005), Cao Fei documented her father Cao Chong'en's process as he completed a commission to sculpt the figure of Deng Xiaoping. According to Hou Hanru, she developed this documentary, disclosing various 'aspects where business intermingles with political and economic interests' in the exchange of art in China by simultaneously 'incorporating installations and performances with her father sculpting on the sites.'[78] The expression of Father involves the multi-dimensions of the realism of the documentary, the cinematic emotionality of the father-daughter narrative, and also provides an insightful view into the artmaking practice that has dramatically shifted in the most political way in just one generation of the Cao family. As a student in art school, Cao had instinctively rebelled against her father's social-realist model for art although she was encouraged by teachers to follow in his successful medium. But as a woman who is still under what she explains as 'China's traditional view ... the son must inherit the father's business ... passed down from generation to generation,' Cao's final aim was to focus her lens on the reality of China's current situation. Hou describes Father as a film that interlaces 'disparate horizons and perspectives' with 'personal familial ties, traditional father-daughter relationships and traditional philosophies.' Ultimately, Cao Fei's artistic labor breaks from the traditional cycle of women's labor, away from a modern history dominated by generations of young women working in factories, from Taiwan to China, to support the education of young men.

Cao Fei has defied the unlikely odds for the recognition of women artists in China – her digital worlds and filmic inventions have taken the art world by storm, having represented the social media generation through her Second Life projects such as *I. Mirror* (2007), the video 'documentary' of the intimate encounters of her avatar China Tracy and Hug Yue, the dashing young avatar created by Ed Mead (see figure 3.3). Cao first embarked on this relationship through Second Life online and Mead was actually a leftist activist living in San Francisco. *RMB City* was the Second Life site where real and cyber worlds converge: 'RMB (Renminbi) is the "people's currency" of the Republic of China and the name of a virtual city created on people's imagination, with no nationalities and no borders.'[79] The city's buildings resembling Beijing landmarks such as the Olympic 'bird's nest' stadium and Rem Koolhaas's CCTV Tower are imaginary, and yet, when Cao presented the project as the 'Great Real Estate Opportunity' at Art Basel Miami in 2007, she was able to obtain a $100,000 property investment from an unidentified collector.[80]

Her opus *RMB City Opera* (2009) (see plate 3), presented at Teatro Astra in Turin, was an interactive live performance with actor-dancers who often emulated the same movements of their avatars, streamed onto the backdrop

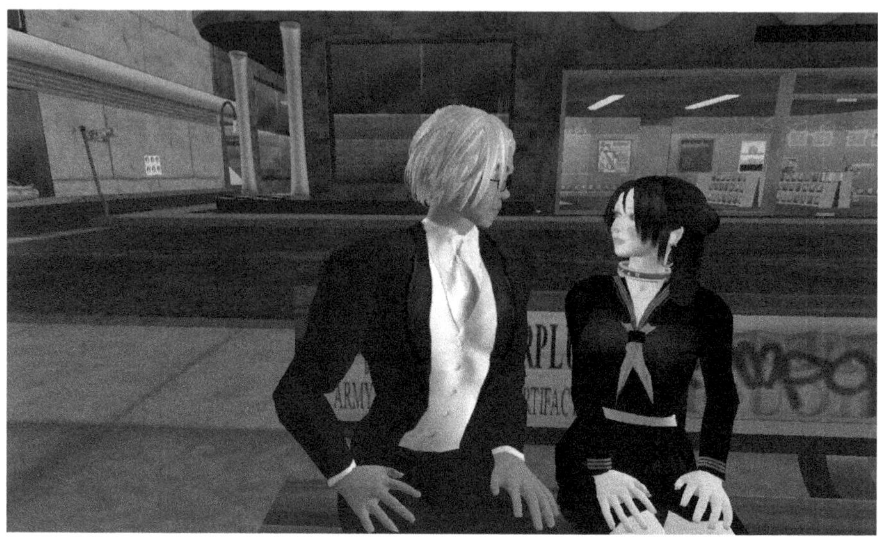

3.3 Cao Fei, *I. Mirror*, 2007, video installation, depicting Hug Yue and China Tracy

from the virtual city – the avatars' handlers on laptops would also appear on stage. Most importantly, the opera was inspired by the characters and aesthetics of *Yang Ban Xi* (the model operas of China's Cultural Revolution). The original 1960s' revolutionary form of live opera and ballet would later be adapted for the cinema, documenting the fantasy of socialist utopia for generations to come. Cao's virtual realities are also conceived as utopian endeavors, where one can choose another identity and live in the location of fantasy, but her works are not just pleasurable envoys into an entertaining game. Instead, they recall China's history through her reflexive use of digital/video media, conveying a new type of witting irony and political critique. Agamben once suggested that the 'close tie between cinema and history' raises the stakes of the 'specific function of the image and its eminently historical character' because history is activated, made significant, and *charged* by the image movement.[81]

RMB City is a reproduction of a metropolitan landscape, a fantasy place in Second Life that not only offers municipal resources such as the People's Palace, the People's Factory, the People's Beach, the People's Temple, and the People's Bank, but also allows others to experience 'different timelines and lifetimes' as described by the avatar Tontong, who encountered Tang poetry and Song dynasty mountain and stream paintings during his visit.[82] *RMB City*'s urban utopia is one that directly contradicts Mao's rural utopia, imagined as the proletariat culture and economic class of the countryside. Since 1949, the Communist alternative to Capitalist inequality was illustrated by the effort to raise up the poorest constituent through elevating the citizens with the lowest status, those of the largest population in the agricultural society of China. Mao's revolution was comprehensive and his movement included elevating the folk arts to represent a national form, such as the *nianhua* new year's posters prints found in every rural household.[83] While *RMB City* is an expression of the utopia of global capitalism instead of socialist equality, Cao's social-media 'second life' exemplifies the new online world alternative (with 50 per cent of China's population obtaining internet access by 2016) that has completely replaced the Communist alternative. Soon to be found in every household is the virtual and imaginary life of cyberspace, the utopic second life for everyone. The virtual life is also an escape from the prevailing government repressions that artist Ai Weiwei continues to expose through his own incarceral experience.

In keeping with the political platform for utopia, Cao published a manifesto for *RMB City* addressing the 'Virtual/Real' of the 'Mirroring City' explaining that

> If what we see and touch are real, what we breathe and feel are virtual; our voice is real, our memory is virtual; fortune is real, poverty is virtual; fulfillment is real, sadness is virtual; resentment is real, affection is virtual; foolishness is real, wisdom is virtual; reigning is real, endurance is virtual; living is real, dying is virtual; the land is real, the sky is virtual ... then, from this moment on, let all the virtual-real conflicts vanish in *RMB City*.[84]

RMB City represents a dialectic of the virtual and the real of social-media life in which Cao's 'imagined community' reconceives and updates Benedict Anderson's political conception of a nation as one that is '*imagined* because the members of even the smallest nation will never know most of their fellow-members, meet them, or even hear of them, yet in the minds of each lives the image of their communion.'[85] However, Second Life is a *global* rather than *national* territory, which is the new socio-political form in which the online community supplants the nationalist politics on the ground. While avatars do meet other members in RMB City, they are, of course, understood to be imaginary encounters, and yet, in the secondary life of social media, there is no denying that relationships and experiences are completely real to members of Instagram, Snapchat, Twitter, and Facebook. Cao explains that she was looking to use a more accessible visual language in order to 'reach a large audience,' which she believed was not the reach of conventional video art 'where you have to know the artist's thinking.' The PDA handheld practice has become a ubiquitous form of expression; as Cao notes, 'everybody uses an iPhone, It's all "new media."' When she opened the *RMB City* exhibition at the Serpentine Gallery in 2008, curator Hans Ulrich Obrist and artist Anthony Gormley were among those who were avatars in the online exhibition.[86] While Cao has achieved this user accessibility, her body of work, taken as a whole, differs from online video entertainment – her digital form of engagement has radically transformed the passive, interpellated subject of cinema through an interactive digital model of theatricality.

The cyber-territory of *RMB City* leads to the most important question: what is the interpellated subject in the digital era of globalization? Identities are always tied to a place, and as Anderson proposed for the analogue representations of twentieth-century nationalism, 'in the modern world everyone can, should, will "have" a nationality, as he or she "has" a gender.'[87] In the twenty-first-century example of *RMB City*, China Tracy could be completely devoid of any of the gendered or ethnic attributes of Cao Fei, illustrating the cover of social media where everyone is someone who they are not. The irony is not lost upon learning that Ed Mead (avatar Hug Yue) was jailed in the 1960s for his violent Communist activism, during the same period that China was experiencing the Cultural Revolution. The political cross currents play into the larger context for global identities, in which *RMB City* reveals how Chineseness, in the digital age, could be defined more distinctly as the future of transnational culture. Inderpal Grewal and Caren Kaplan explain that in the 'borderless world' of globalization 'identities are linked to cultures more than to nations or to the institutions of the nation-state.'[88] Cao's *RMB City* fulfills Grewal and Kaplan's description of the transnational as the 'complex terrain of sexual politics that is at once national, regional, local, even "cross-cultural" and hybrid'; of course, its location or place is an imaginary utopia but, as noted previously, the interaction of the viewer is very real and takes precedence over the representation itself. Indeed, Cao presents an artistic mirror of the utopia for her generation of *trans*-national conditions for *digitally* rather than *cinematically* interpellated identities, located in the liminal space where today's user relies on virtual Google maps to navigate actual physical geographies. And as a woman working in the online gaming world, which still targets the male consumer, Cao has expanded the video vocabulary while innovating the installation form of expression.

Moreover, Cao's image of utopia also mirrors the contradictions of the art world – in reality, the free market of *RMB City* is the patronage of collectors and the institutions of art, and as shown by the Minsheng Museums, they continue to function as corporate and governmental institutions on behalf of a kind of cultural/economic nationalism. Many believe that China's leaders have sold out to the global economic system, which was the very capitalist norm that Mao resisted throughout his efforts to establish the Socialist alternative. In fact, due to the fading of Marxism in the education of China's new generation, Hu Jintao in 2004 initiated the Project of Marxist Theoretical Research and Building (*Makesizhuyi lilunyanjiu he jianshegongcheng*), which was a campaign to introduce Marxism 101 into the education system. The government supported the project through funding and enlisting scholars to teach and write textbooks on the subject.[89] While Marxism (as distinct from Communist authoritarianism) has been reduced to intellectual ideology rather than socio-economic praxis, it is possible that the post-socialist Chinese state has developed 'the largest think-tank community in the world,' according to Kwai-Cheung Lo, who asserts that the 'five hundred research centers with four thousand full-time researchers' at the Chinese Academy of Social Sciences in Beijing alone are 'controlled and disciplined products of the state-party.'[90] Since China now appears more like a country competing for global economic supremacy rather than a fully practicing communist state, theorists such as Lo and Liu Kang suggest that the political project of Althusserian interpellation has *failed*. Liu explains that Althusser had 'tried to elevate dialectical materialism to the status of a metacritical and self-reflexive methodology or a "theory of knowledge,"' which, in hindsight, could be viewed as highly successful, having led the way to the Foucauldian era of power-knowledge.[91] However, interpellation was originally a methodology for making humane 'whole' subjects for a life lived outside of capitalist alienation, the very objective of Mao's socialist alternative.

In today's politics of Chineseness, the specter of Mao has made a resurgence in political philosophy, while at the same time, the old Orientalist conception of China as the 'Asiatic threat' that began during the Opium Wars has reappeared. Badiou in 2005 wrote a controversial defense of China's Cultural Revolution as a 'constant and lively reference of militant activity throughout the world,' particularly in his country of France.[92] His reflection on his participation in the 1960s period in history reveals the way in which French and Chinese ideas were incorporated: 'to live otherwise, to think otherwise: the Chinese – and then we – called that "revolutionarization." They said: "To change the human being in what is most profound."'[93] Badiou was referring to the 1968 Paris demonstrations, whose intellectuals were inspired by Mao's anti-rightist, anti-bourgeois campaigns occurring at the same moment. Many theorists such as Yiju Huang criticized Badiou for glossing over the trauma and violence incurred by the Cultural Revolution, and Slavoj Žižek was openly critical in his reassessment of Mao and his campaigns.[94] In his 2007 essay, 'Mao Zedong: The Marxist Lord of Misrule,' Žižek invokes Hegelian identity politics by rearticulating the 'Asiatic' threat: 'It is THIS Asiatic "radical strangeness" which is mobilized, politicized, by Mao Zedong's Communist movement,' and in the sentences to follow, he associates Hegel's theory to what he describes as the 'female' ambition and ineffective power of Mao: 'woe to a society in which women endeavor directly to influence decisions concerning the affairs of state, manipulating their weak male partners, effectively emasculating them ... Is there not something similar in the terror aroused by the prospect of the awakening of the anonymous Asian crowd?'[95]

Whether referring to the initiatives of Mao's wife Jiang Qing or to the female members of the Red Guard, he suggests that masculine power is the only proper rule of a country. Born in Slovenia in the 'liberal' communist country of Yugoslavia (at the time), Žižek appears to be in complete agreement with Hegel's assertion that military valor among the 'Asiatics' 'is not the calm courage of order' but one that 'passes into effeminacy; allows its energies to sink, and makes men the slaves of an enervated sensuality.'[96] While this kind of thinking appears out of step with twenty-first-century concepts of gender, the dominance of masculine military and governmental power continues today, unabated and unchallenged overall.

Žižek appears to commend Mao's socialist achievement in the same breath: 'his name stands for the political mobilization of the hundreds of millions of anonymous Third World population.'[97] But his identification with Hegel's view of Asiatic otherness stands in direct contrast to the way in which Badiou was himself identified with the Cultural Revolution as 'our political history … I can say "our," I was part of and in a certain sense, to quote Rimbaud, "I am there, I am still there".'[98] Chinese commentators consider both Badiou and Žižek as having misread Mao and the actual conditions of China's Cultural Revolution; however, Badiou's reflection can be construed as a decolonialist gesture of solidarity in the political identity of Chineseness, while Žižek's commentary perpetuates the old Orientalist form of Chineseness whereby the manufacture of otherness supports the stereotype of China as a continuing Asiatic threat.[99] Moreover, Žižek insists that his stereotypical characterization of China established in Hegel's *Philosophy of History* can be found in the writings of Heidegger and Levinas, through the tradition of defending 'the Greek breakthrough, the founding gesture of the "West," the overcoming of the pre-philosophical, mythical, "Asiatic" universe, to struggle against the renewed "Asiatic" threat – the greatest opposite of the West.'[100] The unfathomable use of philosophy here to assert the continuing stereotype of Chineseness is hard to conceive, and it is not an assertion that should be taken lightly. And yet, that is exactly how it appears to be interpreted by Žižek, as either an ironic commentary on China's economic status or an overt perpetuation of the trope of the Asiatic threat. The intellectual challenge to Hegel's nineteenth-century masculinist power and colonialism has been overwhelmingly bypassed and neglected in philosophical discourse. One major way to address the problem would be to encourage the writing of the figure of 'woman' in the transnational texts of philosophy and history.

Conclusion: the futurist utopias of *nuren* (woman) from the Buddhist past

Providing an alternative to Žižek's reductive sign of woman as the perpetual masculinist threat, the figure of Empress Wu has become an important example of politically powerful women in China's history (however short that list may be) and a ruler who should be recognized for her contributions to philosophy. According to Wing-Tsit Chan, the teaching of the *Jin shizi zhang* associated with the Empress from the Huayan school of Buddhist thought was considered the highest, most syncretic development of Chinese Buddhism in the last millennium.[101] Originating from the Avataṃsaka Sūtra in Sanskrit, the *Jin shizi zhang's* metaphysical discourse was one that could show how matter and emptiness are not different, in addition to the way in which 'things arise through causation' at the same time that its 'non-coming-into existence' occurs. By juxtaposing the material forms of bronze and cardboard lions, the *Scavenger* lion can be viewed as a portrayal of these concepts with the paper lion eventually ending at the recycling plant. The goal of the sutra is to grasp perfect harmony, which in Tan's expression can also reflect the environmental goals of the Anthropocene era. Chan's translation of the text acknowledges the materialist meaning: 'the one and the many totally involve each other, we look at one particle of dust and [everything] suddenly becomes manifest. As the "this" takes in the "other," we look at a tiny hair and all things appear together ... when the mind understands, all dharmas can be free and at ease, and because the principle is clear, great wisdom can be achieved.'[102] Perceived through the environmental crisis today, a greater understanding of the causations among all of life in the material world, not just human life, would indeed be transformed if the entire global population is able to grasp those connections.

Empress Wu (often under the name Wu Zhao) was an extraordinary figure, who understood the opportunity she was given to rule as a woman in the patriarchal Confucian system of governance. To establish the honorific terms of her reign, she adopted twenty-three titles for each stage of her sovereign rule and assigned her own archaic names to official state bureaus from the Confucian *Liji Book of Rites* and the *Shujing Book of Documents*.[103] In a society where women were prohibited from showing their faces in public, she changed tradition and refused to manage affairs of the state behind a curtain. She kept male concubines to assert her status and rule as Empress, even as she herself entered the court of Emperor Gaozong as a concubine. It is largely understood that Fazang's support enabled Empress Wu to retain the sovereignty of China, and likewise, her support of the production of large numbers of Buddhist texts is the reason why Fazang remained an influence until his death. Wu is now considered as *The Woman Who Discovered Printing*, the title of Timothy Hugh Barrett's book recognizing the impact of her support of Buddhism.

These are the ways in which Wu Zetian challenged the seventh-century models for women and power, and she is still considered as the only woman to have achieved sovereignty outright. She has been made the subject of countless historical biographies, which to this day, however, have not adequately characterized her by the nobility of her achievements. According to Xianlin Song, she is consistently portrayed as insidious, crafty, diabolical, and cruel – a ruthless concubine and lascivious seductress, who used political trickery and manipulated military power to accomplish those achievements and maintain her rule.[104] The dragon-lady characterization has only recently been challenged, as exemplified by the 2007 book, *Nuren: Wu Zetian* (Woman: Wu Zetian), written by Zhao Mei, whose project was initiated when she answered an invitation by filmmaker Zhang Yimou to develop Empress Wu's biography for a potential film.[105] Song argues that Zhao's biography is remarkable because she addresses the biases in the Chinese language itself in her study of Wu, transforming the gendered structures of meaning in which the very term for empress – *huanghou* – translates to 'one who stands behind the emperor.' Of course, the gendering of every language affixes the signifier of 'woman' to a prescribed social position and the post-Socialist signifier in China is *nuren*, a term that Tani Barlow recognizes as having evolved from the 'national subject *funü* and a defiantly sexualized, retheorized *nuxing*.'[106] Perennially under Confucian protocols connecting gender to kinship and the state, the term *funü* under Mao was a validation of 'female' according to economic class, whereas *nuxing* carried the 'feminine' from a heteronormative sexualization that was complicit with bourgeois commodification. Song suggests that 'women are still being oppressed by the process of signification in history writing' and the solution requires 'inclusion of women both as subjects and as historians [to] change the way in which history is conceived.'[107] Her exhortation is especially relevant for the gendered subjects of art history.

In the age of *global art*, artists such as Cao Fei, Wu Mali, and Yuk King Tan have convened a gendered effort transnationally to create an interpellated subject of Chineseness on film that resists and challenges the intransigence of the old and new patriarchal orders. Their artistic use of the film installation form follows the same deconstructive methodology for understanding how subjects are made by social structures and economic conditions in their redoubling of the concept of ideological 'representation' (the representation of identity, and the representation of the artwork). They have brought into discourse the contradictions of cultural revolution, Maoism, utopia, global capitalism, and labor; and they have provided an alternative representation to counter the 'mythical Asiatic' characterization passed down from patriarchal colonialism. What is at stake is the detrimental notion that China, Chineseness, and 'woman' are inextricably bound to an outdated, yet interminable, Asiatic otherness – if indeed the Hegelian terms for 'effeminacy' continue to reduce the sign of woman to an enervated, weakened political state of affairs.

The importance of Cao, Wu, and Tan's work is in showing the vital complexity of the (eco)feminist subject in a globalized political philosophy. The point of Cao's *RMB City*, for instance, is to acknowledge the ubiquity of the utopia of the China Dream in all of the metropolises, cities, and rural regions of every country implicated by global capitalism. In Hong Kong, Tan's matriarchal subject elevates the status of the elderly and the poor whose labor as recyclers is important work. While Tan's youtube engagement is the digital form of interpellation for the twenty-first century, her objectives can be viewed as aligning with traditional Marxist ideals for recognizing the ragpicker-class of the capitalist world. But as updated by Cao's manifesto, 'fortune is real, poverty is virtual' in the dialectical materialism of cyberspace as Althusser's 'real conditions of existence' have been surrendered to the illusions of virtual life.[108] Cao's dialectics for the virtual and the real are nonetheless compatible with the *Jin shizi zhang*'s metaphysical discourse, in which matter and emptiness are ultimately the same. In contrast, Wu Mali's form of engagement in *By the River, On the River, Of the River* was anything but virtual, as she performatively immerses her viewers by boat into the actual flow of the Danshui tributaries. A life in tune with the cosmos, with existence, as invoked by Jean-Luc Nancy, is comparable to a life aligned with the Buddhist aim for 'grasping perfect harmony' as defined by the understanding that 'all phenomena clearly exist before us and one does not obstruct the other.'[109] The ecofeminist position in the Anthropocene era is differentiated by the privileging of all life, not just human life, and thus relinquishes the power to obstruct the other.

Notes

1 See Moderation(s): Yuk King Tan Tour. Incidents of Travel, website for Witte de With Center for Contemporary Art, Rotterdam. www.wdw.nl/en/our_program/events/moderation_s_yuk_king_tan_tour_incidents_of_travel_hong_kong (accessed 15 August 2017). Yuk King Tan and Chow Chun Fai, *The Limit of Visibility* exhibition, 2P Contemporary Art Gallery, Hong Kong, 15 May–19 July 2012.

2 Jean-Luc Nancy and John Paul Ricco, 'The Existence of the World is Always Unexpected,' in Heather Davis and Etienne Turpin, eds, *Art in the Anthropocene: Encounters among Aesthetics, Politics, Environments and Epistemologies* (London: Open Humanities Press, 2015), 87.

3 See Jinhua Chen, 'More Than a Philosopher: Fazang (643–712) as a Politician and Miracle Worker,' *History of Religions*, vol. 42, no. 4 (May 2003).

4 See 'HK Crowned World's Most Competitive Economy,' *South China Morning Post* (Thursday 1 June 2017) and Benjamin Haas, 'Where the Wind Blows: How China's Dirty Air Becomes Hong Kong's Problem,' *Guardian* (16 February 2017), www.theguardian.com/cities/2017/feb/16/hong-kong-death-trap-dirty-air-pollution-china (accessed 16 October 2017).

5 See Edward Wong, 'On Scale of 0 to 500, Beijing's Air Quality Tops "Crazy Bad" at 755,' *New York Times* (12 January 2013), A16 and Javier C. Hernandez, 'Climate Change May Be Intensifying China's Smog Crisis,' *New York Times* (25 March 2017), A10.

6 *The China Post* (6 January 2017), www.chinapost.com.tw/life/environ ment/2017/01/06/488655/harmful-air.htm (accessed 17 August 2017).

7 Wu Mali, 'Who's Listening to Whose Story?' *World Art*, vol. 5, no. 1 (2015), 190.

8 Boris Groys, 'Politics of Installation,' *e-flux journal*, no. 2 (January 2009), 4.

9 Rey Chow, *Primitive Passions: Visuality, Sexuality, and Contemporary Cinema* (New York: Columbia University Press, 1995), 31.

10 Ibid., 33.

11 Shelden Hsiao-peng Lu had published his 1997 anthology on post-Cold War transnational film studies to track this Chinese subject, one that came to be connected in the twenty-first century among what Shu-Mei Shih characterizes as 'Sinophone communities,' whose spoken text of Chinese language is shared among China, Hong Kong, Taiwan, and diasporic locations. See Sheldon Hsiao-peng Lu, *Transnational Chinese Cinemas* (Honolulu: University of Hawaii Press, 1997) and Shu-mei Shih, *Visuality and Identity: Sinophone Articulations Across the Pacific* (Berkeley: University of California Press).

12 Chris Berry, 'Icy Summer,' in Renate Wiehager, ed., *Cao Fei: I Watch That Worlds Pass By* (Gent: Snoeck, 2016), 216.

13 See, for instance, Michel Foucault, 'The Subject and Power,' *Critical Inquiry*, vol. 8, no. 4 (summer 1982) and Judith Butler, *The Psychic Life of Power: Theories in Subjection* (Stanford: Stanford University Press, 1997).

14 See Zhang Yiwu and Jon Solomon, 'Žižek's China, China's Žižek,' *Positions: East Asia Cultures Critique*, vol. 19, no. 3 (winter 2011), 732–3 and Liu Kang, *Aesthetics and Marxism: Chinese Aesthetic Marxists and Their Western Contemporaries* (Durham, NC: Duke University Press, 2000), 158.

15 Mao Zedong, 'Talks at the Yan'an Conference on Literature and Art: A Translation of the 1943 Text with Commentary,' ed. Bonnie McDougall (Ann Arbor: University of Michigan Press, 1980).

16 Camille Robcis, '"China in Our Heads": Althusser, Maoism, and Structuralism,' *Social Text 110*, vol. 30, no. 1 (spring 2012), 51.

17 See Tani Barlow, 'Theorizing Woman: Funü, Guojia, Jiating (Chinese Women, Chinese State, Chinese Family),' in Joan Wallach Scott, ed., *Feminism and History* (Oxford: Oxford University Press, 1996), 68.

18 Louis Althusser, 'Ideology and Ideological State Apparatuses (Notes towards an Investigation),' *Lenin and Philosophy and Other Essays*, tr. Ben Brewster (New York: Monthly Review Press, 1971), 162.

19 See, for instance, Alain Badiou and Bruno Bosteels, 'The Cultural Revolution: The Last Revolution?' *Positions: East Asia Cultures Critique*, vol. 13, no. 3 (winter 2005) and Jacques Rancière, *Althusser's Lesson*, tr. Emiliano Battista (New York and London: Continuum, 2011).

20 The conventional text for the tacit declaration of the 'death' of Marxism is Francis Fukuyama, 'The End of History,' *The National Interest*, no. 16 (summer 1989).

21 Resources for eco-art include Heather Davis and Etienne Turpin, eds, *Art in the Anthropocene: Encounters Among Aesthetics, Politics, Environments and Epistemologies* (London: Open Humanities Press, 2015) and T.J. Demos, 'Contemporary Art and the Politics of Ecology,' *Third Text*, vol. 27, no. 1 (2013).

22 Description for Édouard Manet, *The Ragpicker*, c. 1865–70, Norton Simon Museum www.nortonsimon.org/art/detail/F.1968.09.P (accessed 9 August 2017).

23 HSBC Lions Fact Sheet, www.hsbc.com/history (accessed 9 August 2017).

24 Enoch Yu, 'From Bullets to Cash Machines, HSBC's 151-Year History is Closely Aligned with the Evolution of Hong Kong,' *South China Morning Post* (Sunday 24 April 2016).

25 www.hsbc.com/about-hsbc/company-history/hsbc-history (accessed 10 August 2017).

26 Mao Zedong, 'US Imperialism is a Paper Tiger,' *Selected Works of Mao Tse-tung* (14 July 1956), www.marxists.org/reference/archive/mao/selected-works/volume-5/mswv5_52.htm (accessed 18 July 2017).

27 Ibid.

28 Emily Lau, 'Paper Lion: Howe's Visit Fails to Placate the British Territory,' *Far Eastern Economic Review* (13 July 1989), 10. UK Mail quoted in Lau's article.

29 Chen, 'More than a Philosopher,' 330.

30 Wing-Tsit Chan, *A Source Book in Chinese Philosophy* (Princeton: Princeton University Press, 1963), 409.

31 Ibid.

32 Ibid.

33 Haas, 'Where the Wind Blows.'

34 Renate Wiehager, ed., *Cao Fei: I Watch That Worlds Pass By* (Gent: Snoeck Publishers, 2016), 234–5.

35 Stacy Alaimo, *Exposed: Environmental Politics and Pleasures in Posthuman Times* (Minneapolis and London: University of Minnesota Press, 2016), 1.

36 Edward Wong, 'Nearly 14,000 Companies in China Violate Pollution Rules,' *New York Times* (13 June 2017), www.nytimes.com/2017/06/13/world/asia/china-companies-air-pollution-paris-agreement.html (accessed 15 August 2018).

37 David Stanway, 'Beijing Bans High-Emission Vehicles in Anti-Smog Move: Xinhua,' *Reuters* (13 February 2017), www.reuters.com/article/us-china-pollution-autos-idUSKB5T00V (accessed 17 August 2018).

38 www.export.gov/article?id=China-Automotive-Components-Market; www.bmw-brilliance.cn/cn/en/pr/shenyang.html (accessed 5 August 2017).

39 Nicholas Jose and Yang Wen-I, *Art Taiwan: The Contemporary art of Taiwan* (Sydney: Museum of Contemporary Art, 1995), 24.

40 Ibid.

41 Katy Deepwell, 'Mali Wu: A Profile,' *n.paradoxa*, no. 5 (November 1997), 49.

42 Ibid.

43 'Vroom Vroom: Cao Fei's BMW Car Unveiled,' *The Art Newspaper* (1 June 2017), http://theartnewspaper.com/news/vroom-vroom-cao-feis-bmw-car-unveiled (accessed 30 June 2017).

44 See Rose Eveleth, 'China is Opening Around 100 Museums Every Year,' *Smithsonian.com* (21 May 2013), www.smithsonianmag.com/smart-news/china-is-opening-around-100-museums-every-year-74842851 (accessed 11 January 2018) and Mao Tse-Tung, *Let a Hundred Flowers Bloom: The Complete Text on the Correct Handling of Contradictions Among the People* (New York: Tamiment Institute, 1957).

45 Barbara Pollock, 'Shanghai's Tricky Museum Transformation,' *Artnews* (March 2014), 70.

46 Tinari as quoted in Ibid.

47 See 'The Museum Boom in China' conference, Columbia University, Graduate School of Architecture, Planning and Preservation, 14 October 2016.

48 Walter Benjamin, *The Arcades Project*, tr. Howard Eiland and Kevin McLaughlin (Cambridge, MA: Belknap Press, 1999), 907.

49 Ibid., 285.

50 https://web.archive.org/web/20120822121136/http://en.bmw-art-cars.de/BMW-ART-CARS/Home (accessed 5 August 2017).

51 Ibid.

52 Giorgio Agamben, 'Difference and Repetition: On Guy Debord's Films,' in Tom McDonough, ed., *Guy Debord and the Situationist International: Texts and Documents* (Cambridge, MA: MIT Press, 2004), 319.

53 Liu Kang, 'The Frankfurt School and Chinese Marxist Philosophical Reflections since the 1980s,' *Journal of Chinese Philosophy*, vol. 40, no. 3/4 (September/December 2013), 564.

54 Ibid., 576.

55 Zheng Bo, 'An Interview with Wu Mali,' *Field, A Journal of Socially Engaged Art Criticism* (winter 2016), 153.

56 Ibid., 161.

57 Larry Shao, 'Interview with Wu Mali,' *Asia Art Archive* (1 November 2010), www.aaa.org.hk/en/ideas/ideas/interview-with-wu-mali (accessed 18 January 2018).

58 Ibid.

59 Reiko Goto, Margaret Shiu and Wu Mali, 'Ecofeminism: Art as Environment – A Cultural Action/WEAD,' *Bamboo Curtain Studio Newsletter* (3 December 2014).

60 Shao, 'Interview with Wu Mali.'

61 Ibid.

62 *The Inside Out: New Chinese Art* was organized by the Asia Society Galleries and the San Francisco Museum of Modern Art, debuting at the Asia Society Galleries, New York, and P.S. 1, Long Island, New York, 15 September 1998.

63 See Cindy Sui, 'Taiwan Kuomintang: Revisiting the White Terror Years,' *BBC News Taipei* (13 March 2016), www.bbc.com/news/world-asia-35723603 (accessed 20 December 2018).

64 Juan Mei-shu, *Yionan chiaolou te ch'isheng: hsunchao 2–28 sanluo te yitzu (Sound of Weeping in a Dim Corner: Looking for the Dispersed February 28 Victim's Families)* (Taipei: Ch'ien-wei, 1992).

65 Elsa Hsiang-chun Chen, 'Wu Mali: My Skin is my Home/Nation,' *Contemporary*

Chinese Art – Another Kind of View, DSL Collection (2008), www.g1expo.com/
fiche.php?id=26 (accessed 18 July 2017).

66 Trinh T. Minh-Ha, 'Documentary Is/Not a Name,' *October*, vol. 52 (spring 1990),
90.

67 Ibid.

68 Ibid., 95. Minh-Ha wrote: 'In its scientific "quest to make meaning," anthropology constantly reactivates the power relations embedded in the Master's confi-
dent discourses on Himself and His Other, thereby aiding both the *centripetal*
and *centrifugal* movement of their global spread.' Ibid., 93. Emphases in original.

69 Aly Song, 'The Women of China's Workforce,' *Reuters* (4 March 2014). https://
widerimage.reuters.com/story/the-women-of-chinas-workforce   (accessed   1
January 2018).

70 Scott, 'Interview with Cao Fei.'

71 Ibid.

72 Jacques Rancière, *Film Fables*, tr. Emiliano Battista (Oxford: Berg, 2006), 18.

73 Kwai-Cheung Lo, *Excess and Masculinity in Asian Cultural Productions* (New
York: SUNY Press, 2010), 35.

74 Ibid. and Kwai-Cheung Lo, 'Sinicizing Žižek? The Ideology of Inherent Self-
Negation in Contemporary China,' *Positions: East Asia Cultures Critique*, vol. 19,
no. 3 (winter 2011), 753.

75 Lo, 'Sinicizing Žižek?' 753.

76 See Jing Wang, *High Culture Fever: Politics, Aesthetics, and Ideology in Deng's
China* (Berkeley: University of California Press, 1996).

77 See Liu Kang, 'Subjectivity, Marxism, and Culture Theory in China,' *Social Text*,
no. 31/32 (1992), 114–40.

78 Hou Hanru, 'Politics of Intimacy – On Cao Fei's Work,' interview, San
Francisco, 25 February 2008, republished online in www.caofei.com/texts.
aspx?id=17&year=2008&aitid=1 (accessed 8 August 2017).

79 Flyer for the *RMB* project, http://arthubasia.org/project/rmb-city-opera-by-cao-
fei-turin-artissima-16-theater-project (accessed 9 January 2018).

80 Chin-Chin Yap, 'The Virtual Muse and her Taxman,' *Art Asia Pacific Magazine*,
no. 57 (March/April 2008).

81 Agamben, 'Difference and Repetition,' 313.

82 Hu Fang, 'Contemplating the City,' in Wiehager, *Cao* Fei, 162

83 See Julia F. Andrews and Kuiyi Shen, *The Art of Modern China* (Berkeley:
University of California Press, 2012), 141.

84 China Tracy, 'RMB City Manifesto (RMB – to be ReMember),' in Wiehager, *Cao
Fei*, 199.

85 Benedict Anderson, *Imagined Communities: Reflections on the Origin and Spread
of Nationalism* (London: Verso, 2006), 6.

86 Scott, 'Interview with Cao Fei'.

87 Ibid., 5.

88 Inderpal Grewal and Caren Kaplan, 'Global Identities: Theorizing Transnational
Studies of Sexuality,' *GLQ: A Journal of Lesbian and Gay Studies*, vol. 7, no. 4
(2001), 664–5.

89 See Lo, 'Sinicizing Žižek?' 751.

90 Ibid., 753–4.

91 Liu Kang, 'The Problematics of Mao and Althusser: Alternative Modernity and Cultural Revolution,' *Rethinking Marxism*, vol. 8, no. 3 (1995), 22.

92 Badiou and Bosteels, 'The Cultural Revolution,' 481.

93 Ibid., 482.

94 See Yiju Huang, 'On Transference: Badiou and the Chinese Cultural Revolution,' *Comparative Literature Studies*, vol. 52, no. 1 (2015).

95 Slavoj Žižek, 'Introduction: Mao Tse-tung, the Marxist Lord of Misrule,' in *Mao on Practice and Contradiction* (London: Verso, 2007), 2.

96 Georg Wilhelm Friedrich Hegel, *The Philosophy of History*, tr. J. Sibree (Ontario: Batoche Books, 2001), 207.

97 Ibid. See also 'Chronology: Slavoj Žižek – His Life' at www.lacan.com/zizekchro. htm (accessed 8 September 2017).

98 Badiou and Bosteels, 'The Cultural Revolution,' 481.

99 See the special volume 'The Chinese Perspective On Žižek and Žižek's Perspective On China,' guest editor Tonglin Lu, *Positions: Asia Critique*, vol. 19, no. 3 (winter 2011).

100 Slavoj Žižek, *On Belief* (New York and London: Routledge, 2003), 11.

101 Chan, *A Source Book in Chinese Philosophy*, 408.

102 Ibid., 424.

103 Xianlin Song, 'Re-gendering Chinese History: Zhao Mei's Emperor Wu Zetian,' *East Asia*, vol. 27 (2010), 370.

104 Ibid., 368.

105 Zhao Mei, *Nuren: Wu Zetian* (Beijing: Tuanjie chubanshe, 2007).

106 Barlow, 'Theorizing Woman: Funü, Guojia, Jiating (Chinese Women, Chinese State, Chinese Family),' 68.

107 Song, 'Re-gendering Chinese History,' 370.

108 Wiehager, *Cao Fei*, 199.

109 Chan, *A Source Book in Chinese Philosophy*, 424.

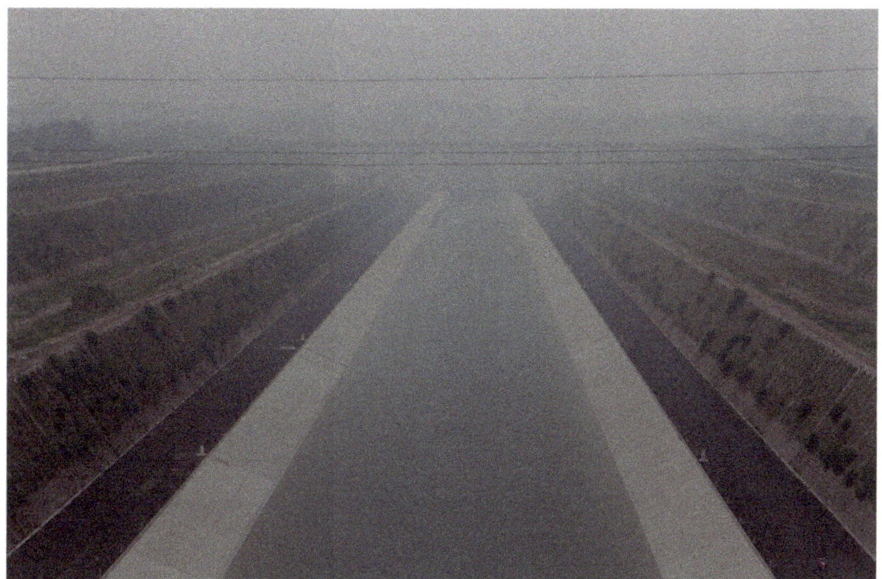

1 Patty Chang, *Configurations*, 2017, still from video installation

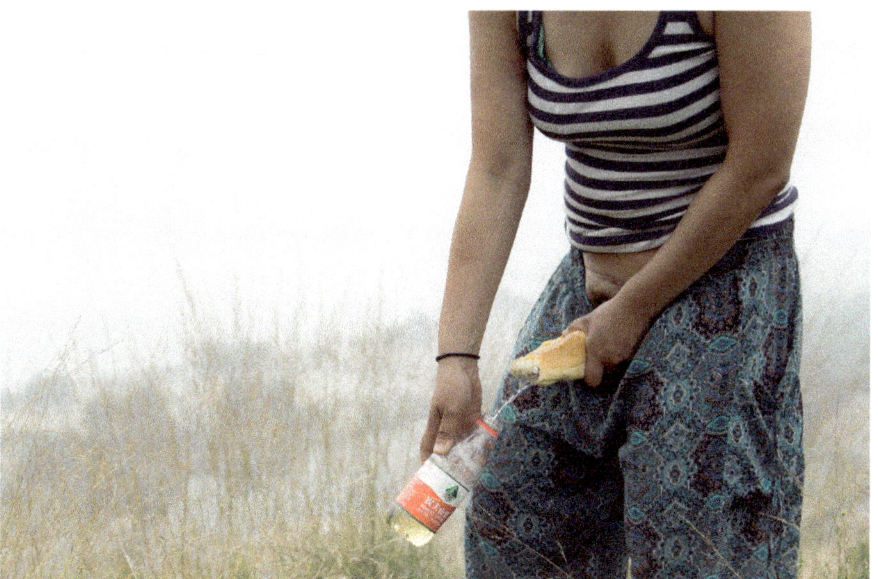

2 Patty Chang, *Configurations*, 2017, still from video installation

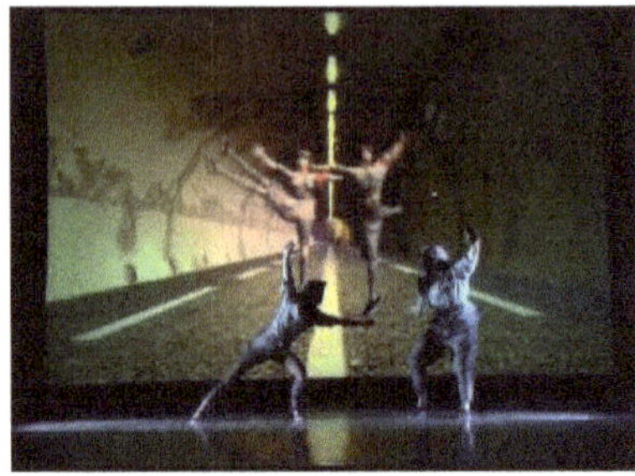

3 Cao Fei, *RMB City Opera*, 2009, film still of live staging at Artissima Art Fair and Teatro Astra in Turin – the world premiere on 7 November 2009

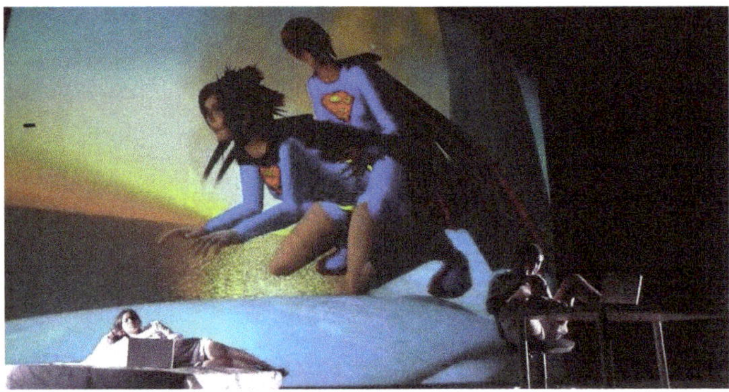

4 Cao Fei, *RMB City Opera*, 2009, film still of live staging at Artissima Art Fair and Teatro Astra in Turin – the world premiere on 7 November 2009

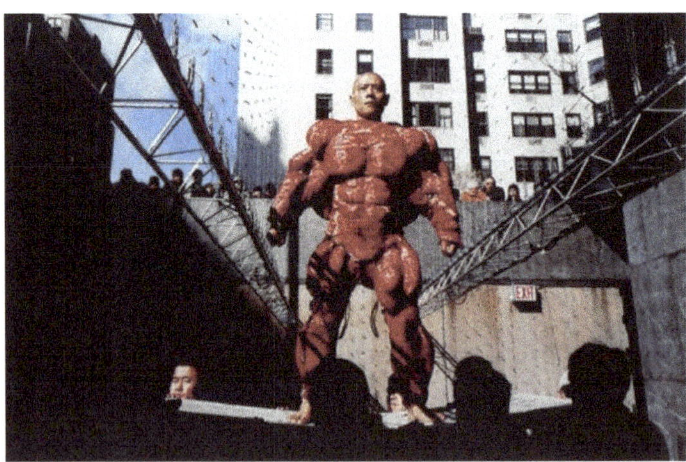

5 Zhang Huan, *My New York*, 2002, the artist wearing a suit of raw meat, presented at the Whitney Biennial

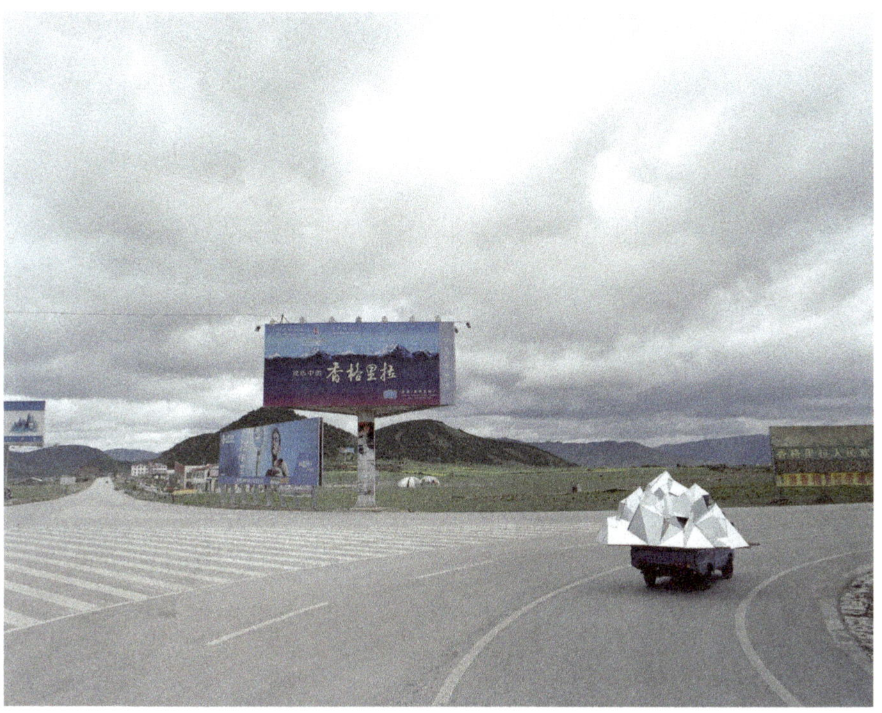

6 Patty Chang, *Shangri-La*, 2005, video still, mirrored mountain on truck

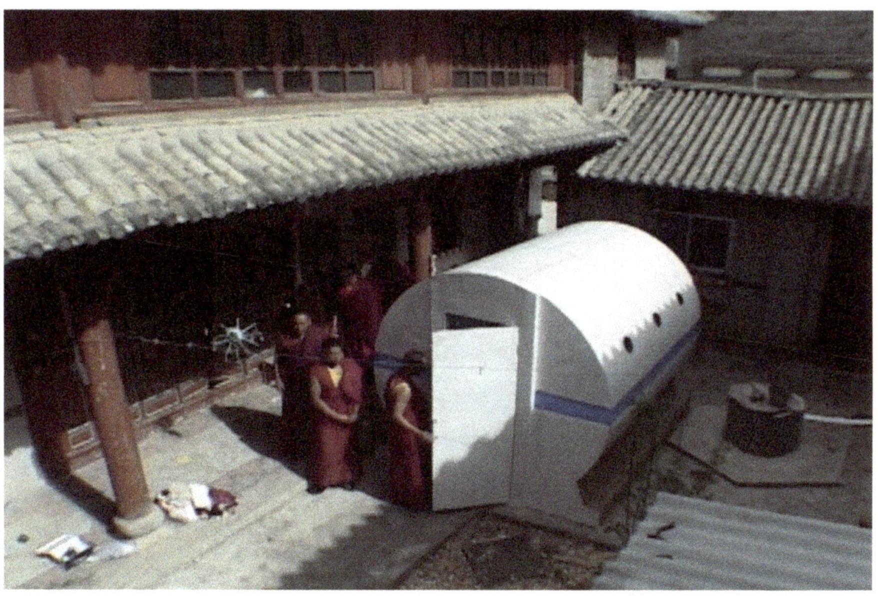

7 Patty Chang, *Shangri-La*, 2005, video still, monks entering oxygen pod

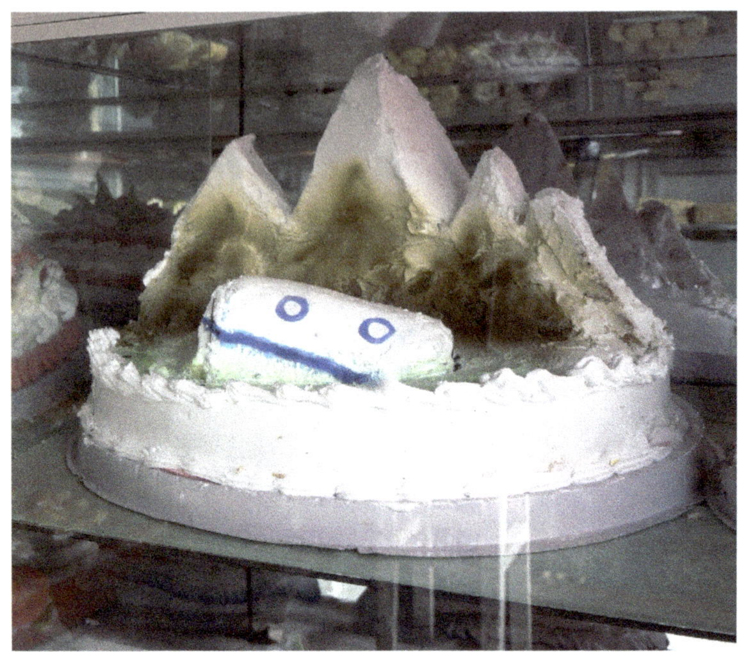

8 Patty Chang, *Shangri-La*, 2005, video still, cake decorated with mountains and pod

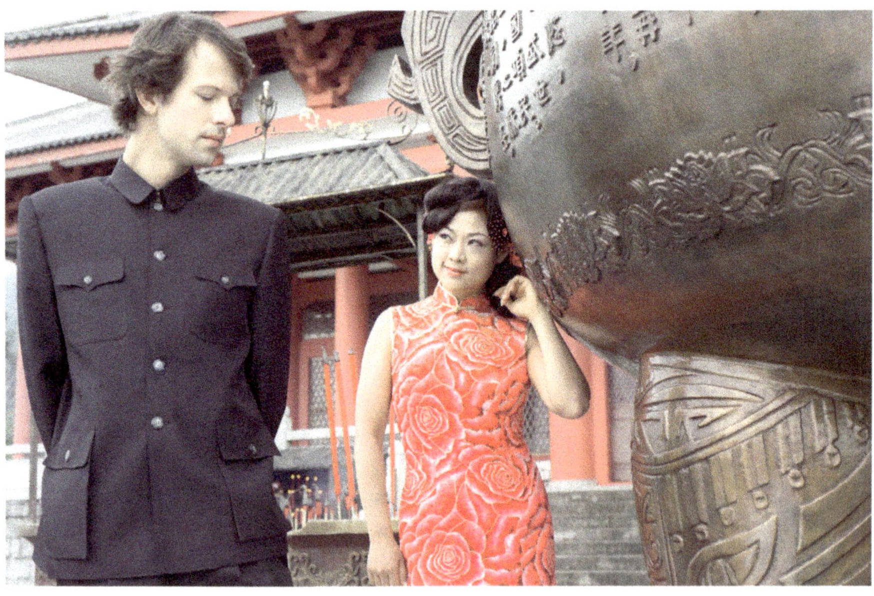

9 Patty Chang and David Kelley, *Shangri-La*, 2005, video, staged in Taiwanese-style wedding photography

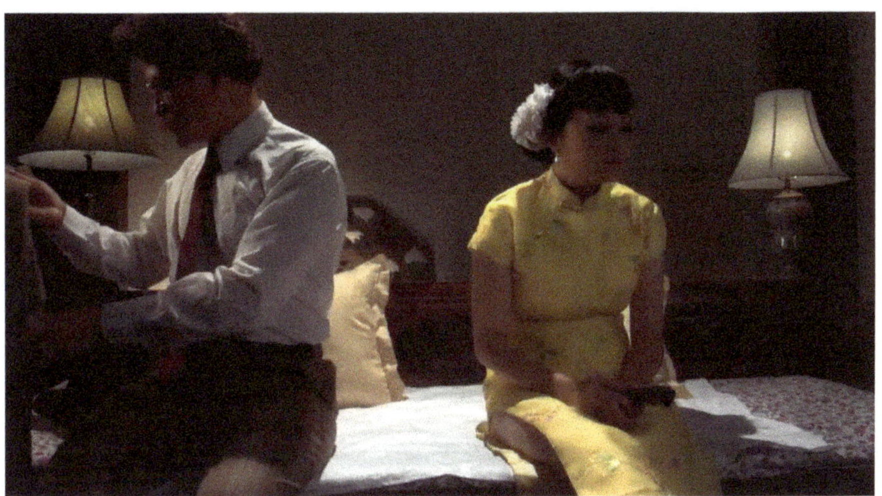

10 Patty Chang, *The Product Love (Die Ware Liebe)*, 2009, still from video installation, Hu Huaizhong as Walter Benjamin and Yi Ping as Anna May Wong

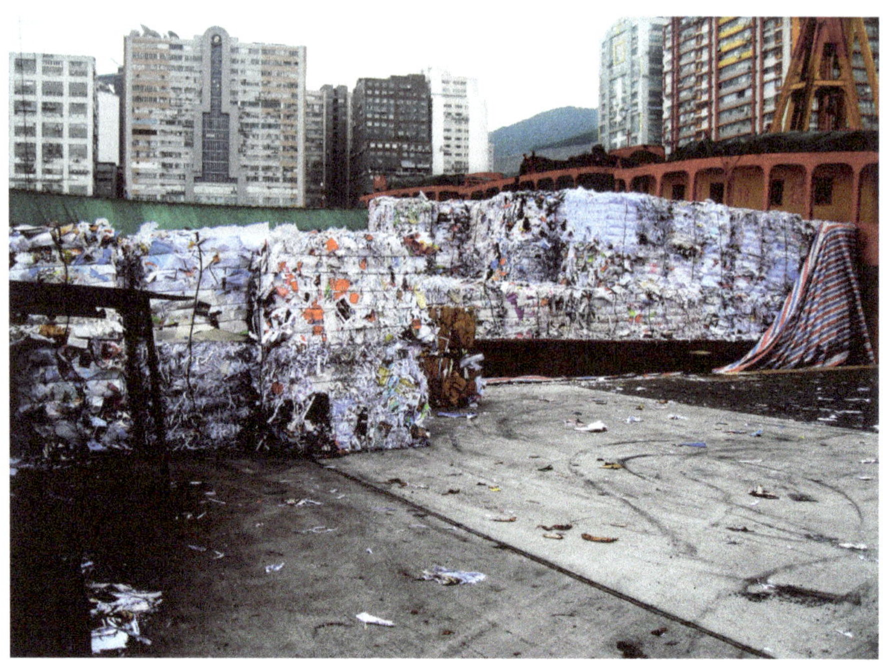

11 Yuk King Tan, *Limits of Visibility*, 2012, still from single-channel HD video loop

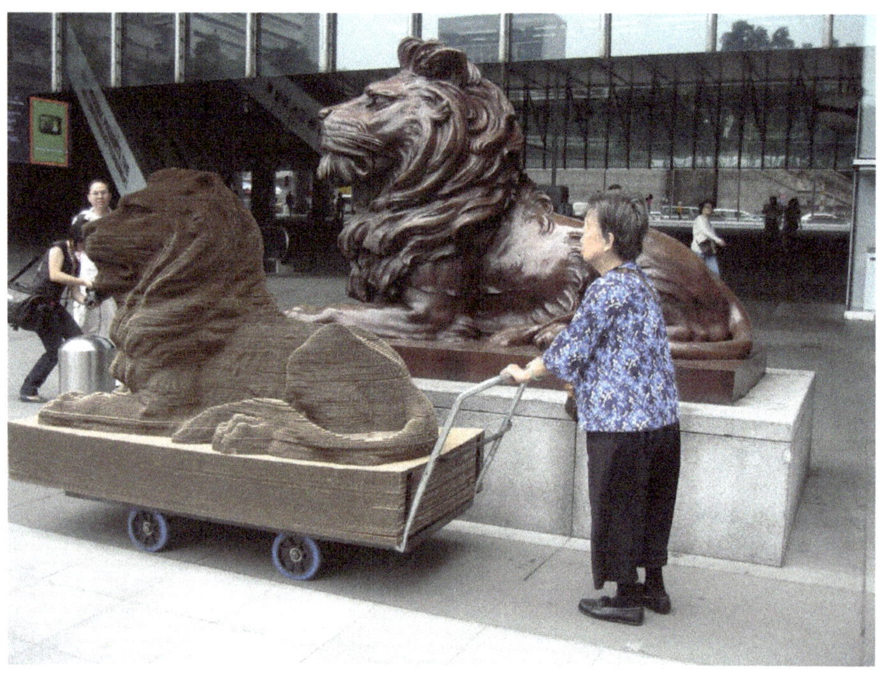

12 Yuk King Tan, *Scavenger*, 2008, still from video

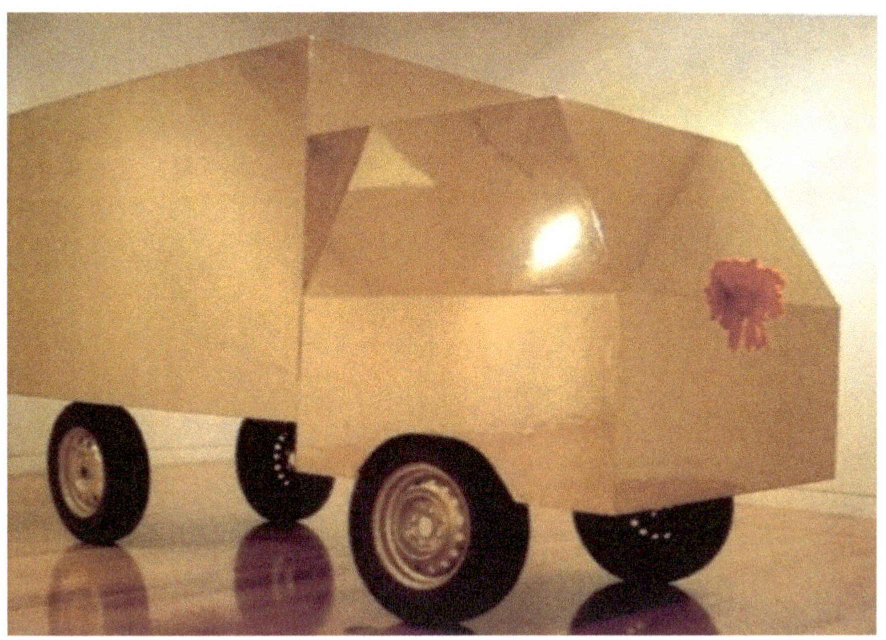

13 Wu Mali, *Prosperity Car*, 1991, mixed media

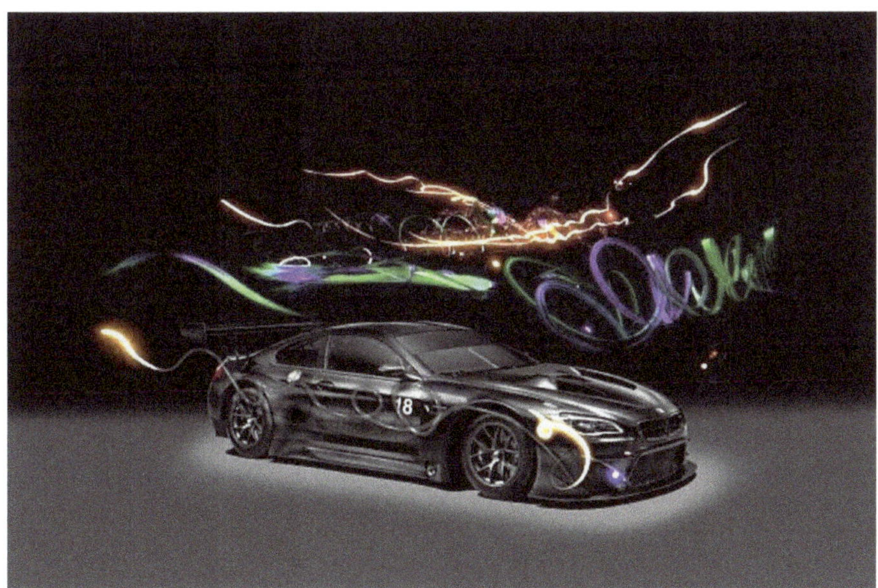

14 Cao Fei, BMW Art Car #18, 2017, designed by the artist, Beijing, Minsheng Art Museum

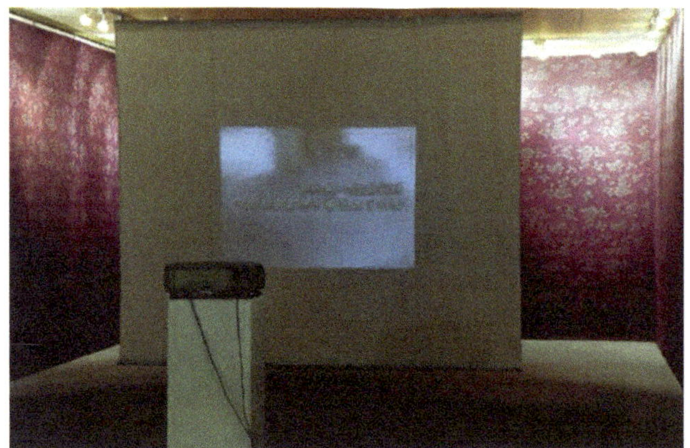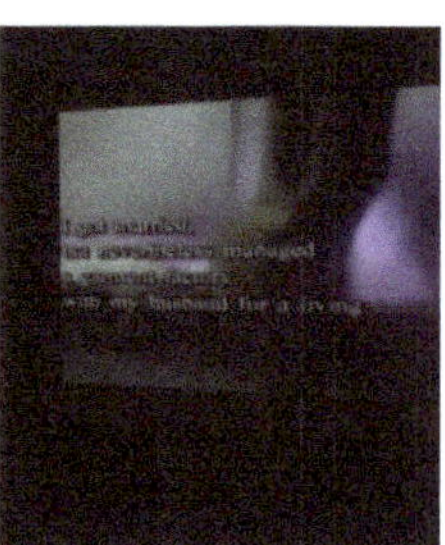

15 Wu Mali, *Stories of Women from Hsin-Chuang*, 1997, video and mixed media installation. Detail: the wall textiles are inscribed with the texts and the film reiterates the voice and texts

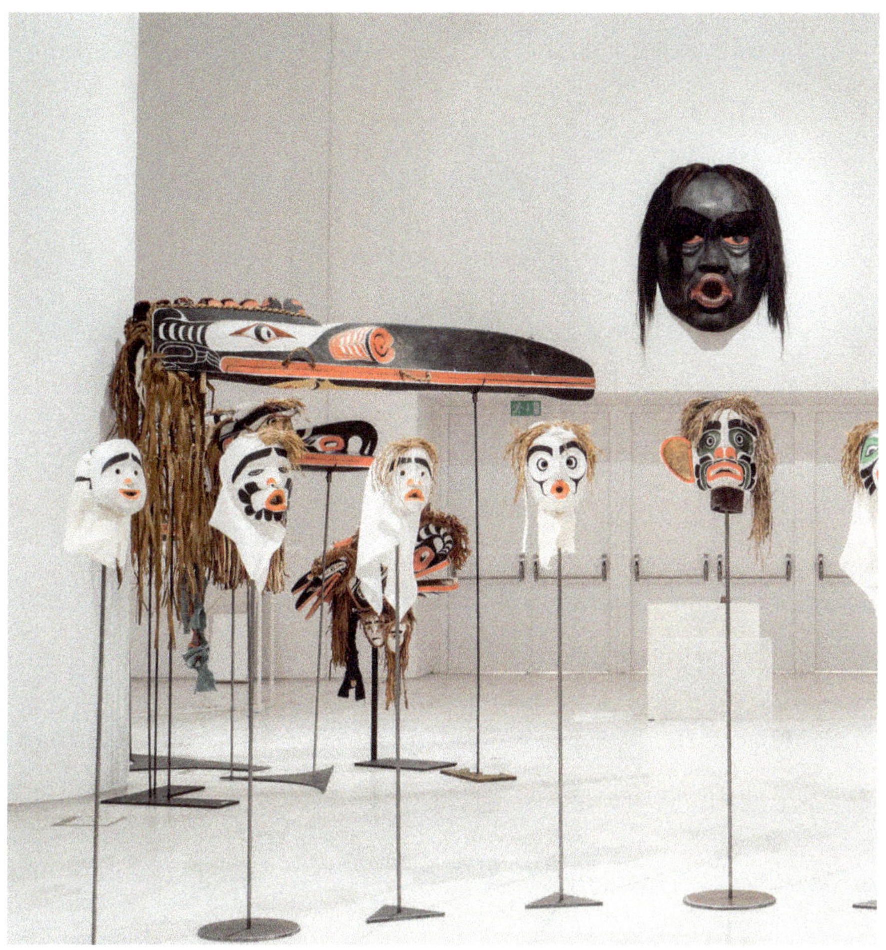

16 Beau Dick, twenty-two masks from the series *Atlakim*, 1990–2012, various materials, installation view, EMST National Museum of Contemporary Art, Athens

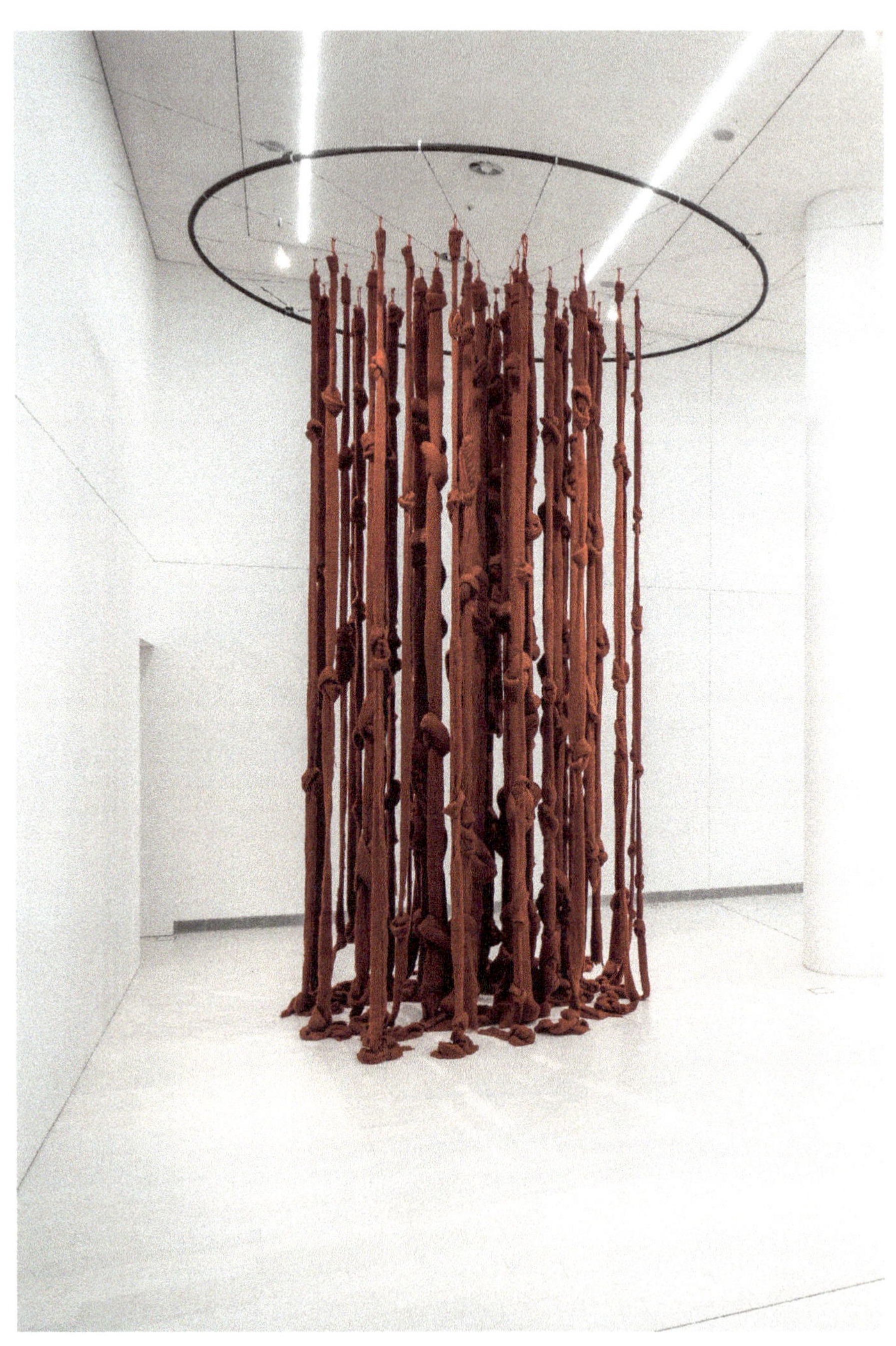

17 Cecilia Vicuña, *Quipu Womb (The Story of the Red Thread, Athens)*, 2017, dyed wool

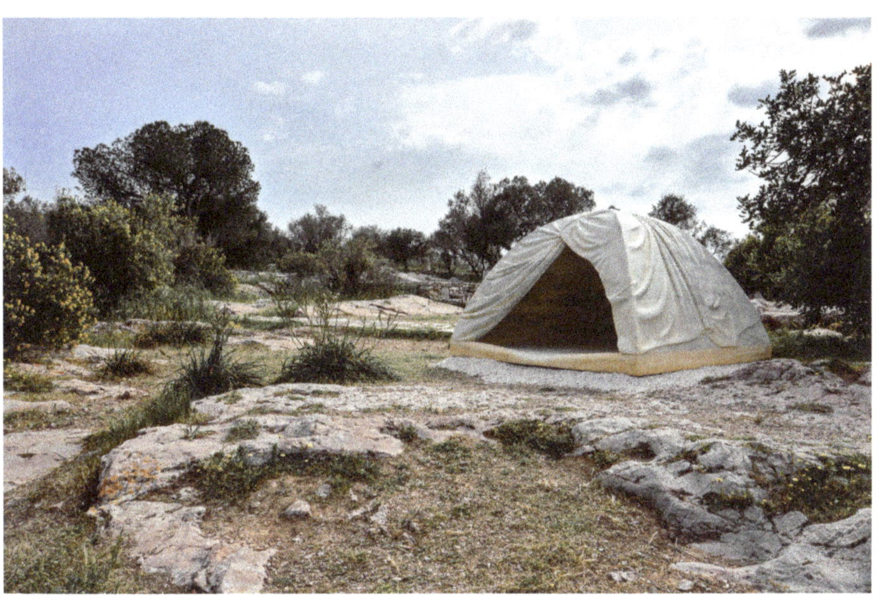

18 Rebecca Belmore, *Biinjiya'iing Onji (From Inside)*, 2017. Filopappou Hill, Athens, Documenta 14

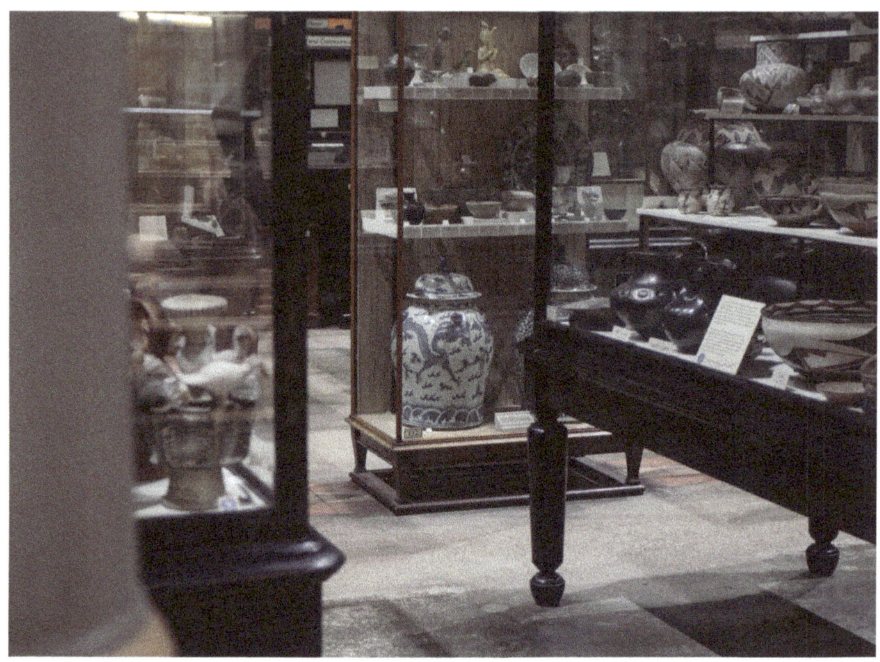

19 Ming dynasty vase at the Pitt Rivers Museum, circa 1500, from the collection of the Rajah of Sarawak, 1923. Detail below: two Ming vases

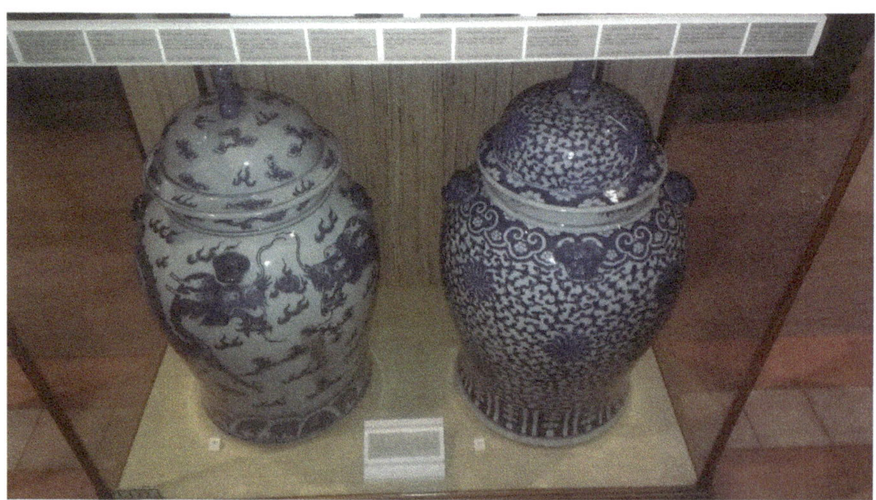

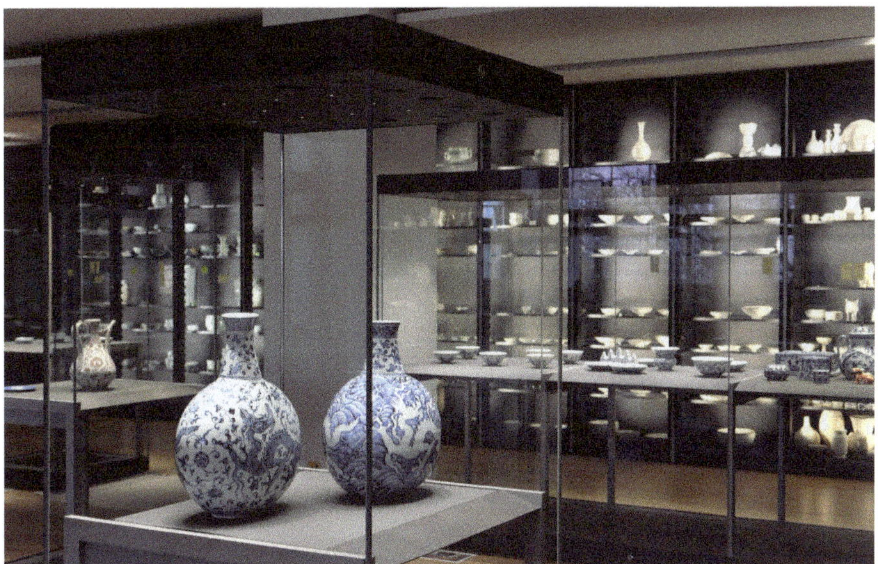

20 Ming dynasty porcelain flasks, circa 1403–24, British Museum, Gallery 95, sideways view, from the David Percival collection

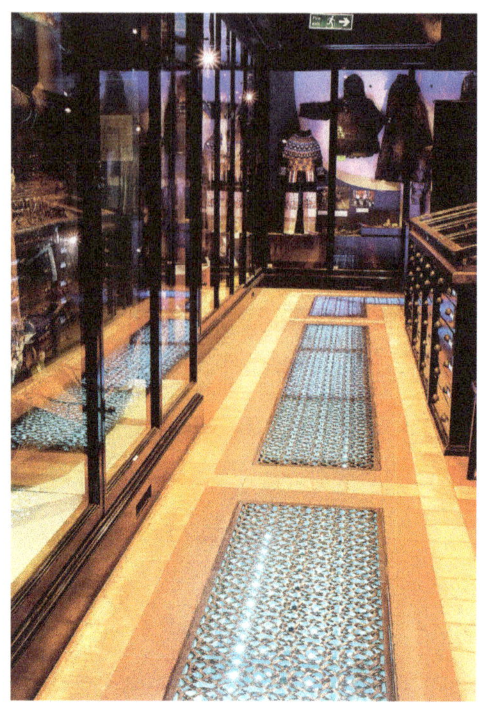

21 Wong Hoy Cheong, *Slight Shifts*, 2004, site installation at Pitt Rivers Museum

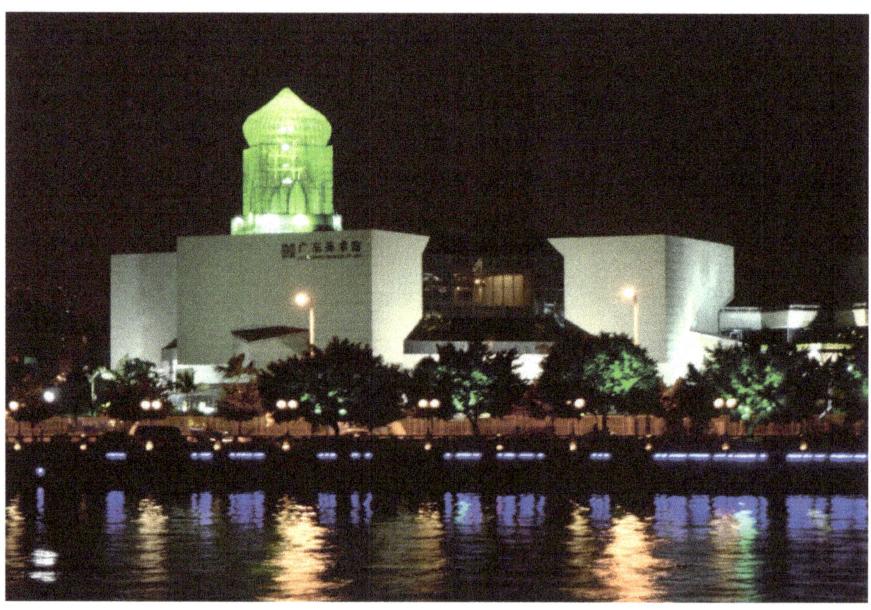

22 Wong Hoy Cheong, *Minaret*, 2005, site installation at the Guangdong Museum of Art

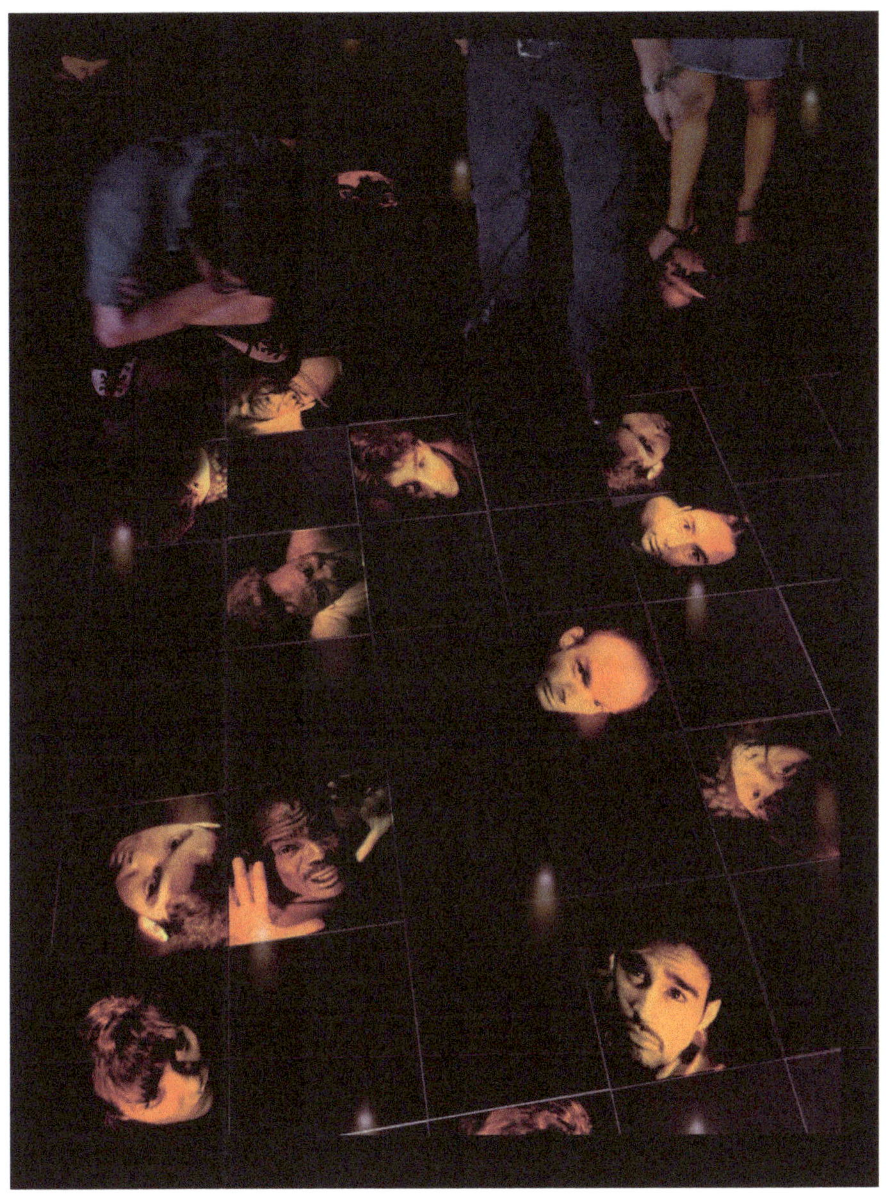

23 Lin Shumin, *Glass Ceiling*, 2001, hologram, glass, and granite installation. 49th Exposition International d'arte

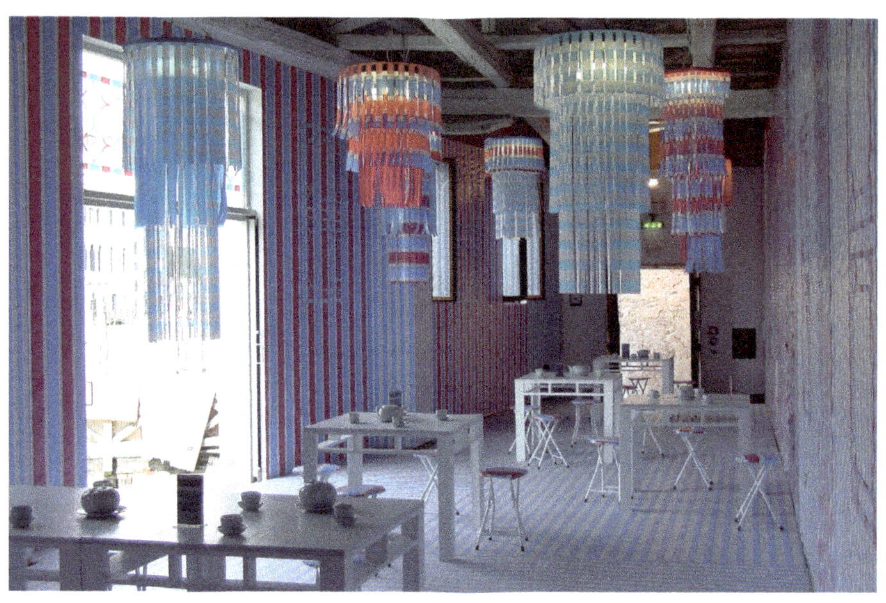

24 Anothermountainman (又一山人Stanley Wong), *redwhiteblue: tea+chat*, 2005, installation, Venice Biennale. 51st Exposition International d'arte

The dialectical image of empire   4

Dialectic of the newest and oldest
  Fashion is a canon for this dialectic also
    The oldest as newest: the daily news
  The newest as oldest: the Empire[1]

The global artfair is considered the new entity of the globalized art institution – biennials and triennials have proliferated across the globe since the 1990s, appearing in a variety of cities such as Shanghai and Guangzhou in China; and in cities from diverse regions including Istanbul, Tanzania, Brisbane, Dakar, Sao Paolo, and Kwangju, to name just a few. These expositions represent the nomadic locations for the new global contemporary art, and they have become an integrated subject of study as exemplified by the myriad of articles and books published recently on 'world's fairs, biennials, and the aesthetic experience.'[2] In theory, they appear as the very example of a de-centered and decentralized institution for art, as they are located in new places when once they were reserved solely for Euro-American states. But contrary to the notion that the biennial is a product of exhibitionary innovation, the expo's organizing principle was first conceived in the nineteenth century. The longest-running artfair, the Venice Biennale, began in 1895 and continues to be held in the Giardini di Castello where it was originally located. This archetypal institution provides a useful genealogy for investigating the structural tendencies that were closely related to the nineteenth-century world's fairs, described by Walter Benjamin as exhibitions that 'create a framework in which its use value recedes into the background.'[3] By 1895, nearly every metropolitan city in Europe and the United States had hosted a world exposition, and nearly all of these spectacular shows of progress included palaces devoted to fine art. The role played by art exhibitions in these showcases of national production was indeed important to the overall function of the fairs in promoting the colonial empire.

This chapter provides a historical foundation for Chapter Five's exploration of the *archive* of Chineseness as the first representation of Chinese artists at the historical editions (1993–2005) of the Venice Biennale as well as the first biennial/triennial expositions held in China in the 1990s. The 1992 Guangzhou Biennial and the inclusion of China's artists in the 1993 Venice Biennale were important 'firsts' in the exhibition of China's *xiandai yishu* contemporary art. In varying ways, the Venice Biennale is the origin-model for all of the new global artfairs, the biennials, triennials, and expositions appearing all over the world in the twenty-first century. An understanding of this phenomenon requires a contextualization of the Biennale's historical principles from which many different forms of nationalisms (artistic, political, phenomenological, and most significantly, capitalist-driven forms of nationalisms) were visualized through the pavilions mapped across imaginary territories. While this study may appear to stray from the focus on Chineseness, its engagement with the historical structures of artfairs contributes to the analysis of the political and symbolic function of contemporary expositions in representing Chinese art and culture. The important ways in which nations and cultures are 'staged' at these expositions provide the institutional context for understanding the global shift attributed to China's contemporary art.

In the decade after China's first participation in the Venice Biennale, the broader emergence of the global terms for art came into use, which problematized the existing cultural categories for art and expositions. Artists and curators began to instrumentalize the pre-existing structures of the biennial/triennials in order to transform the knowledge production that artfairs have perpetuated. The perceivable change occurred at Documenta 11 with Okwui Enwezor's 2002 debut as the first 'non-European art director of documenta' hosting the 'first truly global, postcolonial documenta exhibition'– as recorded in the Documenta archives.[4] Under the title 'Democracy Unrealized,' Enwezor used the opportunity of the quinquennial to stage his five political *Platforms*, which were 'to be seen as forums of committed ethical and intellectual reflection on the possibilities of rethinking the historical procedures that are part of its contradictory heritage of grand conclusions.'[5] The exposition's historical procedures and contradictory heritage were beholden to the structural tendencies for art and nationalism attributed to the world's fairs.

Since Documenta 11, the directors of subsequent biennials and triennials, including Johnson Chang Tsong-zung at the 2008 Guangzhou Triennial, adopted methods that Enwezor first used for addressing social and political issues through the themes of the exposition. Still, it is the historical premise of the artfairs that has enabled curators to utilize its inherent organizing principles to exploit the exposition's new political advantage. Begun in 1955, Documenta has always asserted a sense of political cause in the aftermath of World War II, which contrasted clearly to Venice's nineteenth-century template for exhibiting contemporary art. The postscript in this chapter, 'Learning from Athens,' provides an update to the global artfair by examining

Documenta 14 and director Adam Szymczyk's groundbreaking 2017 presentation of a second location in Athens in addition to the legacy site of Kassel, Germany. As the mythological birthplace for European art history, Athens symbolizes the Classical ideal for art as the foundation for the Kantian relationship between aesthetics and democracy.

As such, Documenta 14's inclusion of the Native American masks of the Kwakwaka'wakw indigenous peoples in the prime exhibition space in Athens, the EMST National Museum of Contemporary Art, was an act that broke from the mythological norm of Art History. The separation of cultures according to art and anthropology was visually constructed by the spaces and architectures of the nineteenth-century world's fairs. As explored in this chapter, the *exposition universelles* were the progenitors of the 1895 Venice Biennale, and they had contributed to the establishment of this art historical norm, one that apparently took over a hundred years to change. In 2017, the pure realism of Athens as the center of the refugee crisis and economic austerity came into conflict with the mythological Greek legacy, and by siting the artfair in the midst of the city's problems, Szymczyk appears to have followed the political example that Enwezor had instantiated with Documenta 11. The use of Documenta 14 as a proscenium stage for the world to see the crisis in Athens extended the practice and function of Enwezor's political objectives for the 2002 quinquennial.

In 2015, Enwezor took the mantle of change again when he was appointed the head of the Venice Biennale as the first African director in the exposition's history. Thirteen years after his debut at Documenta, the veteran curator boldly centered his *All the World's Futures* show on Karl Marx's three volumes of *Das Kapital* (published in 1867, 1885, and 1894 respectively) by enlisting performers to read the entire text from beginning to end on stage every day in the Arena, the Biennale's central pavilion. The live readings were called *Das Kapital Oratorio*, 'a massive, meticulously researched bibliographic project elaborated and directed by Isaac Julien.'[6] Renewed from the spectres of Marx, Enwezor acknowledges the self-critical contradictions of art; as explained in his exhibition catalogue, the 'current art system's casual and unquestioning relationship to power, its love of its trappings and privileges, its very acquiescence to power, perhaps represents not only the utter farcical notion of art's claim to radical autonomy but also its complete powerlessness to be transformative.'[7] Enwezor also invokes Benjamin's premonitions in his interpretation of Paul Klee's *Angelus Novus* (1920), the monoprint, as the example of 'how a work of art can challenge us to see much further and beyond the prosaic *appearance of things*.'[8] In view of this challenge, the historical enormity of artfairs and world expositions tend to prevent us from *seeing* the significance of the fact that it has taken a hundred and twenty years before a black man was given the leadership of the Venice Biennale.

Structural tendencies: the global artfair in Venice

As the legacy art exposition, the Venice Biennale began in 1895 during the 'age of empire' as the period of imperialism, which Lenin once distinguished as having 'economic roots in a specific new phase of capitalism' that led to, among other things, 'the territorial division of the world among the great capitalist powers.'[9] Something like the custodial relic-ruin, the geography of the Venice Biennale still reflects the old imperialism – frozen in time is the mapping of the nineteenth-century economic supremacy of European and North American nations. The exception to the rule was Japan's 1905 victory in the Russo-Japanese war, which led to the country's status as a first-world power, and therefore the country was given 'unofficial' representation in 1897 at the second edition of the Venice Biennale. As the *only* East Asian nation to host its own national pavilion throughout the twentieth century, Japan served in the role of the 'paradigmatic Other of the fine-arts system,' as described by Ignacio Adriasola, since the Japanese 'exception' helped to define the Modern for the institutional logic of the 'world-art' exposition in its early inception.[10] By 1914, the military successes of European nations had resulted in the annexation and rule of every region outside of the 'old' Asian or Spanish empires. The prime territory of the Giardini di Castello acknowledges the ruling victors, demarcated by the official plots reserved for France, Great Britain, Germany, Belgium, Denmark, Switzerland, the United States, and Hungary.

These are countries that have been exhibiting for generations at the Biennale; as announced at the 2015 edition, of the total 'eighty-nine foreign participants, twenty-nine will be in their historical pavilions at the Giardini.' As if suspended in time, this particular mise en abyme has kept in motion a signifying order of the old empire created to sustain fictional territories established on real property. The European pavilions, which are all clustered in virtually the same location decade after decade in the Giardini (see figure 4.1), are the pay-to-get-into pavilions. Included in the paid ticket in 2015 were the sites in the Arsenale added in 1980 where the aforementioned twenty-nine countries, such as China, Italy, Indonesia, and Mozambique, exhibited in this location near the docks. The ticketed pavilions are segregated from the free-to-get-into sites of the remaining forty-four Collateral Events representing countries such as Armenia, Croatia, Mongolia, Cuba, Thailand, and the Ukraine. Many are located in the 'unofficial' gallery spaces among the many piazzas along Venice's famous Grand Canal.[11]

If the Biennale's imaginary community, organized as a hierarchy of nations, appears to follow the scheme naturalized under the Hegelian 'world spirit,' it reflects nonetheless the new priorities of global capitalism. Even as Eric Hobsbawm's treatise of empire has come to represent a twentieth-century Marxist orthodoxy of the past, the twenty-first-century conception

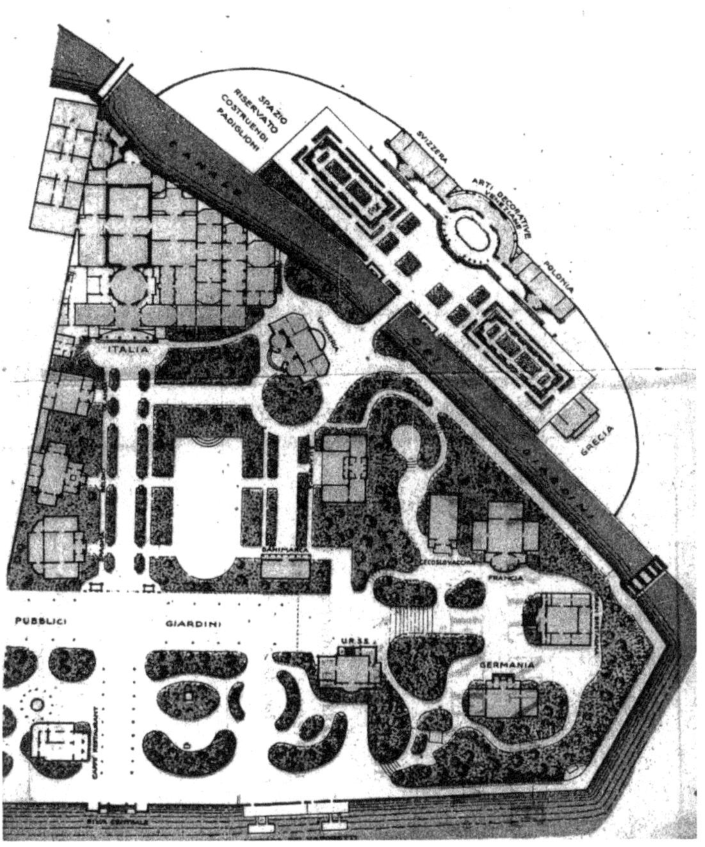

4.1 Layout of Giardini, frontispiece, *La Biennale di Venezia, Storia E. Statistiche*, Con l'Indice Generale, Degli Artisti Expositori, dal 1895 al 1932

of the 'global empire' envisioned by Hardt and Negri retrieves the elements of capitalist power and territorial divisions for articulating the activity of globalization.[12] If indeed Hardt and Negri consider the old nation-statist idea of empire as one that can no longer be used for defining present-day cultures and constituencies, the territorial determination of the artfair remains extrinsically a competition among 'nations' under the civilized aims for art. The mere fact that the Biennale institution survives these two versions of 'empire' tends to reframe the fair as a 'dialectical image' – as a prescient object for historical interpretation. This description derives from Benjamin's study in the 1930s, in which he construes the metaphysical construct of the *arcades* as historical phenomenon, referring to these shopping centers as dialectical fairylands. Benjamin was ahead of his time in his approach to the problem of interpreting history and the conditions of a past epoch. The 'image is dialectics at a standstill,' he wrote, for 'while the relation of what-has-been to the now is dialectical: is not progression but image, suddenly emergent.'[13] Largely understood as Benjamin's critique of the indiscernible social relations forged by capitalism, the architecture of the arcades could visually and tangibly express something about historical processes thought to be progressive.

Likewise, this chapter examines how the artfairs inhabit this particular 'image as dialectics at a standstill' in relation to the history of empire. The idea that the global artfair (such as the Guangdong Triennial or the Shanghai Biennale) introduces a remedy to the old imperial order for the arts requires a better historical understanding of the structures of the artfair itself, which is why Benjamin's dialectical image provides a useful philosophical point of perspective. The Venice Biennale is, by nature, a visual remainder from the time in which it was made, but serves also as an object that bespeaks something different in the present. The 'new' global artfair serves a 'post-Other' artworld in the same way that the utopic 'dream image' of the old arcades served a potential 'classless society' in Benjamin's philosophical undertaking. If his nineteenth–twentieth-century 'wish image' is indeed the desire for the 'dream in which each epoch entertains images of its successor,' a future envisioned from elements of a 'classless society,' then the 'dream' of the twenty-first century is characterized by a future of post-empire multitudes, imagined from elements of a postcolonialist 'raceless' society.[14] To view the Biennale as a 'wish image' of globalization is to transfigure what past artfairs stood for in terms of empire and commodity culture.

Begun in the *exposition universelle*, the fine arts comprised only one exhibition within the grand scale of the world's fair's universe of nationalized products. But shown in its entirety, the exposition engendered the most deceptive relationships, especially in terms of the impact of the classification of the aesthetic because the fairs demonstrated how the 'work of art' was produced solely by Euro-American nations. Conversely, the classification that ascribed the ethnographic artefact to regions subordinate to the empire made it possible for both art and ethnographic objects to be essentialized according to nation. The twentieth-century recognition of 'Western art' in contemporary terms is directly related to 'aesthetic essentialism,' and the fair's model for displaying objects in hierarchical spaces that assign status would endlessly support the sovereignty of the Western aesthetic.

Accordingly, this chapter examines the historical structures by following an analytical development for showing how the enormity of the *world's fairs* as the artfair's progenitor made it possible to instantiate many different conflicting modes of juxtaposition for the future. In visual ways, the fairs' structural tendencies illustrate the earliest conception of capitalist *contradiction*. First, the 'uselessness' of works of art was made clear by exhibiting, for instance, marble sculptures next to manufactured objects like prosthetic limbs. This model for categorizing objects was first introduced at the 1851 Great Exhibition of London, and it served to distinguish the special status of the fine arts as a national inheritance as opposed to the crude money-status of the commodity. Secondly, measuring the value of things in the context of the territorialization of the fairs would enable a way to depict the value of cultures – not only by segregating the 'primitive' cultures into the Midway amusement park area, but also through theatricalized displays of 'primitive' objects, dwellings and even people that were juxtaposed with the 'progressive' examples. The idea of 'progress' was the evolutionary premise of the fair's overarching didactic program.

The national/cultural difference between art and primitive 'fetish' was ultimately validated by an epistemological system that was established by Hegel's philosophy of world history. Thus, artistic or non-artistic production could illustrate the telos of a world history that was an evolutionary process for cultural, racial and/or national epochs. The great impact of the fairs was in their ability to simplify nationalism for the general viewing public through the aesthetic or fetish distinction. By the 1895 inauguration of the Venice Biennale, the world's fair model had proved its useful potential for exhibiting status, progress, and power. As they did in the past, world expositions in China function in the twenty-first century to bolster the country's economic status and to show national allegiance. In this way, the original nation-building purpose and aims are carried over into the new biennials and triennials; even as those historical procedures were reconceptualized by new curators and exhibition organizers in the twenty-first century.

The special 'uselessness' of the fine arts

The 'first fully realized modernist institution,' argues Donald Preziosi, was the Crystal Palace of the 1851 Great Exhibition of London because of the way in which the exposition served as the 'supreme taxonomic and comparative instrument.'[15] By creating a 'landscape of *capital*,' one that is 'coterminous with the landscape of imperialism,' explains Preziosi, the stagecraft of the Crystal Palace was the 'most complete, the most encyclopedic, and the most influential' for installing a 'panoptic and synoptic vision of modernist notions of the subject and of the national social cosmos.'[16] The artifice of the Great Exhibition fulfiled the aesthetic theories that originated with Kant, Hegel, and Winckelmann, working, as Preziosi argues, in service of capitalism and the national and imperial order. Signifying the highest production of the most civilized peoples, the fine art objects of a special status were eventually exhibited in a separate competition of their own with shows that were physically a part of the world exposition but presented in buildings and locations that set them fully apart from objects of industry, craft, and ethnography. This categorical separation by location would have profound impact in determining how 'art' continues to be defined and located to this day.

Treated distinctly as aesthetic production, the fine arts became the 'anti-commodity' in reaction against the commodification of virtually every marketable object at the world exhibitions. The separation of the fine arts was initially conceived and put into practice after the 1851 Great Exhibition of London, and in the competitive context of the international show, the British conflated the low and high status of cultural production as the means of addressing the country's disadvantage in the fine arts, while promoting its excellence in the 'mechanical arts.' During the first half of the nineteenth century, Britain was unrivaled in industrial and colonial power, and the very point of holding the first world exposition in 1851 London was to promote the triumph of the British empire.[17] However, the British fine arts legacy, now viewed as national production, was no match for the French painting tradition – one that extended from the seventeenth-century French Royal Academy of Fine Arts.[18] The measurement of art's non-utilitarian and non-commercial value was established from the commission-based patronage during the Italian Renaissance and extended into the French Salon (the fine arts in modernity understood as inherited by the French).

Art historian Patricia Mainardi explains that throughout the nineteenth century, the French Academy 'maintained a contradictory attitude toward the Salons: it wanted to abolish them ... for they bore the odious taint of commercialism ... the most distinguished artist worked only on commission and would exhibit solely for didactic purposes.'[19] To exhibit work that was for sale was considered as placing painting and sculpture in the position of the artisan/craft class of crass shopkeepers. The British, through the 1851 Exhibition, initiated the model for exhibiting industrial objects in the category of the 'mechanical arts,' highlighting the similarities of these artisan-crafted products, as they were displayed in close proximity to the fine art sculptures. By excluding the medium of painting, the sole representation of sculpture could elevate the 'mechanical arts,' since the elements that went into making sculpture – raw materials, a prototype cast, and assistant laborers – were analogous to the elements of industrial manufacturing. Displayed together, the mutual forms of production of sculpture and industrial objects could be viewed in association.

The effort to elevate the lowest categories of human production by exhibiting them with the highest at the London exhibition was articulated in the

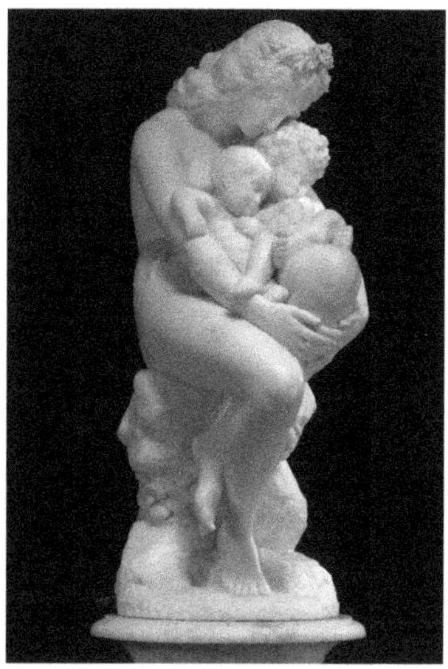

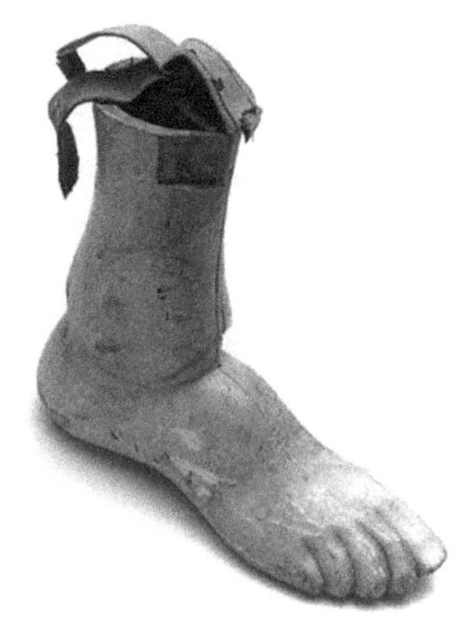

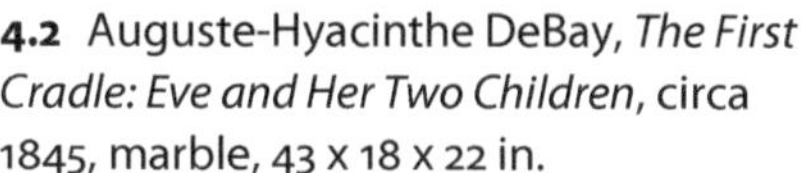
4.2 Auguste-Hyacinthe DeBay, *The First Cradle: Eve and Her Two Children*, circa 1845, marble, 43 x 18 x 22 in.

4.3 Nineteenth-century prosthetic wooden foot

granting of awards as well as in the installation of artworks with industrial works. For instance, the sculptor Pradier was given the Council Medal, the highest exposition award, but his winning artwork, entitled *Phryne*, was listed in the exhibition catalogue among the 'specimens of woolen yarn combed by machinery.'[20] As well, the display of Auguste-Hyacinthe DeBay's sculpture, *The First Cradle: Eve and her Two Children*, was exhibited next to an artificial foot (see figures 4.2 and 4.3). Jules Janin, the French critic, had this to say about the British disregard for the two centuries of effort by the French to retain the high status of the fine arts: 'Go on then, seat the *Venus de Milo* on an anvil; hitch up the *Apollo Belvedere* to a bale of merchandise, make a beer advertisement out of Phidias's *Jupiter*!'[21] It was here at the 1851 display of the prosthetic limb next to the modeled marble foot of Eve that the argument for developing a fine art separation from commodity production could be justified. The special sphere of artistic autonomy would henceforth be reserved for works of fine art.

The concept of the autonomy of art, its special status as a set of objects lacking use value and definitively separate from the social, came into being as a particular product and process of modern history. Art's detachment from everyday life (as Duchamp illustrated by presenting the urinal *Fountain* as his 1917 industrial 'masterpiece') would become the major underpinning of all subsequent avant-gardes and of twentieth-century art discourse in general.

As Peter Bürger observed in his *Theory of the Avant-Garde*, the distinction of fine art as a higher cultural category was supported and reinforced by institutions of modernism. 'Only after art, in nineteenth-century Aestheticism has altogether detached itself from the praxis of life can the aesthetic develop "purely."'[22] The recognition of the aesthetic value of DeBay's *Eve* over the utility of the mechanical foot was the pivotal point in history. The investment into a new form of cultural capital was established, through which the fine arts exchange could appear detached from the crude money capital of the commodity exchange.

In respect of this debate, Benjamin thought that the aesthetic theories of his own period in the early decades of the twentieth century were complicit with the ideology of the 'expression of the base' since, according to Rolf Tiedemann, 'the majority of Marxist art theorists explain culture as the mere reflection of economic development; Benjamin refused to join them.'[23] Rather, he kept hold of the intent of Marx's analysis by suggesting that aesthetic doctrines distort the privileged position for whom they apply. Discontented with the 'now swaggering, now scholastic' theories of art, Benjamin's aim was to continue in the spirit of questioning that Marx had initiated.[24]

How to measure the value of everything

It was the first world exposition that fulfilled the mid-nineteenth-century desire to measure and display the value of things by visually dramatizing the worth of objects (of a different type of capital in exchange for prize ribbons and money). Aesthetic/cultural value would contrast sharply with Marx's 1867 critique – his writings at the time defining the use, surplus, and exchange-value of commodities in relation to other things, most importantly the lives of people who labor to make commodities.[25] The ontological factor of the 'species-being' could never be measured according to the scale of 'economic' value in Marx's analysis. But what has come to light in more recent assessments of the project of empire and capitalist-driven imperialism is that the constituency of the colonized – the natives that were not considered fully 'human' – were believed to be unqualified to share in either class relations or the profits obtained by the surge on raw materials that transformed the 'primitive' world. This 'non-class,' which some have included in Marx's lumpenproletariat, achieved no position or status.[26] Most importantly, the polar-opposite position was exemplified by the quintessential role of the artist, whose labor could not be appraised by moneyed-wages but by god-given genius.

The social meaning of the objects of cultural expression would now involve their function in demonstrating progressive and non-progressive production according to world territories. The world's fairs provided the perfect means to demonstrate the classificatory order in terms of both the status of objects and the status of nations. However, the deliberation of 'race' was the defining evidence for connecting the progressive or non-progressive status to objects and to nations. As Paul Greenhalgh argues:

> Fine art practice at international exhibitions thus had a hierarchical dimension based on race. In social Darwinian terms, the Europeans made fine art; by comparison with Europe India did not, but in the absence of Europe it was allowed to use the label; Africans did not make fine art, but were condemned in advance to be craftspeople only. The category implied then not only an elitism within the visual arts but one within peoples also.[27]

Greenhalgh suggests the fine arts served as the important model for proving what was 'civilized' by juxtaposition next to the displays of what was considered 'uncivilized.' On the highest end of the scale, the presentation of the Euro-American fine arts in the palatial art temples (see figure 4.4) were shown without their art-makers – the works of art were treated as objects of transcendence, unaffiliated with the realm of the anthropological specimen, handicraft, and utility – the primitive arts were commonly known as 'fetish.' The 1889 Paris Exposition Universelle serves as the primary example for setting the trend in which the ethnological villages became an integral part of the world's fairs. The instructive value of the ethnological exhibition (and such objects) was in their function as props in the narratives given by the tableaux for classifying 'primitive' cultures.[28] The 'evidence' underwriting the primitive classification consisted of affinities across broad cultural comparisons made to seem close by the exhibitionary juxtaposition.

The 1889 Paris Universal Exposition went even further than simply allocating pavilions to specific nations by exhibiting different peoples in their 'natural habitats,' staged as geographic locations that represented the position of each place in the ages of human development. Described in 1890 by Otis T. Mason, the anthropological display was the French exposition's

> crowning glory ... It was possible to see there twelve types of Africans, besides Javanese, Tonkinese, Chinese, Japanese, and other Oriental peoples, living in native houses, wearing native costumes, eating native food, practicing native arts and rites on the Esplanade des Invalides side by side with the latest inventions and with the whole civilized world as spectators.[29]

The role of anthropology at the fair was to provide the visual narrative of empire for the visual command of the 'civilized world.'

The row of forty-four dwellings entitled Histoire de l'Habitation (see figure 4.5) designed by Charles Garnier constructed an evolutionary chain of epochal periods.[30] Following archeological conventions, the teleology extended from the Stone Age, to the Pharaohs, up to the modern era. Mason

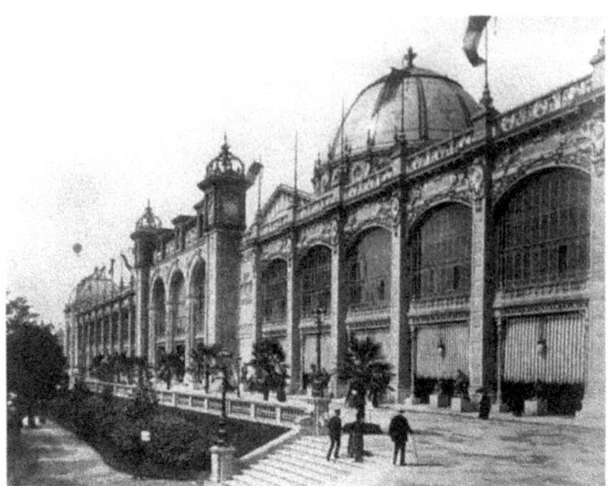

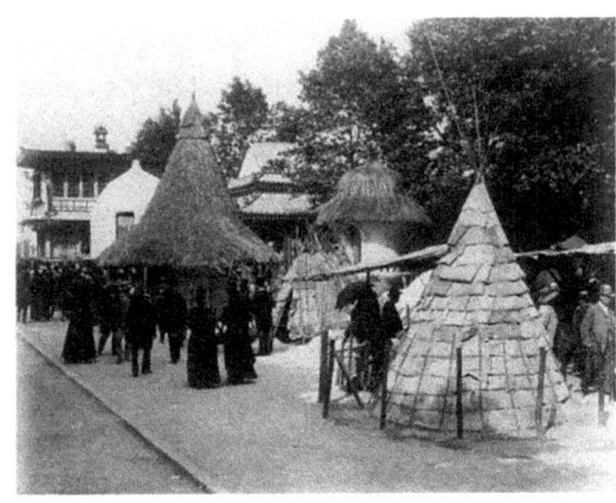

4.4 Palais des Beaux-Arts at the 1889 Paris Exposition Universelle

4.5 Histoire de l'Habitation at the 1889 Paris Exposition Universelle

describes the 'models in actual size of rock shelters, igloos, wigwams, bark lodges, straw hovels, and, without leaving the grounds ... every style of habitation in which human beings have ever lived or ruled or worshipped.'[31] Organized as home, state, and church, the conceptual premise of 'habitations' was, of course, an extension of a broader territorialization. The Habitation exhibition provided the visual alibi for colonial expansion based on the civilizing mission of empire, and the expression of scientific evolution was given through associating cultures with epochs of progress. Mason listed the objects of study in one exhibition, observed as 'groups of men and women, life size; illustrating the first French cave-dwellings, dressed in skin and working with paleolithic implements; the Cro-Magnon man and his wife carving an antler, ancient Mexicans manipulating agave fibre ... a group of Congo negroes, operating with stone tools and monkey-skin bellows.'[32] The nineteenth-century notion that human development followed a course of evolution was also one that produced the tenets of a manifest destiny for certain cultures and 'races.'

While these ideas are now generally blamed negatively on Darwinian determinations, its basic philosophy is credited positively to the Hegelian dialectic. In Hegel's philosophy of world history, the contradictions that exist in human consciousness are perceivable in the collective consciousness of nations. Hegel's famous predetermination about the telos of the 'world spirit' was given in his 1822 conclusion that the 'History of the World travels from East to West, for Europe is absolutely the end of History, Asia the beginning.'[33] This world history is an account of the evolutionary process of consciousness according to cultural and national development in geographic and epochal stages. Hegel's telos in the epoch of European modernity is one that oversees the triumph over the primitive, 'the discipline of the uncontroled natural will, bringing it into obedience to a Universal principle and conferring subjective freedom.'[34] The project of 'universal freedom' was indeed one of the aims of Hegelian *Aufhebung*, which functioned in the master/slave relationship as the sublation of 'the other independent being, in order thereby to become certain of itself as true being … it thereupon proceeds to sublate its own self, for this other is itself.'[35] The constitution of 'freedom' requires a reflection of self in both fear and service, in which mastery results in 'a determinate mode of being; having a "mind of its own" (*der eigene Sinn*)' but 'not over the universal power nor over the entire objective reality.'[36] The contradictions of consciousness that Hegel sought to resolve in and around 1806 Germany were reflexive of the endeavor for Enlightenment 'freedom' in the hypocrisy of the opportunism of slavery in the industrial era of global capitalism. Thus, the master–slave concept in Hegel's *Phenomenology of Spirit* was the political metaphor that Susan Buck-Morss suggests was subliminal to the 'exploitation of millions of colonial slave laborers … accepted as part of the given world by the very thinkers who proclaimed freedom to be man's natural state and inalienable right. Even when theoretical claims of freedom were transformed into revolutionary action on the political stage, it was possible for the slave-driven colonial economy that functioned behind the scenes to be kept in darkness.'[37] Buck-Morss views the paradox as convenient for the construction of coherent national narratives as much in contemporary scholarship as it was in Hegel's era.

The notion of enlightened freedom was, of course, an important nationalist concept in the United States, underwriting the celebration of the 400th anniversary of Christopher Columbus's arrival to the Americas as the theme for holding the 1893 World's Columbian Exposition in Chicago. The explorer's 'conquering' of America would continue to be the respectable narrative throughout the twentieth century, up until the Civil Rights era when the 1964 Red Power Movement staged their acts of protest against broken treaties and genocide. The Chicago fair had perpetuated Columbus's colonialist narrative by staging the 'primitive' in the Midway Plaisance, the section of the fair in which entire groups of ethnic peoples were exhibited under the direction of anthropology departments of leading universities. Fair organizers had followed the earlier example of the 1889 Paris Exposition, where French officials coordinated a village of non-white peoples for display near the Eiffel Tower. Robert Rydell, who has conducted extensive research on world expositions, acknowledges the popularity of the 1889 French ethnological displays that became an integral part of the world's fair: 'No subsequent world's fair lacked a variation on this ethnological exhibit, and for the better part of the next fifty years, such arrangements of nonwhite colonials often bore the name "ethnological villages."'[38] As late as 1933, the Midway delights were advertised in the official guide of the Chicago fair, encouraging visitors to 'Ride the breathtaking roller coaster' at the same place where the spectacles of the '"living wonders," the Siamese Twins, giant people and other "freaks"' that were 'gathered from the four corners of the earth' drew audiences in equal measure to the Midway; however, what also drew them was the day-to-day behavior of ethnic peoples who were now on show.[39] But the consolidation of different 'villages' into the Midway section of the fair functioned to put vastly diverse cultures together in one place, producing the sense that all the various 'tribes' shared something in common by virtue of their difference – the strategy of showing difference by repetition ascribed sameness among them all. Viewed as exotic peoples, foreign novelties, scientific specimen, trophies of colonization, or as traditional craftsmen making 'primitive' things, the people on display at the Midway had little control over the context in which they were being shown. This was the way that 'ethnic bodies' were culturally inscribed at the fairs, and within the limits of their self-representation, they would serve as entertainment for the generally white viewing public.

Organized by Harvard anthropologist Frederick Putnam, the scientific ordering of the ethnological villages at the 1893 Chicago exposition could provide the optimal sense of scientific control over the foreign subject. Putnam's book titled *Oriental and Occidental, Northern and Southern, Portrait Types of the Midway Plaisance* is a work that served also as a photographic guide for viewers to identify the villages of 'Arabs, Singhalese, Javanese, Chinese, Samoans, Hawaiians, Esquimaux, Laps, Soudanese, Turks, Japs, Dahomeyans, Abyssinians, Algerians, Bedouins, Cossacks, Indians, Parsees, Hindoos, Greeks, Egyptians, Syrians, South Americans.'[40] His writings suggest an informed effort to portray these cultures with accuracy and, through Putnam, the project assumed the authority and legitimacy of the scholarly study of anthropology, notwithstanding the Midway's carnival atmosphere. The 'Chinese Village Theater,' for instance, was situated in between the American Indian Exhibit and the 'Captive Balloon Ride.'[41] There, traditional Chinese opera was staged by actors playing several roles as male and female, dressed in full costume, in a drama that was performed largely through music and song. Putnam made a point in his book about employing a decorator/designer to work on the Chinese exhibition named Wong Ki, an émigré from China who resided in San Francisco. He stated that Wong was 'thoroughly Americanized' and this 'good impression' was also received by his wife, Ah Que, who 'at an early age came to California and was taken in charge by the Presbyterian Mission of San Francisco, where she received an education and religious training, she speaks English correctly, and is cultured and refined in manner.'[42] Listing the attributes of the presumably 'civilized' behavior of the Presbyterian Wong Ki and Ah Que, this biographical portrayal of Chineseness defines the cultural criteria by ranking the subjects higher on the scale of ethnological progression – the Chinese are therefore deemed less 'primitive.'

Serving the morals of *Christians* versus the immorality of the superstitious, the concept extended to Hegel's determination of religious use-value for both 'art' and 'fetish' under the concept of individual freedom, notwithstanding the fact that both functioned similarly in the symbolic exchange. In Hegel's 1822 use of the sixteenth-century Dutch term *fetisso*, he defined '*Feitizo*, magic' as an 'object of religious worship' that holds superstitious power with 'a kind of objective independence as contrasted with the arbitrary fancy of the individual' who nonetheless 'remains master of the image it has adopted.'[43] Hegel contradicts himself when he tries to explain the superstitious nature of the 'Fetich' which 'has no independence as an object of religious worship; still less has it aesthetic independence as a work of art.'[44] At first, Hegel states that the beholder, the 'individual,' is the master of the image of religious worship, one that is also an independent object.[45] In the next few sentences, he states that the image cannot be viewed as an object independent of belief nor aesthetically as a work of art. Hegel's reasoning can be understood as functioning through an imperialist objective for derogating the alienating beliefs and 'taste' of foreigners – discussed as a means to define the 'proper' and 'reasonable' (European) approach to objects of religious devotion or of aesthetic purpose.

Hegel's premise is based on the example of the sorcery of the 'Negroes' who do not 'have the idea of a God, of a moral faith' but believe in 'man as the highest power'; the African fetish, Hegel argues, is 'merely a creation that expresses the arbitrary choice of its maker ... which always remains in his hands.'[46] And according to Kant, the difference in the 'religion of our part of the world is not a matter of an arbitrary taste, but is of a more estimable origin. Therefore only the excesses in it and what appertains exclusively to man give indications of the different national qualities.'[47] Excesses are human characteristics such as superstition, which are present in every culture but to different degrees; the degree to which a nation's beliefs supposedly rest on superstition or to which its culture is dominated by the 'beautiful' or the 'grotesque,' then, defines the value of the culture and the nation as a whole; such evaluations are, for Kant, the means to 'judge a nation's judgement,' so to speak. Hegel appears to have cited the evidence in Kant, who also placed Negroes at the lowest rank of taste, by stating that 'not a single one was ever found who presented anything great in art or science or any other praiseworthy quality, even though among the whites some continually rise aloft from the lowest rabble.'[48] The judgment of taste ultimately rested on the idea that beauty could only occur through a moral faith in a monotheistic (European) God, not through superstition. Ultimately, the argument that aesthetics (or, what could be considered as objects of beauty) was somehow a condition of whether the beholder was superstitious or belonged to a moral faith had little basis in logic and functioned primarily to shore up the capitalist mode of exchange. Derogating cultures on the basis of religious difference was a means to define the colonizer's superiority and thus to justify acts of imperial aggression focused toward obtaining advantageous material gain.

The invention of the idea of the ethnographic fetish, then, was simply a way to justify the unethical legacy of the sixteenth-century European traders who engaged in unjust relations with the people whose lands they traveled to. However, the hypocrisy in deciding that only some cultures impute material objects with sacred worth was all too clear between Protestant iconoclasm and the Catholic belief in rosary beads. William Pietz asserts that the 'Protestant denial of any true religious function for any material object was a view well within the horizon of traditional Christian thought. This view, however, was just one of several factors contributing to the first and central theme of the fetish idea: its status as a value-bearing material object.'[49] Pietz explains that the Protestant church eventually separated the two categories when 'material objects came to be identified as proper to economic *as opposed to* religious activity.'[50] The notion of the fetish was, of course, crucial to Marx's theory of economic value. The transformation of the capitalist mode of exchange, as Marx surmised, would frame every circumstance according to money-value. Like the 'misty realm of religion' wrote Marx, the 'fantastic form of a relation between things' is the 'fetishism which attaches itself to the products of labour.'[51] Borrowing the language found in circulating notions of the fetish, Marx acknowledged that the commodity fetish was not unlike the veil of religious reflection which cannot be 'removed from the countenance of the social life-process, i.e. the process of material production, until it becomes production by freely associated men, and stands under their conscious and planned control.'[52] In other words, the commodity fetish would subsume all other modes of assessing value for material objects – with the exception of the special status of the fine arts. This status was something more than cultural capital because it was linked to 'race' – the origins of art emanate from the origins of the artist, and thus, the descendent 'race' and creed of the male European genius.

The official catalogue of the 1889 Paris Universal Exposition had noted that the aim of displaying the work of fine artists was to show the 'stages of human genius.'[53] The nineteenth-century culmination of the positivist and scientific view would include physical and geographic circumstances of the artist's biography in order to substantiate preexisting ideas about artistic traits and the value of certain kinds of artistic production. But journalists reporting on the world's fairs had the power to communicate broad ideologies about art and culture to the greater general public, and they were most influential in the way they simplified the Kantian aesthetic rationale for judging artistic achievement according to essentialist traits. For instance, Lucy Monroe, a critic who wrote about the 1893 Chicago exposition, considered the superiority of works made by American artists to be an effect of 'race and clime' because painting as a product of nation could show 'the influence of birth and heredity – this insistent unconscious patriotism.'[54] The Venice Biennale emerged in part because the fine arts were considered a European legacy and birthright as compared to the heritage of Americans.

Building a nation

The Renaissance legacy of ascribing the aesthetic to national identity was integral to the inscription of artistic status and power at Venice's artfair. However, the mythology of this legacy is clear when viewing the stagecraft of the arts through the perspective of its function in empire and modern nation-building. Italian participation overall on the world stage of nineteenth-century imperialism was considered by Hobsbawm as marginal at best, since Italy's attempt to conquer Ethiopia in 1896 was a failure (although Libya was eventually a successful conquest by 1912). The country was still developing as a modern nation, and according to historian Martin Clark, the notion of national identity in Italy, 'where it existed at all, did not necessarily imply "nationalism," i.e. any demand for a new political structure.'[55] Clark explains that to be 'Italian' or 'even to speak Italian, was to be educated and sophisticated,' and the definition of nation was articulated by the 'high culture' that was 'a major part of the European heritage.'[56] Venice itself was added to the unification of Italy through marriage connections, proving to be an unmodernlike strategy conducted during the Italian Risorgimento. Napolean III in 1858 struck a bargain with Victor Emanuel II to marry off his middle-aged cousin Jerome to Emanuel's fifteen-year-old daughter Maria Clotilde.[57] It was not until the 1920s, when Antonio Gramsci made the case for the subaltern, that the peasant class and the poor of the South, deemed illiterate and superstitious, was regarded as part of the Italian constituency.[58]

The underlying competitive drive for status and power that was pervasive in the late nineteenth century can be seen in the political ascendancy that was involved in the modern development of Venice. The old republican city-state had been taken by Napoleon in the late eighteenth century, which ended the oligarchy of the 'birthplace of capitalism,' the title given by economic historians to the place known for banking and money-lending. The city's powerful reputation in maritime trade, transport, and naval influence was based on its shipping position, at the 'peak of fame' in 1500, when the Venetian passage in the eastern Mediterranean expanded during the rise of the massive Ottoman empire and the opening up of new spice routes into Africa.[59] But by the time that the Venice Biennale began in 1895, Venice was a dilapidated place in need of revitalization. Clark describes a city in the sidelines that, having been ravaged in the late 1840s by cholera, survived nonetheless through its 'promise of universal suffrage and its lack of dangerous social radicalism' and through the 'support of artisans and middle class alike' – notwithstanding the fact that the island city 'had little impact on events elsewhere, even in mainland Venetia.'[60] In addition, as Shearer West argues, the Biennale and the fine arts could function to construct 'cultural identity through the public space of the exhibition' in the aftermath of Austria's 1866 concession of Venice to Italy's unification in light of the 'uneasy place' that Venice found itself occupying in the modern industrial world.[61]

The very purpose of creating the artfair in Venice was to associate and compete with the modern art galleries dedicated to the new state, drawing upon the historical artistic Venetian lineage of Italy[62] (see figure 4.6). In Italy's process of unification, new capital cities were elected by plebiscites, and with each new nomination museums of modern art were erected to commemorate the locality.[63] The first Gallery of Modern Art was established in 1860 in the capital city of Turin. In 1864 the capital city became Florence, and the proclamation of Victor Emanuel's kingship was celebrated by holding the National Exposition of the Kingdom exhibiting the arts with industry, and also by opening the Gallery of Modern Pictures in 1867. Rome was chosen by a plebiscite in 1871, and this new capital of the kingdom of Italy trumped all other capitals that came before by enacting the 1881 Royal Decree of the Royal Gallery of Modern Art. Rome inaugurated the Palazzo delle Esposizioni in 1883, which became the site of the first international exhibition of contempo-

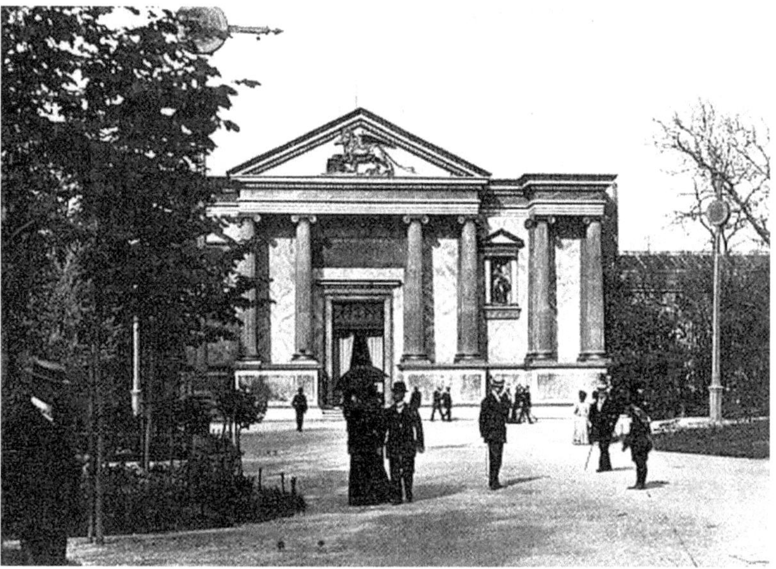

4.6 Palazzo, La Biennale di Venezia, 1895

rary art in the unified Italy. Most of these commemorative galleries were filled with loans from the collection of the king and his royal family.[64]

Whereas the Venice Biennale was decreed as an event to be held every two years to pay patriotic tribute to the wedding anniversary of Queen Margherita, the Gallery of International Modern Art of Venice would open in 1902 to house permanently the gifts of international paintings. But the local administrators strategically used the model of the artfair rather than the permanent gallery to bolster its economic and political state of affairs. Venice took up the methods and means of the artfair to build a tourist economy in order to compete locally in the national bids for artistic recognition and ambitiously brought an international art competition into the city. By the end of the nineteenth century, the world's fairs were an integral part of the international landscape, one in which capital cities worldwide – London, Paris, Brussels, Philadelphia, Chicago – served as representatives of nations.[65]

During the 1930s, when Benjamin was working on his *Arcades Project,* the colonial expositions saw a profound resurgence after a period of decline during World War I. No one at the time could have ignored the ubiquitous expositions that were, by then, becoming controversial; Buck-Morss notes the Surrealist members (Breton, Eluard, and Aragon) had urged the boycott of the 1931 Paris expo 'because it was racist and imperialist, justifying the "millions of new slaves" created by colonialism and the destruction of non-Western cultures in the name of progress, and because the nationalist sentiment it encouraged undermined international solidarity.'[66] But Buck-Morss suggests that Benjamin never mentions the world expositions of his own period, the 'most obvious of "present" images that entered into a constellation with the ur-forms of the nineteenth century.'[67] His silence, she concludes, was 'far from refuting contemporary connections' related to the arcades, but instead, 'supports the claim that the present underlay the project very literally, even if "written in invisible ink."'[68] Not unlike contemporary art biennials and triennials, the fairs were held annually in Paris, Stockholm, Chicago, Brussels, Glasgow, and so forth, because they could bolster markets, create jobs, provide state subsidies, and show allegiance to the state.

Benjamin attempted to redefine the historical through perceiving the arcades as a freeze-frame of an era in which fleeting memories and temporal traces of a society are reflected by the permanence that only architecture could express. He correlated the physical structure of the arcades to the role that the image of construction plays in the collective subconscious, suggesting that the 'new means of production, which in the beginning is still ruled by the form of the old (Marx), are images in the collective consciousness in which the new is permeated with the old.'[69] The arcade image illustrated what Benjamin called 'indefinite affinities' and 'contradictory ties' in evoking a sort of allegory for embarking on a 'voyage … to carry the montage principle over into history.

That is, to build up the large structures out of the smallest, precisely fashioned structural elements. Indeed, to detect the crystal of the total event in the analysis of the simple, individual moment.'[70] Not unlike the arcades, the visible and tangible structure of the old global artfair created the wish image of a 'new' global order that is really a mirror of the same.

Thus, the appearance of the new and the recurrent dialectical image is one that Benjamin described as 'ambiguity.'[71] His 1935 and 1939 exposés 'Paris, Capital of the Nineteenth Century' treated more concisely the themes that were found throughout *The Arcades Project*, which included the panoramas and the world's fairs.[72] He used the word 'phantasmagoria' to suggest that the dazzling deception of the fairs was the means to distract from the commodity function of these landscapes of nationalist production and power. That is, the propaganda that served both politics and industry depended on the visitor's 'state of subjection' as the experience of being captivated by the entire universe of amusements and 'specialties.'[73] Likewise, the romantic and timeless landscape of Venice enchants the participant of the contemporary Biennale in the manner that Benjamin renders poetic the fairyland image of the arcades. The 'glittering distraction' here is from the recurrent vision of the 'old' Baroque-like but indeterminate era of Venetian architecture. The 'new' monumental billboards that represent contemporary works of art hang from the loggias and cover the facades along the Grand Canal (see figure 4.7). The

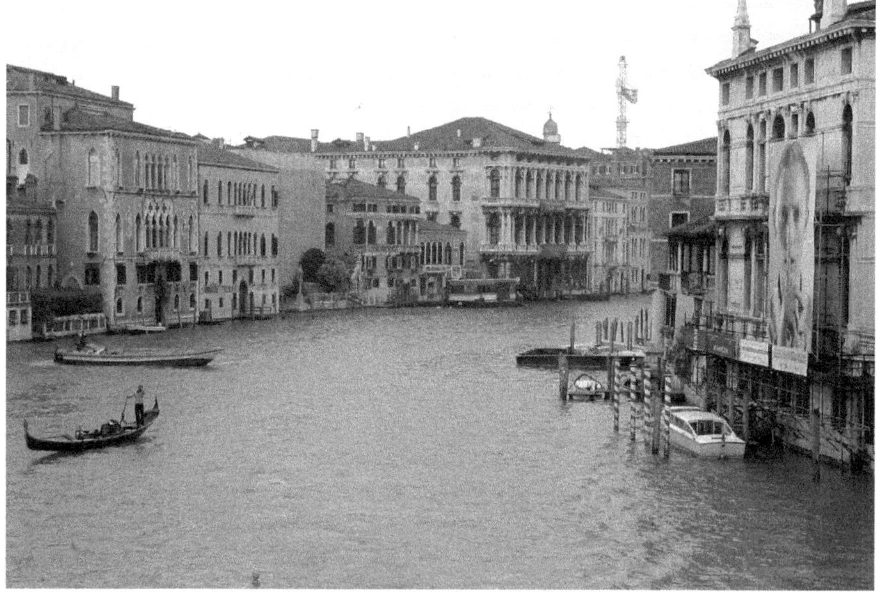

4.7 Grand Canal, Venice 2005

newness of the 'art scene' juxtaposed next to the old tends to overshadow the relations of power implied by the partitioning of the artfair's territorial sites.

In this context, the fairs were crucial to an aesthetic that could exemplify objects that were antithetical to the industrial, the crude bourgeois, and the primitive. The legacy is one that continues in a material art object that could engender social meaning. And, in the reversals of the postmodernist championing of the industrial readymade, the 'everyday,' and the dematerialized conceptual art object, the meaning of art is considered as no longer residing in the material object but derives from the artist and viewer's consciousness. However, the question as to how the nationalist pedigree of the 'Western' aesthetic was able to prevail, even as artistic innovation requires constant cultural synthesis, has only recently begun to be addressed in the last several decades or so of art historical inquiry. As Benjamin suggested, 'the relation of what-has-been to the now is dialectical,' and to invoke the notion of a 'Western art' today is to raise the specter of an 'aesthetic essentialism' understood as a nationally inherited artistic potential. As I have argued in this chapter, these indiscernible social relations were made visible by the fairs, and like the arcades, the Biennale maintains an aura of the past by retaining the architectural structure of a nation-statist topography. Even more of a dialectical fairyland to this day, the artfair functions at a 'dialectical standstill,' projecting the 'indefinite affinities' between old imperialisms and the 'suddenly emergent' image of globalization.

Learning from Athens

At Documenta 14, the masks of the Kwakwaka'wakw indigenous peoples created by the hereditary chief Beau Dick dominated an entire gallery in the new EMST National Museum of Contemporary Art in Athens (see plate 16). Held for the first time in a second location, the museum in the iconic city of Greece served as the main site of the 2017 quinquennial, while the Fridericianum in Kassel, the legacy Documenta venue, was 'given over to the public collection of Greek and international contemporary art of the National Museum of Contemporary Arts, Athens (EMST).'[74] Since the inauguration of Documenta 1 in 1955, the contemporary art exposition has been housed in the Fridericianum, where the bombed out World War II ruins of the seventeenth-century Hessian museum served as the political emblem for the founding curator Arnold Bode – his first show for the German public was a showcase of works denounced by Hitler as 'degenerate art.'[75] *Learning From Athens*, the title of Documenta 14, was also groundbreaking in many other instances, among them the way in which the Native subject was celebrated as a work of contemporary art to the diminishment of its historical categorization as a work of ethnography. Announced in the mainstream press, 'the curators said the idea was to erase the border between the art historical and the ethnographic, and to start conversations about how art can take on anticolonial resonances even in colonial museums.'[76] Displaying Beau's masks in the art museum in Athens and also in the Documenta Halle, the dedicated museum in Kassel, was an effort to change the ethnographical classification of the artist's two series, *Undersea Kingdom* (2016–17) and *Atlakim* (1990–2012).

Several other artists at Documenta 14 also carried the anthropological signifier into the global art exposition, including Cecilia Vicuña, whose *Quipu Womb (The Story of the Red Thread, Athens)* (2017) (see plate 17) was a textile sculpture created from ancient Peruvian techniques of knotting, and also Khvay Samnang, known for creating his eleven masks of woven vine, *Preah Kunlong (The Way of the Spirit)* (2017), while living and working among the indigenous Chong community in the forest of Cambodia. But neither of these exhibits could be as strictly interpreted as anthropological works in the way that Beau Dick's Kwakwaka masks could be construed conventionally – Beau's birth name, Walis Gwy Um, means 'big, great whale.' Nonetheless, critic H.G. Masters, writing for *Art Asia Pacific*, questioned what it meant to install Samnang's work, along with a mural by indigenous Australian artist Dale Harding, in the Naturkundemuseum im Ottoneum, which was dedicated as a Documenta 14 site in Kassel. 'Doesn't it seem almost classically ethnographic,' inquires Masters, to show their works 'in a natural history museum?'[77] The museums designated by art and by anthropology have long determined the difference between the two categories. The system of typological ordering for aesthetic modernity was represented by art, while the scientifically primitive was represented by anthropology. Ever since James Clifford challenged the juxtaposition of the 'tribal' Kwakiutl mask next to Picasso's 'modern' *Girl Before a Mirror* (1932) in the Museum of Modern Art's 1984 *'Primitivism' in 20th Century Art* exhibition, the way in which museums determine what is tribal and what is modern has been challenged and reconceptualized with varying degrees of change to the model of exhibition.[78] As this chapter has sought to acknowledge, the historical development of this system of exhibition was greatly influenced by the example of the world's fairs, and the idea that the Guangzhou Triennial and the Shanghai Biennale prove that the model has changed is far more complex than it appears.

Kwakiutl is often the name given to Beau Dick's Kwakwaka'wakw community from British Columbia, and the history of their representation in the world's fair is entirely significant for understanding the importance of his masks exhibited in 2017 at Documenta 14. At the 1893 World's Columbian Exposition in Chicago, the Kwakwaka'wakw created a major controversy when the young anthropologist Franz Boas – coincidentally a German émigré to the United States – sponsored their exhibition at the fair. At this 400th anniversary celebration of the arrival of Christopher Columbus, the displays of Native American cultures in small villages were organized according to regions, such as, the 'Crees from Manitoba, Penobscots from Maine, Iroquois from New York.'[79] The ethnographical narrative of an obsolete peoples, destined for extinction under Social Darwinism, was visually narrated to show the waning 'primitivism' of the Natives. Boas was a student of Frederick Ward Putnam, the aforementioned presenter of the ethnographic shows, and author of *Oriental and Occidental, Northern and Southern, Portrait Types of the Midway Plaisance*. Boas broke from the scientific racism of his colleagues in the Ethnology Department at Harvard, and assisted eight Kwakwaka performers in presenting a *hamatsa* or cannibal dance at the fair, which would stun the viewers.[80] Toward the end of the event, the Native interpreter George Hunt took out his knife, cut into the backs of the two performers named Two Bites and Strong Back, and then proceeded to thread a length of rope through their incisions. Howling with wolf-like cries, Two Bites would eventually fasten his teeth on Hunt's arm and bite off a piece. Historian Anthony Hall asserts that 'the Kwakwaka'wakw performance was treated as a grave affront and as a matter of humiliation for many officials of church and state,' which effectively led to the legislation of the 1885–1951 federal *Indian Act* by which the Canadian government would 'outlaw several forms of traditional dance and potlatch giveaways that were seen to counter the work of Christian evangelization on Indian missions.'[81] But in truth, the Kwakwaka's shocking drama was staged by the Native community as an act of protest against the subjugation of Indians that the fair symbolized – even as the act confirmed the 'savage' stereotype. Other historians suggest that in the context of the fair, the primitivist ethnographical discourse would work to the Kwakwaka'wakw's advantage, since the Native was always considered as an outsider to the national history of the colonialist, and thus the government and the church were exposed for their efforts to destroy the community's 'primitive' way of life.[82]

A century later, Beau Dick would continue in the Kwakwaka's role as an activist and a leader of his community. On 27 March, just months before his exhibition would open at Documenta 14, Beau died from an illness. Candice Hopkins wrote his memoriam and recounted how he had often confronted federal policy makers and conducted ceremonies to call out the broken treaties and continuing degradation of Indigenous rights. Hopkins conveys the way in which the artist addressed the connection between the Native condition and the exhibition of Documenta in Athens by acknowledging the

> intersections between Kwakwaka'wakw governance systems and the origins of democracy in ancient Greece as well as ideas of citizenship. It was well-known that Beau had eschewed any official form of Canadian government ID as he did not recognize the legitimacy of the federal government to not only dictate his identity as a 'status Indian,' but also as a Canadian.[83]

Hopkins suggests that Beau's connection to Documenta was specifically in relation to the place of Athens and through the shared experience of the migrant's loss of homeland. Greece was the emblem of the migrant's refuge in 2016 and this refuge was one of the primary considerations for siting Documenta 14 in Athens. 'Beau wanted to travel to Athens so that he could speak with people who have had to leave their homelands. For him, the loss of one's homeland rendered culture, language, and tradition vulnerable.'[84] A descendant of carvers, Beau's grandfather apprenticed him from an early age, and he was faithful to his culture and his tradition by assisting in the carving of totems and by following the ritual form. One of the last masks he made was a self-imaged Orca whale 'action figure' with grey hair and his signature hat. But Beau also broke from tradition by presenting his work in museums and expositions, including the Museum of Anthropology at the University of British Columbia – historically understood as the site of ethnographic artefacts rather than of artistic self-representation. As noted in my essay published in *Global and World Art in the Practice of the University Museum*, 'the museum, especially the anthropology museum, is an archive of [the] relentless reciprocity' of the colonizer and the colonized, 'retaining important material evidence of the institutional violence of the past.'[85] Beau's ability to move among the spaces of his community, the anthropology museum, and now the contemporary art exposition, can be viewed symbolically as acknowledgment of the colonized coexisting with the colonizer amidst the potential for institutional change. His exhibition of 'anthropological artefacts' as self-expressive works of art in Documenta 14 provided clear evidence of institutional change.

However, Director Szymczyk's decision to host *Learning from Athens* in the European Union's strongest and weakest states was highly controversial, since Germany was thought to have dictated the 2015 austerity measures that kept the Greek people and economy in monetary crisis. And many in Greece were skeptical of Documenta because they blamed the 2004 Olympics in Athens for its role in the country's debt crisis. Angela Merkel has long been viewed in Greece as the economic punisher who was against bailing out what the German media condescendingly calls the *Schuldenland*, the 'debtor's country.'[86] Nonetheless, by 2016, Greece had accepted close to one million migrants from Syria and elsewhere, which began to change the perceptions of the country in the eyes of Merkel and the EU. As the primary entry point for Middle Eastern asylum seekers, Greece was left alone to deal with tens of thousands coming into their camps as European countries voted to tighten their borders. Merkel was also increasingly alone in continuing to welcome refugees into Germany, and by March 2016, Greece became the largest recipient of the 700 million euros in humanitarian aid granted by Europe. But in August 2017, Germany, France, the UK, the Netherlands, and Norway had moved to send back asylum seekers to their port of entry in Greece.[87] When

Documenta 14 officially closed the exhibitions in Athens on 16 July, protests in the city erupted against the return of refugees back to Greece from Germany, along with the stalled transfer of approved asylum seekers still waiting to join their families in Berlin. Szymczyk's daring approach to Documenta 14 was played out in the real time of the migrant crisis.

Amidst the heated politics of holding Documenta 14 in both Greece and Germany, there are multiple conflicting historical relations that extend from the legacy of Western culture and art history, beginning with the Greek Classical ideal in art and the influential development of eighteenth-century Neoclassicism in Germany. As led by J.J. Winckelmann, his systematic writing of the history of art would become the canonical model, described by Preziosi as the construction of 'an entire national artistic tradition – that of ancient Greece – from its birth through its historical decline and demise.'[88] After World War II, the 'Greek miracle' was instituted by historians such as E.H. Gombrich, whose elevation of Greek art, representing the 'dawn of history, and classical scholarship,' had firmly established the mythology of Western art history, the development appearing 'quite natural that the awakening of art from primitive modes' began in Greece.[89] Gombrich's 1950 publication *The Story of Art* is considered the most-read art book of all time among the general public and also the most definitive guide to Western art.[90] In essence, the Greek miracle in art was a German contribution to the mythology. Yet, in view of the twenty-first-century conditions for geopolitics and global art, the symbolic siting of Documenta 14 in both Greece and Germany is one that ultimately challenges and puts into question the whole 'story of art.' The entire Western teleology for art begins to erode, especially since the 'primitive modes,' such as Beau Dick's expression, have come to be represented by the new mythology in 'global art.' Paradoxically, *Learning from Athens*'s involvement in the realpolitiks of the refugee situation and the economic crisis in Greece reignites the ideals of Athenian democracy as symbolized by the Parthenon, the very monument to the Western ideal.

Documenta was always an exposition emblematized by the bombed-out Friedericanum's postwar restoration of Hitler's 'degenerate art' rather than following the Venice Biennale's model for 'imperial fairylands' as national pavilions on fantasy real estate. The 1955 vision created by the founding director Arnold Bode for the first Documenta was to develop Kassel into a place that would always communicate the specter of World War II and Hitler's legacy in Germany – the ultimate event for signifying the displacement of peoples in Europe. The exhibition of art could function to convey the symbolism of a place/nation as it related to the important epochal moments and signature events through the exhibition's location and site itself. This was the legacy conveyed by Szymczyk's title *Learning from Athens*, which also takes after the philosophy of urban planning initiated by Robert Venturi,

Denise Scott Brown, and Steven Izenour in their seminal 1972 study *Learning from Las Vegas*. The iconography of postmodernism was interpreted by the authors, who not only conceived of 'Las Vegas as a communication system' of billboards that are buildings, and of advertising as landscape, but also analyzed taste and value as a historical system of class relations in architecture.[91] *Learning from Athens* boldly asserts the iconography of post-migrancy by suggesting Athens could serve as a communication system for the landscape of humanity, one in which the Greek society, impoverished by governmental austerity, would become one of the few democratizing places for the asylum seeker. If postmodernism confronted the conflicting visual signifiers of capitalism in urban planning, then postmigration exposes the aftermath of asylum-seeking and exile in the era of placelessness for the refugee.

The contradiction, however, was expressed by the local populace of Athens who accused the administrators of Documenta of exploiting the city on behalf of 'crisis tourism.' The prestige of the powerful Documenta institution as representative of the high-brow legacy of Western art assumed the position of cultural hegemony – precisely the reason why graffiti in Athens hailed the artfair as 'Crapumenta,' covering the city with statements such as 'Dear Documenta, I refuse to exoticize ... to increase your cultural capital.'[92] The criticism was aimed at the exposition's role in the city as a form of institutional colonization, one that circumscribed modern Greece to the primitive subject of homelessness and poverty. At the same time, Szymczyk was very strategic in his financial dealings, since he was also well aware of the privilege that Documenta could signify. Rather than collaborate with Athens's wealthier private art museums, the director 'opted to work with public institutions,' according to reporter Jason Farago, and a 'fair chunk of Documenta's 37 million euro budget (about $40 million) has gone into nearly bankrupt Greek art organizations, which you can think of as an artsy stand-in for the eurozone transfer payments that Germany continues to resist.'[93] Other relationships were also revived through Documenta's occupation of Athens, with locals and newcomers forging new collaborations with the visiting art world. But overall, the diversion of funds to Athens's public art institutions through the Documenta enterprise was the most astonishing socio-political move taken by an artfair.

Not a foregone conclusion

At Documenta 14, Rebecca Belmore's *Biinjiya'iing Onji* (*From Inside*) (see plate 18) is a sculptural representation of a refugee tent made out of marble, an emblem of the social conditions in Athens. Belmore, an artist from Sioux Lookout in the Anishinabe territory of Ontario, Canada, was one of the first Indigenous Native women represented at the Venice Biennale.[94] Her marble tent is a monument to those seeking shelter from the oppressive forces against them throughout time. If *Learning from Las Vegas* used the urban model of Florence and Rome to define Las Vegas as the locus of postmodernism, then *Learning from Athens* looks to the marble of the Parthenon to symbolize the post-migrant ideals of democracy. Documenta 11's theme, *Democracy Unrealized*, led by Okwui Enwezor in 2002, was appropriately the forerunner to Szymczyk's political use of the artfair to bring attention to a social system. Enwezor's program opened the way for Szymczyk by expanding the locations of engagement through 'transdisciplinary "platforms" devoted to different themes' presented on four different continents the year prior to the 2002 opening: 'Democracy Unrealized' (Vienna, 15 March–20 April 2001; Berlin, 9–30 October 2001), 'Experiments with Truth: Transitional Justice and the Processes of Truth and Reconciliation' (New Delhi, 7–21 May 2001), 'Créolité and Creolization' (St. Lucia, 13–15 January 2002), and 'Under Siege: Four African Cities, Freetown, Johannesburg, Kinshasa, and Lagos (Lagos, 16–20 March 2002). Enwezor articulated his vision in his subtitle, 'Art is the Production of Knowledge,' explained further in the exhibition material as the questioning of 'unspoken hierarchies of attention in the Western exhibition scene' such as the 'denial of the legitimacy of the West's exoticizing view of "the foreign," and the confrontation of that perception with those artistic activities that conflict with our projection ... The "foreigners" were once the object of our gaze—now they are looking back.'[95] The difference between the high pedigree of the aesthetic in Western art history and Enwezor's use of the signifying practices of the exposition site can be seen in Szymczyk's development of Documenta 14. The repetition of Enwezor's political model is perceivable in the contentious political space that Szymczyk created for his exhibition, amidst the homelessness and poverty that Greece and the refugee crisis has come to signify.

In conclusion, Enwezor's choice to stage the reading of Marx's *Capital* every single day of the 2015 Venice Biennale was a speech act that openly acknowledged the matrix of capitalism, nationalism, and money-status that art and the Biennale institution signifies. Enwezor included in the *56 esposizione* catalogue a series of photographs of frontispieces taken from multiple volumes of *Das Kapital* in translation, editions in Bengali, Serbian, Czech, Dutch, Yiddish, Persian, Russian, Thai, Indonesian, Kazakh, Uyghur, and Telegu. Marx's 1867 text had become historically global and as the central subject for his *All the World's Futures* exhibition, Enwezor explains the way in which 'the aura, effects, affects and specters of Capital will be felt in one of the most ambitious explorations of this concept and term.'[96] As the Biennale's first black curator, his curatorial statement describing his radical objectives for the 56th edition was a return to the nineteenth-century text. In the same way, the organizing structure of the pavilions and the ancillary exhibitions remain the same as they did since the nineteenth century. The Biennale president Paolo Baratta defended the unchanging real estate of the exposition: 'I am glad I did not listen to the forlorn considerations expressed by those who in 1998 told me that the notion of an exhibition made up of national pavilions was outmoded.'[97] He went on to suggest that the alternative would have been a 'white cube ... within which our history was to be effaced.'[98] In his self-defense, he cites the pluralism of the voices of curators who organized the different pavilions and who engaged in the exposition's history through the 'free dialogue' of the arts. Enwezor also acknowledged the Venice Biennale as something more than 'just a fairground for an exhibition, the Giardini represents, in miniature, a scene of processes of national determination and social upheaval.'[99] In a scene more hopeful than idealistic, Enwezor articulated his vision by suggesting that the Giardini has always been a *Garden of Disorder* and his intervention through *Reading Capital* was his strategic way forward for *All the World's Futures.*

Notes

1 Walter Benjamin, 'Materials for the Exposé of 1935,' *The Arcades Project*, tr. Howard Eiland and Kevin McLaughlin (Cambridge, MA: Belknap Press, Harvard University Press, 1999), 907. A shorter version of this chapter was published in 'The Global Art Fair and the Dialectical Image,' *Third Text*, vol. 24, no. 6 (November 2010), 719–34.

2 Caroline Jones, *The Global Work of Art: World's Fairs, Biennials, and the Aesthetics of Experience* (Chicago: Chicago University Press, 2016).

3 Benjamin, 'Paris, Capital of the Nineteenth Century; Exposé (of 1939),' *The Arcades Project*, 17.

4 See Documenta 11, 8 June–15 September 2002, Platform 5: Exhibition www.documenta.de/en/retrospective/documenta11 (accessed 4 January 2018).

5 Okwui Enwezor, 'The Black Box,' in Okwui Enwezor et al., eds, *Documenta 11_ Platform 5* (Ostifildern: Hatje Cantz, 2002), 43.

6 Okwui Enwezor, 'The State of Things,' in Okwui Enwezor, *La Biennale di Veniezia, 56th International Art Exhibition, All the World's Futures* (Venezia: Fondazione La Biennale di Venezia), 19.

7 Enwezor, 'The State of Things,' 20.

8 Ibid., 19.

9 Eric Hobsbawm, *The Age of Empire, 1875–1914* (London: Abacus, 1994), 60.

10 Ignacio Adriasola, 'Japan's Venice: The Japanese Pavilion at the Venice Biennale and the "Pseudo-Objectivity" of the International,' *Archives of Asian Art*, vol. 67, no. 2 (October 2017), 215. For a comprehensive study of Japan and the contribution of the Tokyo Biennale (1952–90), see Reiko Tomii, *Radicalism in the Wilderness: International Contemporaneity and 1960s Art in Japan* (Cambridge, MA: MIT Press, 2016).

11 The language of the 'official/unofficial' sites at the Biennale has been diminished slowly since 2005; however, the determination was based on whether works were accepted into the main show. Collateral events must also submit to a Biennale process and must be fully funded. See Sarah Hyde, 'How to Get a Satellite Show During the Venice Biennale,' *Artnet*news* (8 February 2017), https://news.artnet.com/art-world/satellite-show-during-venice-biennale-849362 (accessed 8 September 2018).

12 Michael Hardt and Antonio Negri, *Empire* (Cambridge, MA: Harvard University Press, 2000).

13 Benjamin, *The Arcades Project*, 285.

14 Ibid.

15 Donald Preziosi, *Brain of the Earth's Body: Art, Museums, and the Phantasms of Modernity* (Minneapolis: University of Minnesota Press, 2003), 132–3.

16 Ibid., 139. Emphasis in original.

17 See Peter Stearns, 'British Industry through the Eyes of French Industrialists (1820–1848),' *Journal of Modern History*, vol. 37, no. 1 (March 1965), 50.

18 Patricia Mainardi, *Art and Politics of the Second Empire: The Universal Expositions of 1855 and 1867* (New Haven: Yale University Press, 1987), 8.

19 Ibid., 10.

20 Ibid., 26.

21 Ibid.

22 Peter Bürger, *Theory of the Avant-Garde*, tr. Michael Shaw, 11th ed. (Minneapolis: University of Minnesota Press, 2004), 22.

23 Rolf Tiedemann, 'Dialectics at a Standstill: Approaches to the *Passagen-Werk*,' in Gary Smith, ed., *On Walter Benjamin: Critical Essays and Recollections* (Cambridge, MA: MIT Press), 279.

24 Ibid., 465 (N4a, 2).

25 See Karl Marx, *Capital: A Critique of Political Economy*, tr. Ben Fowkes, vol. I (New York: Vintage, 1977), 125.

26 See Peter Stallybrass, 'Marx and Heterogeneity: Thinking the Lumpenproletariat,' *Representations*, no. 31 (summer 1990).

27 Paul Greenhalgh, *Ephemeral Vistas: The Expositions Universelles, Great Exhibitions and Worlds's Fairs, 1851–1939* (Manchester: Manchester University Press, 1988), 209.

28 'Feitizo magic' was the term used by Hegel in Georg W.F. Hegel, *The Philosophy of History*, tr. J. Sibree, *Great Books in Philosophy* (Buffalo: Prometheus Books, 1991 (1822)), 94.

29 Otis T. Mason, 'Anthropology in Paris during the Exposition of 1889,' *American Anthropologist*, vol. 3, no. 1 (January 1890), 31.

30 Richard Guy Wilson, 'Challenge and Response: Americans and the Architecture of the 1889 Exposition,' in Annette Blaugrund, ed., *Paris 1889: American Artists at the Universal Exposition* (Philadelphia: Pennsylvania Academy of the Fine Arts, 1989), 100.

31 Mason, 'Anthropology in Paris during the Exposition of 1889,' 32.

32 Ibid.

33 Hegel, *The Philosophy of History*, 103.

34 Ibid., 104.

35 G.W.F. Hegel, *The Phenomenology of Mind* (New York: Harper Torchbooks, 1807), 229.

36 Ibid., 239.

37 Susan Buck-Morss, 'Hegel and Haiti,' *Critical Inquiry*, vol. 26, no. 4 (summer 2000), 822.

38 Robert W. Rydell in introduction to Smithsonian Institute, *The Books of the Fairs: Materials about World's Fairs, 1834–1916, in the Smithsonian Institution Libraries* (Chicago: American Library Association, 1992), 4.

39 A Century of Progress, *Official Guide, Book of the Fair 1933, Chicago, Century of Progress International Exposition* (Chicago: A Century of Progress, 1933), 121.

40 F.W. Putnam, *Oriental and Occidental Northern and Southern Portrait Types of the Midway Plaisance* (St. Louis: N.D. Thompson Publishing Co., 1894), introduction.

41 See map of grounds on index page in *Official Catalogue of Exhibits on the Midway Plaisance, Colombian Exposition Group 176* (Chicago: W.B. Conkey Company, Publishers to the Exposition, 1893).

42 Ibid.

43 Hegel, *The Philosophy of History*, 94.

44 Ibid.

45 Ibid.

46 Ibid., 93–4.

47 Immanuel Kant, *Observations on the Feeling of the Beautiful and Sublime*, tr. John T. Goldthwait (Berkeley: University of California Press, 1960), 107.

48 Ibid., 111.

49 William Pietz, 'The Problem of the Fetish, ii: The Origin of the Fetish,' *Res* 13 (1987), 40.

50 Ibid. Emphasis in original.

51 Marx, *Capital*, 165.

52 Ibid., 173.

53 Ibid., 209.

54 Lucy Monroe, 'Chicago Letter,' *The Critic*, vol. 22, no. 588 (27 May 1893), 351.

55 Martin Clark, *The Italian Risorgimento* (New York: Longman, 1998), 42.

56 Ibid.

57 Ibid., 73. The prominent member of the Bonaparte family would marry into one of the oldest houses of Europe in a contract that ceded Savoy to France and united the French in an alliance to ward off the Austrian occupation of Italy. In exchange, Venice would be relinquished by Austria to become part of the unified Italy. Although Victor Emanuel II in 1861 would be given the title of the first king of modern Italy, he was married to Adelaide, the archduchess of Austria. By 1878, Umberto I had ascended the throne of his father Victor Emanuel II. In 1868, Umberto I had married his own cousin Margherita, the princess of Savoy.

58 Gramsci's acknowledgment of the lowest class, the subaltern, has been understood in current political theory as the 'third-world' designation of peoples. Antonio

Gramsci, 'Some Aspects of the Southern Question,' in *Selections from Political Writing: 1921–1926* (New York: International Publishers, 1978).

59 Frederic C. Lane, 'Recent Studies on the Economic History of Venice,' *Journal of Economic History*, vol. 23, no. 3 (1963), 315.

60 Clark, *The Italian Risorgimento*, 54.

61 Shearer West, 'National Desires and Regional Realities in the Venice Biennale, 1895–1914,' *Art History*, vol. 18, no. 3 (1995), 405. For analysis of conditions of Venice's late addition to Italy's 1861 unification, see Clark, *The Italian Risorgimento*, 87.

62 Shearer West's overall argument was based on this point that Venice drew from its arts heritage to support a national position. See West, 'National Desires and Regional Realities.'

63 J. Pedro Lorente, *Cathedrals of Urban Modernity* (Aldershot: Ashgate, 1998), 183.

64 See ibid.

65 For descriptions see Wolfgang Friebe, *Buildings of the World Exhibitions*, tr. Jenny Vowles and Paul Roper (Leipzig: Edition Leipzig, 1985).

66 Buck-Morss, *The Dialectics of Seeing: Walter Benjamin and the Arcades Project* (Cambridge, MA: MIT Press, 1989), 323–4.

67 Ibid., 323.

68 Ibid.

69 Benjamin, *The Arcades Project*, 4.

70 Ibid., 269 (first notes for *Passagen-Werk* N2, 6).

71 Ibid., 10.

72 See Benjamin, 'Paris, Capital of the Nineteenth Century (1935),' *The Arcades Project*, 3–13.

73 Ibid., 10.

74 Paul Teasdale, 'Documenta 14 Kassel: The Overview,' *Frieze* (7 June 2017), https://frieze.com/article/documenta-14-kassel-overview (accessed 4 January 2018).

75 See 'Documenta Kassel 16/06-23/09, 2007,' www.documenta12.de/index.php?id=d1&L=1 (accessed 4 January 2018).

76 Rachel Donadio, 'German Art Exhibition Documental Expands into Athens,' *New York Times* (5 April 2017), C1.

77 H.G. Masters, 'Documenta 14, Kassel (Part 2),' *Art Asia Pacific* (9 June 2017), http://artasiapacific.com/Blog/Documenta14KasselPart2 (accessed 10 September 2017).

78 James Clifford, *The Predicament of Culture: Twentieth-Century Ethnography, Literature, and Art* (Cambridge, MA: Harvard University Press, 1988).

79 Anthony Hall, *Earth into Property: Colonization, Decolonization, and Capitalism* (Montreal: McGill-Queen's University Press, 2017), 54.

80 Paige Raibmon, 'Theatres of Contact: The Kwakwaka'wakw Meet Colonialism in British Columbia and at the Chicago World's Fair,' *The Canadian Historical Review*, vol. 81, no. 2 (June 2000), 157.

81 Hall, *Earth into Property*, 56.

82 Raibmon, 'Theatres of Contact,' 185.

83 Candice Hopkins, 'In Memoriam: Beau Dick (1955–2017),' *Documenta Notes*

and Works (4 April 2017), www.documenta14.de/en/notes-and-works/17052/in-memoriam-beau-dick-1955-2017 (accessed 7 September 2017).

84 Ibid.

85 Jane Chin Davidson, 'Global Art and World Art: An Update on Art and Anthropology in the University Museum,' in Jane Chin Davidson and Sandra Esslinger, eds, *Global and World Art in the Practice of the University Museum* (New York and London: Routledge, 2017), 59.

86 Jason Farago, 'Documenta 14, a German Art Show's Greek Revival,' *New York Times* (10 April 2017), C1.

87 See Helena Smith and Philip Oltermann, 'EU States Begin Returning Refugees to Greece as German Reunions Slow,' *Guardian* (25 August 2017).

88 Donald Preziosi, *The Art of Art History: A Critical Anthology* (Oxford: Oxford University Press, 1998), 17.

89 E.H. Gombrich, *Art and Illusion: A Study in the Psychology of Pictorial Representation* (New York: Pantheon, 1961), 118.

90 See William Skidelsky, 'Picture Perfect,' *Guardian* (16 May 2009).

91 Robert Venturi, Denise Scott Brown, and Steven Izenour, *Learning From Las Vegas: The Forgotten Symbolism of Architectural Form* (Cambridge, MA: MIT Press, 1977), 8.

92 Helena Smith, 'Crapumenta! ... Anger in Athens as the Blue Lambs of Documenta Hit Town,' *Guardian* (14 May 2017).

93 Farago, 'Documenta 14, a German Art Show's Greek Revival.'

94 Charlotte Townsend-Gault, 'Rebecca Belmore and James Luna on Location at Venice: The Allegorical Indian Redux,' *Art History*, vol. 29, no. 4 (September 2006), 725.

95 See *Documenta 11 – Retrospective* – documenta website, www.documenta.de/en/retrospective/documenta11# (accessed 19 January 2018).

96 Okwui Enwezor, *All the World's Futures 56th International Art Exhibition: La Biennale di Venezia 1* (Venice: Marsilio, 2015), 94.

97 Ibid., 17.

98 Ibid.

99 Ibid., 92.

The archive of Chineseness: the global exposition and the museum

In 2012, the Shanghai Biennale opened at the new mega museum, the Power Station of Art, the massive seven-story, 450,000-square-foot former electrical plant that was transformed into a museum in the model of London's Tate Modern. Museums have become important civic centers and tourist sites for international cities such as Shanghai and Beijing, contributing to the rapid development of China's metropolitan areas, and attaining the symbolic status that they have long had in Europe, the United States, and other industrialized nations. While the global artfairs in China represent the globalized art institution, here in Shanghai, the biennial in the maturity of its ninth season inaugurates the new contemporary *museum* that also opened in 2012 – it is the biennial that is the historical exhibition. Declared by Amy Qin to be 'the first state-owned contemporary art museum in China,' both the Power Station and the Shanghai Biennale have become 'landmark events' for the country.[1] Qin notes that at Shanghai's tenth edition held two years later in 2014, the head curator Anselm Franke from Berlin was, for the first time in the Biennale's history given free rein to select the show's focus and theme. The administrators state that the future aim is for the event to 'be more international,' and so prominent intellectual figures were enlisted to serve on the museum's advisory committee. The combined site of the art expo and the contemporary museum represents a paradoxical shift from the symbolic function of these institutions, in which artfairs are considered as the dynamic displays for the staging of contemporary art, while museums are thought to be static repositories for historical objects.

In the 1990s, the implementation of artfairs would serve as the means in China to operate within the new economic system to bypass political restrictions for exhibiting art. A review of select art biennials/triennials in this chapter, such as China's ground-breaking Guangzhou Biennial held in 1992 and the subsequent inclusion of artists from China and Taiwan for the first time in the Venice Biennale in 1993, can show how this formative period was important to the very definition of the new global contemporary art. The most unique set of contradictions emerged from the growth of the art scene in China in direct contrast with the repressions of China's government; and this was happening around the same moment that the biennial/triennial was becoming the site for staging political platforms and interdisciplinary forums, as exemplified by Okwui Enwezor's theme *Democracy Unrealized* for Documenta 11 in 2002. The objective of this chapter is therefore to track a particular development of the biennials and triennials in an attempt to comprehend the political and discursive contradictions that pertain to the 'archive' of Chineseness. The 'paradoxes and conundrums' are those that also pertain to the discourse of contemporary art as a whole, and as Nikos Papastergiadis argues, the 'complexity has intensified due to the massive expansion of people and practices that are now considered as being part of the global art world. To make sense of this diversity and complexity it is necessary to develop wider conceptual and historical frameworks.'[2]

Contributing to a wider framework for archival practices, this chapter's contextualization of the discursive domain of expositions and museums for representing Chinese states is conceived as a study of the 'performative archive,' a concept that shares affinity with Gunhild Borggreen and Rune Gade's notion of 'performing archives' described as 'the moment or situation where the archive is transformed into a dynamic and self-reflective medium that intervenes in and challenges its own ontology.'[3] The record of the expositions in Guangzhou reveals the self-reflexive challenge, from the inception of the first 1992 Guangzhou Biennial to the politics expressed in the theme *Farewell to Postcolonialism* for the 2008 Guangzhou Triennial. While Enzwezor's 2002 platform was premised on the use of postcolonial critique to challenge Documenta's eurocentric legacy, the relevancy of the postcolonial itself would be contested just six years later at the Guangzhou Triennial. The curators of the 2008 Triennial argue that the postcolonial was yet another concept produced by the West, and that China was never truly subjected to Euro-American influence or power during Mao's governance in the twentieth century. This conception is dependent on the belief that the cultural contexts of Revolutionary China (1949–76) had somehow insulated Chinese culture from Western power relations – even as socialist realist painting was a product of "the West." But in the aftermath of Deng Xiaoping's 1980s *gaige kaifeng* (reforms and openness), any purported cultural insularity has been relinquished to the processes of transnationalism, especially after the 1997 return of Hong Kong as a Special Administrative Region of China. The discrete, whole subject of China on the basis of an authentic Chinese identity has been put into question, which is the very premise of this book's examination. As illustrated by the history of China's biennial/triennials, art expositions since the 1990s have played a part in the country's globalization processes.

My own engagement in this debate looks to decolonial practices for reconciling the ideologies of the colonial and the postcolonial through this study of museums and global expositions, especially the inaugural representations of China, Hong Kong, and Taiwan at the Venice Biennale. The postcolonial issues of appropriation and synthesis of Chinese culture were integral to the 1990s debates articulated in Rey Chow's seminal essay 'On Chineseness as a Theoretical Problem.' The contradictions embodied by the term are therefore conceivable as Orientalist appropriations of the past that contribute nonetheless to the present-day syncretism of the Euro-American formation of global art. In the context of identity, contradiction is a unique problem and Chineseness provides a conflicted reconciliation much in the way that Édouard Glissant uses the language of *creolization* to convey the chaotic and creative disorder of the experience of border-crossings, immigration and exile. Showcased in Platform 3 of Documenta 11, Glissant's poetic philosophy establishes the model for an analysis of geographical consciousness as conceptualized for the global art exposition. Manthia Diawara explains Glissant's 'new vision of difference' by citing his key concepts of 'relation, opacity, creolization, and disaffiliation. The Martinique-born writer and thinker was, of course, the first philosopher of post-filiation, by which I refer not only to his rebellious thesis of disaffiliation, in the sense of breaking with a genealogy and tradition of Western and non-Western philosophies concerned with binary opposition and contradiction.'[4] Much in the way that Diawara argues for a break from both West and non-West binaries, the concept of Chineseness shares in the mutual recognition of dis-affiliation in which the Orientalist language of the past and the global nationalisms of the present are inevitably reconciled in the decolonial vocabulary of mondialization and world-making.

As such, the study of the archive of Chineseness can be understood through the historical record *and* a performative reflection of the metaphorical space of the global exposition and the artists who are represented by it. The chapter begins by reviewing the remarkable period that commenced in 1992 with the first Guangzhou Biennial and then the 1993 inclusion of the first artists from China/Taiwan in the Venice Biennale. To follow is the contextualization of two significant Guangzhou *Triennials*, the first in 2002 titled *Reinterpretation: A Decade of Experimental Chinese Art 1990–2000*, and the third in 2008 titled *Farewell to Postcolonialism*. The political contradictions of the artfair-versus-museum discourse are traced to the ideological shift of global art (and the postcolonial) as the creation of the binary opposition to world art (and the colonial). As examined in Chapter Four, the nineteenth-century world's fairs had distinguished the separation between objects of art and objects of anthropology, and ever since, cultures had been defined by museums of fine art and museums of anthropology. By tracking the sixteenth-century Ming vase in the collection of the Pitt Rivers anthropology museum, the contradictions can be perceived through juxtaposing the contemporary subjects of Chinese artists with the museum's historical objects.

The provenance of the sixteenth-century Ming vase at Pitt Rivers is traced to the Sarawak, a Malaysian Chinese community, which represents a diasporic Chineseness. In 2004, Malaysian Chinese artist Wong Hoy Cheong created a site-specific and performative installation also at the Pitt Rivers Museum, and his juxtaposition with the Ming vase in the same galleries exposes the artificial inscriptions of art and science, of cultural relics and living cultures.

The individual case studies in this chapter offer an analysis on how cultural and national identities are performed and produced through the metaphorical spaces of the exhibition. The historical objects collected by anthropology museums in Europe and the United States have come to represent the colonialist past, and its archival methodology is made apparent by the temporary displays of those very same cultures exhibited in global artfairs worldwide. If they are shown in the same space at the Pitt Rivers, how is it possible to call the Malaysian Sarawak culture an example of colonialist world art while the Malaysian Chinese culture is considered as a contemporary global representation? When viewed in the context of the performative archive of Chineseness, the embodiments of Chinese contemporary artists in direct contrast to the representation of Chinese vases can be understood as the enactment of disaffiliation from the norm of binary oppositions, including the idea of Europe and its Others, and/or China and its Others.

Global expositions, global art, and the postcolonial

The 1992 Guangzhou Biennial can be reviewed as a key example of a performative archive, a dynamic and self-reflective activity of an important moment in history. Curator Lu Peng selected 400 works by 350 contemporary artists for this first biennial exhibition held at the Guangzhou Central Hotel, developed as an independent, commercial endeavor funded with private resources.[5] Often referred to as a painting biennial, the new generation of artists included Mao Yan, Shang Yang, Zhou Chunya, Shu Qun, and Wei Guangqing.[6] Lu was completely aware of the shift that the Biennial had represented during this critical moment after Deng Xiaoping's 1992 Southern Tour of the country, whereupon, the chairman solidified his principle for '"one central task, two basic points"; planning and market forces are not essential difference[s] between socialism and capitalism.'[7] The political climate had shifted from hard-line resistance toward bourgeois capitalist economics. Lu conceived his inaugural exposition as an entrepreneurial venture, and explains the significant changes to exhibitions in China that it had affected, by which

> the 'sponsorship' of the past has been replaced by 'investment,' in terms of operations, the cultural organization of the past has been replaced by a company; in terms of process, the administrative 'notices' of the past have been

replaced by legally binding contracts; in terms of academic underpinnings, the old ad hoc, artist-run 'artwork selection teams' have been replaced by jury committees run by art critics; in terms of goals, the old monolithic, narrow and always argumentative goal of artistic 'success' has been replaced by efforts towards comprehensive economic, social and academic 'effectiveness.'[8]

The curator oversaw the incoming new standards for art initiated by Deng's reforms, whereby Mao's dictates for *culture created for the sake of culture* was being replaced with the idea that *culture must be produced for sale.* Under these conditions, the artfair's useful form and function as a cultural status-making enterprise was apparent. As Lu explains, 'we spent over CNY 30,000 to invite *Flash Art* editor Francesco Bonami to the "Guangzhou Biennial" ... in hopes that international society could learn about local Chinese contemporary art.'[9] Indeed, Lu's efforts proved successful, as shown in the following year when fourteen artists were invited by director Achille Bonito Oliva to participate for the first time in the 1993 Venice Biennale. Oliva had included fourteen artists from China – Ding Yi, Wang Guangyi, Zhang Peili, Geng Jianyi, Xu Bing, Liu Wei, Fang Lijun, Yu Hong, Feng Mengbo, Li Shan, Yu Youhan, Wang Ziwei, Sun Liang, and Song Haidong in the section called 'Passagio a Oriente' – in addition to Taiwanese artist Lee Ming-sheng who was included in the international group show.[10]

Even as Oliva's title reflected the Orientalist obsession, the potential for drawing attention to a culture, a nation, outside of the European context could be engaged through the biennial concept and its art-by-nation organizing principles. The status-making function may have been useful for Lu Peng's 1992 initiative, but as discussed in Chapter Four, it is actually a structural premise from the world's fair, an integral part in the nineteenth-century event created as an industrial competition that was useful in the shift to market changes in China. The significance and innovation ascribed to China's contemporary art in 1992 can also be attributed to artists who were seen as avant-gardists negotiating the pressing circumstances and repressions that culminated in the 1989 Tiananmen Square demonstrations (as a process of Deng Xiaoping's *gaige kaifang* political reform). Lu explains the impact of the 1989 events, in which many artists and critics left China for other countries in order to obtain political independence, financial means, and exhibition opportunities to continue their work.[11] For those who stayed behind, the aim was to bring the 'art industry' to China, which inspired the organizers to develop the first contemporary artfair amidst the political difficulties of that period. As Wu Hung asserts, 'a prevailing view among advocates of experimental art in the early and mid-1990s was that this art could be legalized only when it could realize its economic potentials.'[12] The ability to create monetary advantages through art expositions was instrumental to negotiations with

China's officials, and by the late 1990s, semi-official exhibitions and art galleries in Beijing and Shanghai would slowly become acceptable. The important point is that the inception of the art biennial paved the way for the development of art museums in post-1989 China.

By 1996, Shanghai would boast two museums – the Shanghai Museum housing Chinese antiquities and the Shanghai Art Museum devoted to exhibitions of contemporary and modern art. Barbara Pollock asserts that in the years to follow, 'Shanghai tourists have a choice of no fewer than ten contemporary-art museums, most of them private ventures supported by individual investors. According to the latest government statistics, China is building approximately 100 museums a year, an increase from fewer than 2,500 in 2001 to more than 3,500 a decade later, with 390 opening in 2011 alone.'[13] In a matter of decades, the exponential growth of biennial expositions and museums had transformed the conditions for representing art in the country – after the first Guangzhou Biennial was held in 1992, the first Shanghai Biennale opened in 1996, and the first Shenzhen Ink and Wash Painting Biennial in 1998.[14] As an entrepreneurial enterprise, the biennial distinguishes China's new exhibitionary form in which expositions held in Beijing in 1996 and 1997 were also groundbreaking in their innovative context.[15] In achieving this new ideal, *xiandai yishu* (contemporary art) contributed to the twenty-first-century formation of the global institution *inside* of China as well as contributing to the international system for global art. The biennials and triennials, however, were the first and perhaps the most influential in establishing China's status as a member of the international art community.

Ten years after the first Guangzhou Biennial, the first Guangzhou *Triennial* was curated by Wu Hung, Huang Zhuan, and Feng Boyi to reintroduce works for the theme, *Reinterpretation: A Decade of Experimental Chinese Art 1990–2000*, exhibiting between 18 November 2002 and 19 January 2003. In hindsight, the *shiyan meishu* experimental art movement was a phenomenon ascribed to the last two decades of the twentieth century. Wu explains that the triennial's 'main purpose is not just to showcase a group of works of Chinese experimental art from the 1990s; it is, more importantly, to *reinterpret* this art through various means.'[16] Initiated and organized by the director Wang Huangsheng for the Guangdong Museum of Art, the biennial/triennial form was indeed one of the new tools that enabled this reinterpretation. Wu acknowledged the exposition's function in helping to 'construct the global context of 1990s experimental art.'[17] He suggests that by the 1990s, the art community in China was 'thoroughly globalized' rather than endemic of the country's local culture since artists, critics, and curators had all traveled outside of the country to create and exhibit their work internationally. This development came at a moment when 'global art' came into prominence, particularly as the network of biennials, triennials, and artfairs enabled the advance of China's art and their role in the 'globalized art institution.'[18]

In the convening years, curators and organizers of biennials/triennials in China would also use the exhibition's institutional format to serve as a platform, largely for political purposes. If the First Guangzhou Biennial in 1992 was able to bring the European artworld to China for the first time, the third Guangzhou Triennial in 2008, just sixteen years later, would boldly declare that the relations of national power had been transformed and reversed. The idea that the eurocentric classificatory order had shifted was articulated by the exposition's title *Farewell to Postcolonialism*. Curators Gao Shiming, Sarat Maharaj, and Chang Tsong-zung hosted '181 artists from over 40 countries around the world, including 50 films/videos from the Middle East, Southeast Asia and Africa under the projects "Middle East Channel," "East-South: Out of Sight" and "Africa: Personal Poetics."'[19] The exhibition's showcase of a greater global range of artists and the organizing of symposia exemplified the new cultural strategy for the global artfair.

As noted earlier, the utilization of the art exposition as an overt political platform was principally a new endeavor, propeled by Okwui Enwezor's political strategy for Documenta 11 under the 2002 theme *Democracy Unrealized*. The curators of the third Guangzhou Triennial (GZ3), Tsong-Zung and Gao Shiming, adopted Enwezor's 2002 use of Documenta's 'platforms' by hosting a series of events that prefaced the exposition – Enwezor had looked to the 'artistic and intellectual possibilities' of the biennial/triennial concept through his series of five different platforms, with the first four held as 'conferences, debates, and workshops that preceded the exposition in five locations: in Europe (Vienna and Berlin), Asia (New Delhi), the Americas (St. Lucia), and Africa (Lagos).'[20] The 2008 Guangzhou Triennial was launched in the same way, and the 2007 *Farewell to Postcolonialism* conference preceded the opening of the exposition while the series of discussions and forums were carried over into the closing symposium *Towards a Post-Western Society* in November 2008.

There was a major difference, however, between the visions of Enwezor and Tsong-Zung/Gao, since the Documenta director emphasized a postcolonialist strategy for the politics of his groundbreaking project: 'Postcoloniality, in its demand for full inclusion within the global system and by contesting existing epistemological structures, shatters the narrow focus of Western global optics and fixes its gaze on the wider sphere of the new political, social, and cultural relations that emerged after World War II.'[21] Documenta 11's radical shift in perspective has often been cited as enacting the irrevocable change to the globalization of the arts. While Enwezor saw the potential of the postcolonial for transforming the Western global system for art, as evidenced by his own role as the first African curator in the history of Documenta, the paradox in which just six years later the curators of the 2008 Guangzhou Triennial would declare the end of postcoloniality proposes a political contradiction.

The effort to define the globalization of the arts was the apparent motivation for Enwezor, Tsong-Zung, and Gao, but each interpreted the postcolonial in different ideological ways. Gao explains how the triennial's curatorial focus on 'self imagining' was an attempt to reframe the epistemological premise for contemporary art in general. And to break from the preconceptions that encircled global art and art history, Gao conducted 'an exercise in negation,' an endeavor that is

> neither Western nor non-western [*sic*]; neither global nor local; neither international nor national; neither left nor right; neither the third world nor the third space; neither tourist spectacle nor ethno-scape. Not cosmopolitanism; not multi-culturalism; not tribalism; not post-colonialism; not identity politics; not sociological report; not relational aesthetics; not a regime of the other; not alternative modernity; not hybridity; not a showcase of new stars.[22]

From this position of 'negation,' Gao elicited ideas and responses from curators, critics, and artists through a 'questionnaire exercise,' which he included in the triennial's platform, a polling of attitudes that sought to expose and then to bypass the binaristic approach to postcolonial terminology. His effort to transcend artistic ideals, however, echoes the negative dialectics of Adorno and his analysis of historical materialism using the concept of 'non-identity' as a resistance to Hegelian consciousness. Adorno's aim included a challenge to Hegel's 'all-subjugating identity principle,' his 'world spirit ... defined as permanent catastrophe.'[23] Arguing that this 'universal history must be construed and denied,' Adorno's exile from Germany's violent identity politics is the important factor for understanding his *critical negation* of that rationalist, idealist, progressive view of history,' as described by Susan Buck-Morss, the perspective that ultimately led bourgeois society to accept Hitler's totalitarianism: 'Enlightenment is totalitarian.'[24] Perhaps Gao, like Adorno, wanted to do away with the idealist progressive view of history in his own time period; however, Gao's version of negation seems strangely forgetful of the authoritarian politics that Lu Peng strove to overcome through his first Guangzhou Biennial in 1992.

Tsong-Zung's explanation for *Farewell to Postcolonialism* was more decisive, although his reasoning was solipsistically based on the proliferation of the artfairs themselves, citing the emergence of hundreds of biennials over the course of a few decades. As exemplified by the Guangzhou Biennial, global expositions had appeared in all parts of the world since the 1990s, from the Gwangju Biennale begun in South Korea in 1995, to Dak'Art – Biennale de l'Art Africain Contemporain begun in Senegal in 1996. Tsong-Zung argues that the expositions had opened up greater opportunities for countries like

China to 'foster a local urge to engage the globalised world from their own vantage points, take possession of international artistic discourse, and eventually forge visions of their own.'[25] The political platform of the biennial/triennial provided the means for engaging a self-referential logic in which the very proliferation of the world expositions was used as evidence of the shift in power through the self-representation of cultures and nations. Tsong-Zung conceives of the cultural change in art as a marked shift away from the 'clear division between the West and "the margin,"' a move that he suggests began with the initiation of cultural diversity at the 1989 *Magiciens de la terre* exhibition at the Pompidou Centre.[26] 'Magicians of the Earth' was considered as the significant effort to counteract the Euro/ethno-centered divisions perpetuated by the art world, as curator Jean-Hubert Martin attempted to transform the Paris Biennial.[27] And thus, according to Tsong-Zung, the proliferation of biennials and triennials substantiates this shift in the subsequent years of the Pompidou show. His argument that the period of postcolonialism is essentially over was based on these exhibitions, but he also points to the 'anticipated rise in influence of Asia' as an outcome of the 2008–9 banking crisis that connected failed mortgage loans to economies around the world.[28] Tsong-Zung perceives a 'new sense of mutual dependency' among nations in the period after the 'exhilarating Asian season of international exhibitions followed by the meltdown of the world financial system.'[29] The context for distinguishing the end of the postcolonial period was primarily the portentous relations of power between Asia and the West.

The extent to which the triennial's platform was a farewell to postcolonialism, however, was often contested by the participants of the event who published their responses in the aftermath. In 'Some Notes on the Road to the GZ3,' Gertrud Sandqvist suggests that the theme was devised more as a provocation to explore the 'different situations of the Chinese historical situation' as distinguished from the type of postcolonialism 'thought, taught, and discussed at prestigious academic institutions in the West.'[30] She pointed to the statement made by Triennial Director Wang Huangsheng: '"Postcolonialism is an inevitable, highly controversial avant-garde cultural theory in current politics and culture." To a certain extent, the GZ3 both introduced and abandoned post-colonialism in the same event.'[31] The discrepancies in the understanding of the *postcolonial* has long been a part of its academic scholarship – for instance, the difference between postcolonialist theory and the conditions of the postcolonial period, marked by the end of British rule in India in 1947, can be construed as intellectually disparate subjects, especially since many believe that colonial and neo-colonial states around the world are continuing their political occupations through ongoing governance over natural resources among other capitalized forms of power. Arguably, China has never been colonized, with the exception of Hong Kong; however, the capitalist enterprises established by foreign industrialists as part of the concessions of the Opium War (1839–60) are well-documented.

At the same time that the end of postcolonialism was being heralded at the 2008 Guangzhou Triennial, the conception of a contemporary *global art* as distinct from a historical *world art* was being shaped by historians and global art proponents. In this discourse, the new production of works by non-Euro-American cultures has been attributed to a new global contemporary order that is considered to be the final break from both the modernist system for art and the postcolonial order. Hans Belting, for instance, declares the ideological divide is represented by the arrival of global art as differentiated from the *colonialist* production of world art.[32] The new biennials/triennials as exemplified by Tsong-Zung and Gao's exposition asserting the end of the postcolonial era played a seminal role in this debate, promoted as an obvious 'contemporary' form of global representation outside of the historical circuit of museums and Euro-American art institutions.

Global art theorists such as Belting argue that there is no ideological compatibility between studies of contemporary global art and those of historical world art – Belting defines the latter as encompassing 'most cultures beyond the West whose heritage was preserved in empire type museums,' explaining how world art was for a long time 'primarily owned by Western museums, where it existed as an expatriated and contested treasure from colonial times.'[33] The critique of these cultural biases in the museum has been ongoing since the 1984 *'Primitivism' in 20th Century Art: Affinity of the Tribal* exhibition at the Museum of Modern Art – the 'great modernist art pioneers' displayed next to primitive ethnographic specimens – and as Tsong-Zung suggests, the impactful 1989 *Magiciens de la terre* exhibition was not only the answer to MOMA's *Primitivism* show but was also the point of departure for the new equality of cultural representation. Here, the global art expositions – biennials and triennials, such as *Farewell to Postcolonialism* – appear as the alternative to the colonial through representing global art, *not world art*, even as 'Africa' is included in both categories. Belting views global art as differing 'profoundly from world art in that it is always created as art to begin with, and that is synonymous with contemporary art practice, whatever the art definitions may be in the individual case.'[34] In essence, he defines the discourse split along the classificatory order that has long separated the scientific artefact of world art and the aesthetic fine art object, reinscribed as global art. While his analysis may appear promising for the prospect of all cultural objects attaining the high art category, the world art objects ascribed to colonial history remain under occupation of the colonialist inscription. The problem remains in the redoubling of the value judgments made against world art as works that were originally castigated from the criteria and standards of Western art.

Museum, world art, and the colonial

In light of the critical difference between world art and global art, the *exchange* of the object itself needs to be re-examined in respect of the circuit of exhibition, from the colonial collection to the museum. The subject of the Chinese vase, for instance, can illustrate the problem in a revealing way, since it has been an object of growing interest in the art market. In 1995, the artist Ai Weiwei had brought attention to the value and meaning of vases in his performance/photograph *Dropping a Han Dynasty Urn*. During the late 1990s, Ai was traveling around China's countryside collecting antique vases – some of which appear to be as old as from the Han period as far back as third century BCE. He explains that at the time he was able to purchase these relics on the open market in various places.[35] Staged for the photograph, he performs the dropping of the ancient urn in an act of destroying something that has withstood the millennia of time, which is enough to make the viewer feel the emotional sense of loss. The performance constitutes a memorial for the symbolic function of Han vessels, supported by photography's gesture that 'embalms' the subject, as Roland Barthes once described. Long before the glorious Han dynasty, the work of art assisted in a ritual process in order that a Chinese community abides by the rule of heaven. The emperor who conducts the rites with vessels and ceremonial objects was the Son of Heaven over the living and the ancestral dead. The gestural break from tradition was performed in the most literal way by Ai when he dropped the antique vase.

But fifteen years later in 2010, the stakes were raised for Chinese porcelain when a Qing dynasty vase was sold in London for a record-breaking 69.5 million dollars. The vase was not dated to the antiquity of the Han but to the period of the emperor Qianlong in the 1700s, acquired by a collector in the 1930s. The sale had elevated the profile of Chinese art overall, but adding to this new status, the controversy emerged around vases made by potters from the celebrated porcelain capital Jingdezhen who were able to create amazing replicas, knock-offs of dynastic ware that could not be discerned from vases dating to the earliest imperial ceramics. Researchers such as Maris Gillette have studied these workshops in Jingdezhen that actually date back to the Han dynasty.[36] But here, it is important to point out that this particular Qianlong vase was thought by some to be among the treasures looted by British troops during the second Opium War from 1856 to 1860 when they sacked the imperial palaces in Beijing.[37] Based on this colonial provenance, the history of such looted objects has come to represent the very example of Belting's critique of the world art object. The meaning and value of the work and the historical relevance of the vase tends to be overshadowed by the history of empire. If indeed global art can represent cultures in less problematic ways than world art's 'expatriated and contested treasure from colonial times' as exemplified by the Qianlong vase, what role then can these objects play in the greater context of the history of art and the discourse of vases?

The representation of history is oftentimes neglected in the oversimplified analysis of colonial objects in the world art category. Take, for instance, the most treasured of Chinese vases, the Ming dynasty vase, particularly the two uniquely large examples dating to the early 1500s displayed at the Pitt Rivers Museum (see plate 19). The Ming vases staged in this museum are considered as world art objects, not fine art objects, and in this anthropology museum, works are exhibited according to typology. As discussed in my co-edited volume, *Global and World Art in the Practice of the University Museum*, no other museum is quite like the Pitt Rivers, with its Victorian system of densely packed cabinets containing diverse objects, from farm tools to exquisite works of art. The galleries were built in 1887 as an annex next to a natural history museum at Oxford University. The Ming vases were acquired from the collection of the White Rajahs in Sarawak in the Malaysian State of Borneo, the place where Chinese and Malaysian people currently comprise the largest population. Between 1841 and 1946, Sarawak was occupied by the British dynasty of White Rajahs, the lineage instituted by the founder James Brooke and continued by his descendants.[38]

Distinguished as exportware, these Ming vases were made in China in the 1500s, ostensibly for export to Sarawak and not for the imperial class of appreciators in China. Trade between China and Borneo had existed since the tenth century, and by the nineteenth century, possession of these great Chinese pottery jars, not unlike the possession of livestock in their barter economy, was a 'sign of aristocracy as well as of riches' among the Sarawak community.[39] The jars were considered foremost as status objects, as finery that was carefully guarded, but they were also functional objects used for storing things. It was stated that 'to be forced to surrender one is the severest of punishments.'[40] Before the British Rajah occupation, the Sarawak population was thought to be nomadic in moving and residing across the interior of Borneo. The vases would have been carried from place to place, and in this metaphorical depiction of its nomadic function, the vases represent a particular concept of Chineseness illustrated by its border-crossing aesthetic. The Malaysian Chinese ritual practice is completely different from the imperial expression usually associated with the Ming vase. Their exchange in the Sarawak barter system also reflects a very different model for the acquisition of imperial works. But Sarawak's economy changed tremendously with the incoming occupation of the White Rajahs who opened up the country to Western capital through exploiting Sarawak's mineral resources.[41] Glissant had noted the difference in lifestyle of the nomadic transiency of peoples during the pre-colonial period, a time when relations of power determined by the boundaries of center and periphery meant nothing. It was not until the fixing of nations, the conquests and declarations of territories, that the fundamental 'subject races' would come to be established by the British in Sarawak. The Ming vases embody this history as expressed by provenance, ownership, and the status of cultures.

Ultimately, the status of the commissioning party, the collector, in regard to what was originally made for the Chinese dynastic class as opposed to the nomadic Sarawak, contributes to the current connoisseurship of the aesthetic or money value of the vases. The Ming vases in the Percival David collection in the British Museum, by contrast, are imperial vases found in the court of the last Qing emperor. The collection is named after the celebrated figure who acquired the imperial works in 1927 after the fall of the last dynasty of China in 1912. Sir Percival David was a baronet, an honorary advisor to the National Palace in Beijing in 1928 before the onset of Japan's invasion in Manchuria in 1931.[42] This aspect of the exchange of world art is yet another example of the expatriation process criticized by Belting as an object that is 'owned' by empire-type museums.[43] At the British Museum, the representation of the imperial status of the David collection is supported by the well-lit, glass-encased exhibit of the vases (see plate 20), exemplifying modernist precious objects and engaging important signifiers of both aesthetic and money value. Vastly different, the Pitt Rivers showcase of the Sarawak Ming vase offers no apparent hierarchizing narrative about its value above anything else in the galleries – each object is just another heterogeneous object without distinction. This typological arrangement for world art is now informed by a newer sort of self-aware sensibility, which is the postmodernist alternative to the modernist aesthetic exemplified by the British Museum.

As museums transform their exhibitionary aims and practices, and acknowledge their ethnographical gaze toward world art objects, the importance of the history of imperialism puts into focus their role in museumifying the colonialist past. The idea that 'collecting is a form of conquest and collected artifacts are material signs of victory over their former owners' has been the subtext of the anthropology museum's function as collectors of world art.[44] While repatriation of objects has become one of the goals of the Pitt Rivers practices, the logic behind their system of exhibition can also be understood as the important endeavor to retain the traces of the museum's history, including the practices of colonialism, while acknowledging the conceptual science of portraying objects according to typology. At the Pitt Rivers, the vase is just another thing in the collection, waiting for researchers to find a new perspective for looking at them. The Ming vases at the museum provide a clear example for locating diasporic difference in the history of the Sarawak, and a decolonial perspective toward its cultural production would oversee the break from the nation-statist text – the 'Ming vase' of the nomadic Sarawak on the margins of China and Malaysia transcends the nationalist convention and better represents Chineseness. In their symbolic service, the useful and honorific life of these two vases becomes a metaphor for the diversity of a historical Chinese culture that does not have to serve an authentic culture or the Han dynastic legacy. Instead, until the White Rajahs governed Sarawak, the vases carried with them the traces of the original Confucian concept for honorary vessels that were engaged in both a ceremonial and useful function. Chineseness acknowledges the Malaysian use of Chinese art in the long tradition of ceremonial objects, created for the service of the spiritual rites under the mandate of heaven.

Performing Chineseness: globe, world, Malaysia

In 2004, artist Wong Hoy Cheong created a site-specific installation titled *Slight Shifts* for the Pitt Rivers Museum, proposing a clear challenge to the ostensible difference between the scientific artifact and the artistic treasure on display. The Malaysian artist, who has resided in the United States and Malaysia provides a transnational contrast to the preconceptions of the Ming vase in his expression of diasporic difference. Well known for addressing subjects of colonialism and postcolonialism, Wong has also been recognized as a global artist represented in multiple biennials and triennials. For *Slight Shifts*, Wong restaged the Pitt Rivers's displays and Victorian era vitrines with multicolored sensor lights, transforming the densely packed galleries to shine color onto the ethnographical objects organized by type (see plate 21). As described in the museum educational materials,

> visitors walked through corridors of light filtered up through the cast-iron gratings or projected from corners. Boats were returned to turquoise oceans and an unnoticed ceiling opened to the skies above. The play of light revealed new dimensions to objects and transformed visitors' experiences, making their exploration of the Museum both physical and contemporary.[45]

The viewing engagement with *Slight Shifts* is conceptual and performative, renewing the aesthetic tradition by using the gallery's three-dimensional space to create its effect, since 'real space' has proven to be more powerful than the illusion of three-dimensionality in art.[46] Wong provides a clarification of his artistic aims: 'In this time and day of globalization, with a flattening of experiences, I think provocations of the senses are needed.'[47] The movement and emotion of light and color draw on the viewer's senses but the illumination cast upon the objects in the galleries, including the Sarawak Ming vases, illustrates the full dimensions of the colonialist past that the anthropology museum encompasses. Wong's symbolic expression was meant to cast light on the archive of colonialism through this particular engagement, as the refraction of this light on the body of the viewer was a form of social implication for self-reflection. Rather than disavowing objects from ethnographic history, discarded along with their colonialist past, Wong refocuses the viewer's gaze toward them and literally spotlights their staging in the anthropology museum.

Hou Hanru characterizes *Slight Shifts* as conceptually different from Wong's longstanding focus on issues of colonial and postcoloniality. When the show *Days of Our Lives: Wong Hoy Cheong Selected Works 1998–2010* was presented at the Eslite Gallery in Taipei in 2010, questions about the debates raised by *A Farewell to Postcolonialism* at the 2008 Guangzhou Triennial had deferred to the subject of Wong's early body of work on the postcolonial. For instance, his video installation titled *Re:Looking (2002–3)*, selected by Hou Hanru for the 2003 Venice Biennale, merged factual and fictional content in regards to the subject of Austrian migrants working in Malaysia. In the video, Wong interviews the Austrian migrants who 'talk about how they hate Muslims, Turks and Malaysians,' and yet, the Europeans were originally the occupiers of the country; 'Malaysia wasn't a colonizer or aggressor. Instead *we* were victims of colonization.'[48] The postcolonialist approach to the elision of the violence of the colonial is one that acknowledges the history of the vanishing present. Wong's 2005 exhibition at the Second Guangzhou Triennial titled *Minaret* marked an aesthetic change to his work, described by Hou as an expression 'still related to migration, history and religion, [but] more related to globalization as having a long history. As something not new.'[49] *Minaret* was a scaffolded minaret tower made from bamboo and construction netting that was built as a temporary structure on the roof of the Guangdong Museum of Art (see plate 22). The minaret hails from a tradition of Islamic mosque architecture, and while Wong was inspired when he 'discovered that the oldest mosque in China was in Guangzhou,' he also viewed the symbol as a marker of a thousand years of globalization.[50] The artist had initially approached the imam at the still-functioning Huaisheng Mosque to complete the project there at the original site, but in the end, his structure would be built at the museum.[51] The glowing minaret cast in green light was visible for miles at night.

As a global artist who has exhibited in the Pitt Rivers Museum, the 2003 Venice Biennale, and the 2005 Guangzhou Triennial, Wong's Malaysian Chinese subjectivity represents an exemplary transnational Chineseness in the context of global exhibitions. When juxtaposed with the colonialist provenance of the Sarawak vases at the Pitt Rivers Museum, the contradiction between categorizing the world art of the past and Wong's global art of the present can be understood in more specific ways. Reflecting the long syncretic history of Chineseness, Wong reinscribes the Islamic symbol by re-creating the Minaret at the Guangzhou site of the Triennial. The Ming vase in the anthropology museum carries the same diverse history in the legacy of wares made in China for export to Sarawak in Borneo. Whether articulated as world art or global art, identity attributed to Chinese art/artefacts/objects will always be contingent on an artificial system of inscription, one that pertains equally to representations in anthropology museums as they do in biennials and triennials. The discursive conflicts, contradictions, and paradoxes of representation through any system of display that categorizes objects by nation, culture, or ethnicity will ultimately prove to be insufficient for the processes of identification. The very use of the term *Chineseness* in this book represents the contradictions among the destabilized, unfixable meaning of 'Chinese' in relation to art, particularly in globalized contexts for the staging of *exhibitions*.

Worldmentality

The terminology of the *globe* and the *world* requires further contextualization in the larger scope beyond the art discourse, since the archive of both world art and global art in the Euro-American context is still associated with the effects of empire. The term *globalization* refers politically to trade in a global economy, periodized by the formation of global corporations in the 1990s and the trade agreements conducted through the newly founded World Trade Organization. The reach of global capitalism in the twenty-first century extends to the flow of people as well as goods, as globalization refers to the ways in which the system of capital affects the labor and migration of people in all parts of the world. The ideology of the *global* emerged as a response to capitalist globalization whereby the distinctions between signifiers of the globe and the world are often viewed by the difference in the industrial demands of the past and the present. Papastergiadis explains the current sociopolitical order of the 'global' and its 'programme of integration and unification':

> In a globalising world, everything ultimately becomes the same. Standardisation brings efficiency and greater connectivity not just in commercial transactions, but also in the delineation of cultural values and political rights. In this singular organisational regime ... a uniform language is imposed on all places, so that one place merges with another. The space of the globe (rather than world) becomes a continuous and smooth surface where all relations between past and future, near and far, foreign and familiar, have to submit to the regime of integration.[52]

Papastergiadis looks to the concept of *mondialization* as the alternative to the commercial flows of the global in alignment with the marxist-informed arguments made by Kostas Axelos and Jean-Luc Nancy. In their analyses, a mondialized worldview is different from the capitalist regimentation of the global view, conceived also as a position of *worldmentality* that looks to the interconnected mapping of the world – one map is always contingent upon and connected to the other map. They remind us that global capitalism is human-centric, and not unlike the position of the Anthropocene, the world, the planet, exists outside of human intervention.

Moreover, *worldmentality* is often attributed to the work of Glissant, whose French Caribbean approach to culture, as noted earlier, was represented as a theme of Documenta 11's Platform 3, Créolité and Creolization. Glissant's articulation of the mixing and intertwining of peoples and cultures was expressed through his philosophy of poetry, focusing on language and the vernacular dialects of speech that break from discrete and cohesive ethnicities. The discourse of Chineseness shares the distinctions articulated in theories of creolization, especially in the spoken vernacular of Sinophonic film expressions as described by Shu-Mei Shih. The changing definition of transnational Chineseness consists not only of multiple Chinese identities across an expanse of diasporas but also includes what Glissant describes as 'the mutual mutations generated by this interplay of relations,' contributing to the 'principles of creoleness.'[53] Chineseness shares affinity with Glissant's idea of a regression 'more or less innocently' toward 'negritudes ... Frenchness, of Latinness, all generalizing concepts.'[54] Enwezor acknowledges Glissant's 'discontinuous, aleatory forms' that are consistent with an artistic context that is 'constellated around the norms of the postcolonial' at the turn of the twenty-first century.[55] At the same time, Glissant's approach fully agrees with Papastergiadis's analysis of the homogenization of culture that comes with capitalist globalization.

However, the clear distinction can be recognized by what creolization could actually mean for the analysis of art objects, when conceived as a *visual* text that needs to be differentiated from Glissant's *métissage* of linguistics, languages, and translations. Perhaps the most important question that Glissant raises is whether art history could be decolonized at all, particularly whether the decolonial process could really change the art historical methodologies for writing the text of cultural production. Here, Enwezor's reminder that 'the history of modern art has been inextricably bound to the history of its exhibitions' was essential to his theory that 'exhibitions have evolved from the presentation of singular perspectives' into the 'frightening *Gesamkunstwerk* evident in mega-exhibitions globally that seem to have overtaken the entire field of artistic production.'[56] The curator argues that the exhibition now functions as a 'dialogical forum' among heterogenous 'actors, publics, and objects' and that the entire mega-exhibition framework requires further exploration and analysis.[57] Much more than just a simple display of objects, the dialogical forum consists of a visual exchange of complex subjectivities within cultures as well as among heterogenous participants of the expressions. Enwezor's call for exploration and analysis is precisely what is needed for obtaining an understanding of the actors, publics, and objects of Chineseness through the exhibition. And based on this need, the forthcoming segment addresses the embodied models of expression by some of the first artists representing Chinese states at the mega-exhibition of the Venice Biennale.

Chineseness at the Venice Biennale[58]

In contrast to the staging of vases and objects found in museums, the difference between national identity and cultural identity can be understood by reviewing the staging of the artists at the Venice Biennale. In the effort to emphasize the *human subject* that Chineseness ultimately represents, the forthcoming analysis focuses on artists who *perform* the aspects of individual expression whereupon national identity is defined by the artist's affiliation to Chinese states while cultural identity constitutes the fluidity of Chineseness as their lived experience. The artists Lee Ming-sheng, Lin Shumin, Wu Mali, Ho Siu Kee, Stanley Wong, Zhang Huan, and Cai Guoqiang are those selected for the case studies because they employ the *repertoire* of artistic practices, the 'embodied memory: performances, gestures, orality, movement' that Diana Taylor defines as forms of 'ephemeral nonreproducible knowledge.'[59] In the conflict in which artists are made to embody nationalist identities at the Venice Biennale, the expression of the human subject-as-art-object is key, since the artists are distinctly marked by the politics of geography in relation to the territorial states of Taiwan, Hong Kong, and China. While their geographic origins from these Chinese states provide a distinct form of identifying with the social and political influences of the local/regional place, the individual expressions of the artists emerge from completely separate personal aims, motives, memories, emotions, ideas, and narratives.

The documentation of these inaugural works contribute to what Taylor describes as an 'archival memory' contained by 'documents, maps, literary texts, letters, archaeological remains, bones, videos, films, CDs, all those items supposedly resistant to change.'[60] As explored in Chapter Four, the Giardini site of the Biennale in Venice is in itself the archeological remainder of the original place in 1895 from where the art festival evolved into a prestigious contemporary art exposition. To this day, its mapping of the buildings and spaces for art could be seen as the permanent archival context for the constructed geographies accorded to territories of city/nation/state. Taylor distinguishes between the archive's record of the event and the production of the living repertoire of *undocumentable* experiences. Rather than separate the repertoire of the cultural subjectivity of Chineseness from the archive of the inaugural nation-statist event, I argue that the Biennale does not simply collect a body of work but functions as a 'performing archive,' defined by Borggreen and Gade as a process that is 'formative in shaping history and thus perform human beings, structure and give form to our thoughts and ideas.'[61] The Biennale can be viewed as an empirical stage for the emergence of Chineseness in the global context for contemporary art, and the aim of this study is to distinguish between expressions of 'nation' and 'culture' rather than to encyclopedically document and define the first representations of diasporic Chineseness from 1993 to 2005.

More importantly, I argue that national identity and cultural identity are not binaristic in their expression of Chineseness, since a person's identity cannot be separated, which is the reason why bodily-oriented and performative works are so important for this study. Both forms of identity have also intertwined in the transnational context of political philosophy in Chinese history. When Wang Jingwei published his definitive 1905 essay on modern nationalism in China, 'Minzudi guomin' (Citizens of a Nation), he still conceived of a common genetic kinship, history, language, and beliefs.[62] The modern meaning of the 'Chinese nation' will inevitably carry the traces of the Confucian definition of culture and community in which the fundamental concept of *xiao* (filial behavior) as explained by Feng Xin-ming, in his translation of the Confucian *Xiao Jing*, defines 'being good to parents and ancestors' as 'not only a way of life for individuals, but also a way of ordering the entire society.'[63] The political ideology uniting the family and the state kept the imperial order in power ever since the Han ethnicity of the Chinese people was instituted during the Han dynasty (206BCE–220CE). Political authority was enmeshed with cultural authority as premised on the Confucian concept of *li*, in which art and ritual facilitated the moral authority of the ruler through ceremonial access to the ancestors and the gods. This complicated Confucian political system came to a symbolic end with the transformation of imperial China in 1911.

Under Mao, the campaign against the 'Four Olds' (*si jiu*) during the Cultural Revolution (1966–76) was a push to eradicate Confucian beliefs as superstitions, but the shift to Deng Xiaoping's ideals for economic reform would actually renew the old political order.[64] Deng's *yiguo liangzhi* 'one country, two systems' policy enacted in 1984 was a development of economic nationalism that clearly has roots in the Confucian hierarchy, articulated as 'there is only but one China and under this premise the mainland adheres to the socialist system while Hong Kong, Macau and Taiwan may retain their capitalist systems over a long time to come.'[65] The edict was as much nationalist as it was culturalist in its political objective, as confirmed by scholars of the post-1980 discourse in China. Wang Yichuan had defined the *Zhongguo ren gongtong ti* as the longstanding reflection of the 'Chinese cultural rim' (distinguished from the Pacific Rim) by returning to a Confucian order for the four layers of Chinese culture: mainland China as the core, Taiwan, Hong Kong, Macao comprising the second layer, overseas ethnic Chinese as the third, and the Chinese in East/Southeast Asia as constituting the fourth.[66] Central to the current politics of diasporic Chineseness, the impact of 'one country, two systems' has only increased in significance in the twenty-first century, especially after Hong Kong's 1997 return to the sovereignty of the People's Republic of China. The idea that capitalist economics would secure the nationalist connection among the three Chinese states today underscores the political difference from the old Confucian moral authority for the Chinese community.

The focus of the forthcoming case studies of historical works therefore begins with Taiwan and three Taiwanese artists who emphasize cultural identity, particularly the Confucian identity explored in the work of Lee Ming-sheng and Wu Mali and then the Buddhist identity in the work of Lin Shumin. Their expression of culture and ritual differentiates from the political turmoil occurring within the Chinese states during the 1990s. At the time, the broader inclusion of non-European states at the Biennale also reflected the changing conditions for contemporary art in the global context.[67] Following the study of Taiwan, the focus shifts to Hong Kong's nationalist identity of economic characteristics as explored in the work of Ho Siu Kee and Stanley Wong. By reviewing their respective 2001 and 2005 Biennale exhibitions, the acknowledgment of the 'shopping capital of the world' enables an understanding of what it means to be a 'citizen-consumer' of the island-city. The final study of this chapter examines both the cultural and nationalist identities of China as expressed in the work of Zhang Huan and Cai Guo-Qiang at the 1999 Biennale. Through expressions of cultural memory, Zhang invokes the vernacular narratives extending from the Confucian *Classic of Poetry*, while Cai reproduces an iconic Cultural Revolution monument. At the end of the twentieth century, artists such as Zhang and Cai were emigrating to live in other parts of the world and yet they were representing the nation of China at the Biennale, putting into question the relevance of the nation-statist model for artistic representation.

Taiwan

As introduced earlier in this chapter, Taiwanese artist Lee Ming-sheng was among the very first artists from Taiwan and China to have represented Chinese contemporary art at the Venice Biennale. Director Achille Bonito Oliva invited Lee and fourteen artists from *China's New Art* show to participate in the 1993 *Aperto* international group show.[68] The nationalist identities of the artists themselves, from Taiwan and from China, were distinguished by their separate representations in the same group show. During this critical moment, after the 1989 protests at Tiananmen Square brought attention to the repressions of the Communist Party, the greater focus on artists from China was inextricable from the country's complex political situation. As explained by Lu Peng, the growing but 'infinitesimal international community' for *Zhongguo xiandai yishujia* contended with artistic practices that 'were completely incompatible with the demands of the official state art apparatus.'[69] But the historical period was just as impactful for artists in Taiwan although conditions there were overshadowed by China's dramatic upheaval. Chao-yi Tsai explains that the 'turning point of qualitative change in art' in Taiwan can be attributed to the 'lifting of martial law in 1987,' since it was 'a critical release point setting long-repressed social forces in motion.'[70] Chiang Kai Shek's occupation of the island-state had prolonged effects and the dynamics of *Sheng Jieyan Ling* (martial law) from 1949 until 1987 coexisted with Taiwan's exponential industrial growth during the 1980s and 1990s. Needless to say, the political conditions produced a conflicting set of circumstances for artists from both Taiwan and China in relation to a nation-statist identity.[71]

Offering a clear expression of *cultural* identity, Lee Ming-sheng's presentation of his installation/performance *Fire Ball or Circle* at the 1993 Venice Biennale produced an entirely different narrative from the nationalist subject. The new global art production is still linked to a ritualized practice associated with the historical vessels of world art whereby the contemporary performance artist returns to the ceremonial purpose of expression. In this very first representation of Taiwan at the contemporary artfair, Lee uses his own body as the focus of the work of ritual, renewing the moral function and the funerary tradition of the work of art. As one of his early 'green' works, Lee created an enormous tree trunk out of nearly two and a half tons of throwaway paper which he installed in the space of the *Aperto* international group show. He then performed a funeral ceremony for the tree which he describes in this way:

> I read from the eulogy ... I took off my green monk's robe and climbed onto the 'paper tree trunk' ... I took a mixture of 500cc of my own blood, five gallons of cow's blood and high volume spirits and poured it a scoop at a time over my own head ... My body writhed in the waves of blood, twisting and turning ... I put my green monk's robe on once more and stepped off of the 'paper tree trunk' ... I made a final bow to the audience.[72]

At the historic site of Venice's iconic location, the performance of such a provocative image of blood and the body creates an intensity for understanding the 'death' of the environment unlike any other work of art. The visceral image of the human figure immersed in blood draws viewers in through a heightened sensory perception. The viewers become emotionally involved as they participate as spectators of the ritualized work of mourning for the environment. But Chinese art in the long tradition of vessels and *liqi* ceremonial objects was created for the function of ritual, which Lee invoked through his embodied role as the monk.[73] During ancient times, the work of art assisted in the ritual function in order that a Chinese community abides by the rule of the emperor who is the Son of Heaven over the living and the ancestral dead. As a time-honored form of Chinese reverence, performance itself is predicated on ritual action, which Thomas Berghuis explains as taking 'part in a process that aims at maintaining and enriching the community as a whole ... applied to aspects of the everyday life of Chinese citizens, including those governed by law, moral systems, and the social conventions of society at large.'[74] The artistic use of *contemporary* performance art innovates the ritual tradition that once functioned to facilitate the moral order, expressing now for the entire global community beyond the Chinese community. Global warming and climate change are moral issues, since they are directly caused by human activity, and Lee's performance proposes a ritualized perspective toward the problem that affects all humans. Whether enlisting the body of the viewer or expressing through body art, the human subject in the work of art reveals the potential for representing a communal process by creating the borders of the self as the borders of a community. Glissant had forewarned that we need to 'make drastic changes in the diverse sensibilities of communities by putting forward the prospect – or at least the possibility – of this revived aesthetic connection with the earth.'[75] He explains that a poetics of relation involves the shared 'passion for the land where one lives' lest we end up inhabiting what he describes as a *Museum of Natural Non-History*, which is where global warming and climate change is headed.[76] Decolonization will not have done its work until these relations go beyond the limits of the colonial.

Ritual, in the cultural context of Chineseness, is a historical Confucian practice and in Taiwan's population of over twenty-three million people, 93 per cent consider themselves as Confucian, Buddhist, or Daoist – oftentimes all three.[77] Confucian kinship is perhaps the most distinguishing philosophy for defining a cohesive Chinese cultural identity, and the most convincing argument on this account was made by none other than the feminist artist Wu Mali whose remarkable contributions to Ecofeminism are discussed in Chapter Three. At the Venice Biennale, she challenged the Confucian patri-archal order through the presentation of her installation titled *Library* (1993) (see figure 5.1), exhibited in the pavilion for the 'Republic of China in Taiwan' organized by the Taipei Fine Arts Museum.[78] *Library* at the Biennale con-sisted of a simple double-stacked book shelf containing a collection of 'pulp fiction' that Wu created by literally taking 'influential books from the past,' shredding them into tiny bits, and then, reconstituting them to fill the insides of a set of acrylic boxes that were made in the shape of books.[79] Wu destroyed and re-constituted the Confucian canon of the *Four Books* that were formally dated to the fourth century BCE as well as the *Five Classics* as they were organ-ized during the Han dynasty (206 BCE–220 AD) (although the individual texts were thought to have originated during the Zhou dynasty as far back as 1100 BCE).[80] As one of Wu's *Five Classics*, the *Yijing* divination texts included the hexagram for the logic of filial piety as the basis for the family-as-nation:

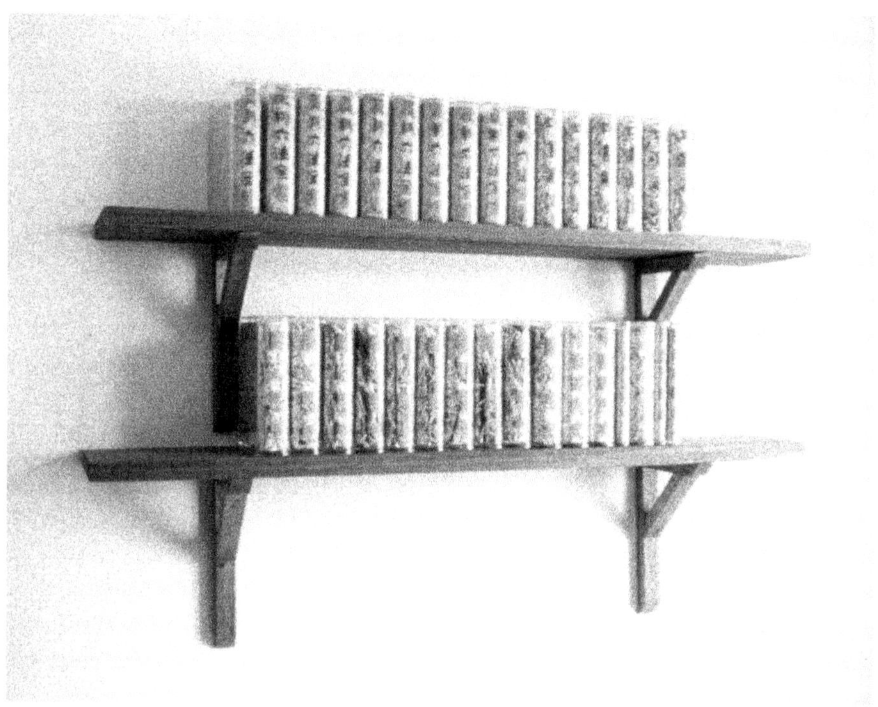

5.1 Wu Mali, *Library*, 1993, books, shelves, wood, Plexiglas, gold paper, installation

if family relationships are in order (if a husband is a husband, and a son is a son) then the entire empire on heaven and earth would be in order. Females, of course, remain outside of the ancestral lineage and the belief in the male heir required the birth of sons to carry on the Confucian order. Wu's obliteration of the classical text literally destroys its readability and challenges the Confucian patriarchal foundation that determines Chinese lineage and thus Chinese identity. The reconfiguration of the material properties of the book into mere pulp filler for an empty plastic shell renders meaningless the contents of the book (both literally and metaphorically). Through this iconoclastic act, Wu's focus on the all-male authorship of books in her library reminds the viewer of the patriarchal Chineseness that has kept in place the *Zhongguo ren gongtong ti*. Some of the most divisive moments in the history of modern China had occurred through organized challenges to the textual traditions of Confucian teaching. The 1919 May Fourth Movement was an insurrection of intellectuals and writers who took to the public their message of transforming an education system that fostered illiteracy by privileging only males of a certain class. As noted earlier, the Red Guards of the Cultural Revolution (1966–76) demolished the 'Four Olds' as the outward forms of Confucian ideology, including the educational institutions. And yet, Confucian values are at the very core of defining the Han Chinese community, considered as the primary unifying concept for Chineseness.

In addition to the Chinese Classics, Wu selected an overall body of works which have been recognized as canonical 'but the authority of which has been much disputed, or works that have become outmoded and no longer influential.'[81] Her library came with a system of classification in which the viewer could peruse books according to the six orders that she called: '1. the World of Art, 2. Encyclopaedia, 3. Chinese Classics, 4. Science and Civilisation of China, 5. Nobel Prize in Literature, and 6. Godfather (books on or by great men).'[82] The spine of each 'book' was affixed with the gilded gold lettering of the original book title. The installation emphasizes the politics of textual canonization and the archive of an overwhelming patriarchal knowledge that underwrites all of the traditions of essentially every culture. As the site of textual beliefs, Wu suggests her installation has an air of the gruesome 'because the *Library* smelt of the last vestiges of ancient civilisations.'[83] The artist renewed her *Library* exhibition by presenting another installation under the same title at the 1997 Venice Biennale in which the work was further enhanced to create a space that felt even more like the reverential experience of time-honored libraries. In providing an artistic space for looking at objects, she describes her interest in the library space as an obsession 'with the idea of fusing the word and the image, two different media, which implicitly describes the possibility of multiple intersections' of ways to produce meaning.[84] Through the performative experience of viewing the work of art, audience members are therefore involved in the ritualized and embodied experience of the library.

A reverence toward patriarchal ancestors could easily be interpreted as the subject of Lin Shumin's video installation titled *Glass Ceiling* (see plate 23). Lin was selected for the 2001 Taiwan Pavilion along with four other artists represented at the Venice Biennale.[85] In his hologram installation projecting images of human faces onto the ground of the gallery space, Lin uses the human figure most eloquently to express the negotiation of the self between the physical and virtual world. But the artist aligns with Wu Mali's critique of the Confucian patriarchal order, since he includes images of both female and male people between the ages of seven and eighty-one from over forty different countries. The three-dimensional images projected onto the glass tiles of the *Glass Ceiling* create a convincing illusion of moving bodies viewed sixty centimeters deep that seem to be trapped. The people appear to be looking up through individual squares that constitute the tiles of the exhibition's floor whereas viewers in the pavilion must look down at their 'ceiling.' From this commanding position standing on the level above, the viewers' posture becomes an ironic gesture because they are actually in a humbling position bent over in the gallery.

Glass Ceiling expresses through the bodily-oriented practice which enables Lin to propose the belief that 'we will all come back to inhabit a body which may be of a different gender, nationality, or even species than the one we currently inhabit.'[86] The work reflects the Ch'an teachings of the Buddhist Altar Sutra which specifies that the final 'true bliss of Nirvana where there was neither birth nor death' would end the need for reincarnation.[87] The way in which this belief is performed by *Glass Ceiling* is contingent on the response of the viewer, who comes face to face with the mutable and fleeting instance of life itself in the engagement with the mutable and fleeting images of people on the hologram. In the concept of the afterlife, whether from the Confucian perspective of worshipping ancestors in the other realm or from the Buddhist belief in returning to earth as reincarnate in another body, the concurrent presence of the dead and the living is generally the accepted idea in Chinese tradition. The Buddhist and Daoist 'state of calmness' and 'eternal stillness' is the state in which 'all sentient beings would not differ from inanimate objects' like that of the 'grass, plants, tiles and stones.'[88] Overall, *Glass Ceiling* takes the perspective of the Buddhist illusion to its logical conclusion, which is philosophically how the viewer conceives of and responds to human life in the visible world. And this is perhaps a perfect alternative to the conceits of nationalism that art for so long has been confined.

Lin implicates the viewer who participates further in the work by having to walk around or on top of the faces and bodies in order to look down on them in the darkened room. The hologram images disappear and reappear according to the movement and position of the viewers' gaze and the location of their bodies. The Taiwan Pavilion is located in a former Venetian prison, which adds to the drama of *Glass Ceiling*, and as described by Lin, 'In a way, the piece creates the malicious feeling of walking on someone's head or face.'[89] He suggests the spectator's intrusion is a 'kind of negation of the other, which occurs in human behavior on a physical level, as well as on a psychological level.'[90] This negation also occurs when viewers' shadows obscures the faces on the holograms. As such, viewers walk gingerly across the tiles in a self-conscious manner as if they are being looked at by the people below the glass ceiling.

The transparent 'glass ceiling' is, of course, the metaphor for the barrier that prohibits access to the top levels of employment in Europe and in the United States – refusing opportunity to females and people of color according to exterior identifications. *Glass Ceiling* can be viewed as a counterpart to Wu Mali's *Library*, since Lin's depiction of the well-worn phrase reviews the hierarchical processes and the relations of power that affect all human subjects. In representing Taiwan, both Lin Shumin and Wu Mali presented works at the Biennale that placed the viewer's body in the critical role of constructing the meaning of the work of art. Overall, both artists look at the ways in which tradition and history affect the self of Chineseness in contradiction to the political enmity among the ruling parties of Taiwan and China as represented by the Nationalists and the Communists since 1949. On one hand, Lin reveals a common thread of subjectivity in his expression of Confucian, Buddhist, and Daoist values that pertain specifically to Chinese culture, whether in China, Taiwan, or elsewhere. On the other, Wu critiques the very foundation of those values as inscribed by ritual and the patriarchal text. Nonetheless, they are using conceptual media and practices under the Western form that 'contemporary art' generally signifies, and in this way, their work exemplifies Chineseness as a confluence of philosophy and practice.

Hong Kong

Artists Ho Siu Kee and Stanley Wong provide a more conventional understanding of Chineseness through portraying the *nationalist* identity of Hong Kong at the Biennale. Assessment of a nation is usually measured by the country's economic activity, and Hong Kong's status as the shopping capital of Asia – the 'shopper's paradise' and the 'world's emporium' – constitutes a longstanding international image of mercantile culture. During the 1950s and 1960s, the island city was a free-entry port for the movement of goods from China, and from the 1980s onward, it became one of the largest cargo terminals for the circulation of shipping containers. As explained by Janet Ng, 'while Hong Kong is despised for its shallow materialism, blatant consumerism, and lack of historical culture, it is also admired as a true capitalist holdout in a region that saw much communist insurgence and victory in the middle of the twentieth century.'[91] But the depiction of the historical culture of Hong Kong by its mercantile identity is one that originally emerged in association with the Opium Wars and its ceding to the British by China in 1841 as a concession of defeat. The hostilities were first initiated during the late eighteenth century when China thwarted British mercantile opportunism through restrictive customs and tariffs.[92] Ever since, Hong Kong has functioned as a political space of democratic negotiation inextricable from its compromise on behalf of capitalist endeavors – even more so in the era of globalization. When Hong Kong returned to China's sovereignty in 1997, its nationalist identity of consumerism would suddenly and paradoxically become mirrored by the cities of Beijing and Shanghai as they began their ascent as rival shopping capitals of the world. The rapid transformation of China's 'Capitalism with Chinese Characteristics' would put into question the meaning of the *yiguo liangzhi* system, especially if taken outside of the context of China's authoritarian rule.

Still, the consumer culture of Hong Kong symbolizes a democratizing practice that is oppositional to Communist ideology. According to Ng, 'there is a direct equation between being a good Hong Kong citizen and being a good consumer, since consumption is more than individual participation, but is a 'state' project of survival.'[93] The civic programme of consumerism is associated with Hong Kong citizenship, and both Ho and Wong in different ways take up the national identity of the citizen-consumer through their artistic expressions at the Biennale.

The selection of artist Stanley Wong, a creative director for an international advertising agency, was therefore an appropriate choice for the 2005 Hong Kong pavilion at the Venice Biennale.[94] Organized by Sabrina Fung and the Hong Kong Development Council, Wong created a performative installation titled *redwhiteblue: tea+chat* (see plate 24) that covered the exhibition space with the material of the cheap plastic red, white, and blue nylon bag. Wong explains how he selected the carryall that has served many Hong Kong emigres who return to the mainland with gifts and foodstuffs that one must bring to friends and relatives on such a visit.[95] The highly durable bags are found everywhere around the world due to their common usage in the cargo and shipping industry. According to Wong, the vernacular usefulness of the material supplants the cheapness of the product in such a way that almost everyone across all lines of class, gender, and caste have used the bag.

Wong had also incorporated the red, white, and blue motif in his advertising poster designs as well as in his art installations. The commercial sign and patterning functions to echo the 'industriousness and struggle of the Hong Kong people;' Wong states that this is because during 'the 1960s, starting out with nothing, they succeeded in constructing the metropolis that is present-day Hong Kong with their fortitude, positivity and adaptability.'[96] Bringing this 'Hong Kong spirit' to the Hong Kong Heritage Museum, Wong views the motif as a connective aesthetic, one that can be received by anyone through the positive perception of a commercial throwaway product.

At the Biennale's pavilion, Wong's installation was a re-creation of a teahouse enveloped in the plastic material. Audience members become performers themselves when they were invited to partake of tea on the red, white, and blue covered tables and chairs. At both ends of the exhibition space were computers and webcams for viewers to connect to others on the internet. The installation was meant to foster the human interaction of 'drinking tea,' deemed to be an element in the constitution of Chineseness as an identity. Wong suggests that the idea of having 'tea' is to spend long hours in the afternoon eating many courses of dim sum and enjoying long conversations with friends in a relaxed manner – to cook, dine, and share meals with others is the most outward show of affection among one's relations. He bemoans the ritual's diminishment in the quick pace of everyday life in Hong Kong, and his tearoom at the Biennale sets out to capture the sense of those contemporary ubiquitous spaces where similar relations to the effect of 'tea' might occur. Here, Wong questions how technological forms of communication are adapted to fit social rituals as humans become physically distanced from each other – a question that resonates even more in the ten years after Wong's show. *Redwhiteblue: tea+chat* evokes how technological communication is deeply a part of the patterning of commodity culture, and rather than simply opposing the effects, he connects the entire complex circuit of commodity, technology, and human ritual.

Going by the name anothermountainman, Wong refers to Bada Shanren (the mountain man of the eight greats), the seventeenth-century painter whose life and work are considered as representative of the tumultuous shift from the Ming dynasty to the Qing.[97] In Wong's expression of social media incorporated into the consumerist signifiers of everyday life, his artistic practice defies the political past of China's old party line for resistance against bourgeois materialism and Mao's negation of art for art's sake – 'politically independent art [does] not exist in reality' – as much as Western art's avant-garde legacies in Marxist criticism.[98] Hong Kong's identity as the shopping capital of the world has become the metropolitan model for China in the twenty-first century, the clear path for the future of Chineseness.

At the inaugural exhibition of Hong Kong at the 2001 Biennale, curated by Chang Tsong-zung, the video installation of artist Ho Siu Kee's almost-naked body is presented through a life-sized video projection in the space of the Hong Kong pavilion at Schola di Sant Apollonia.[99] The title *Golden Proportion* (see figure 5.2) refers to the mathematical concept of *phi*, the equation based on the principle ratio used in measuring proportionate parts of the human anatomy. The video shows Ho in the act of conducting various experiments, questioning what the golden proportion actually means in 'man is the measure of all things,' recalling Protagoras's philosophical inquiry associated with the citizen of the Greek polis in fifth-century BCE. Thought to have begun with Euclidean or Pythogorean mathematical concepts, the use of *phi* in art was attributed primarily to Leonardo Da Vinci's compositional strategies for drawing the figure in respect of the pictorial plane. Ho's expression celebrates

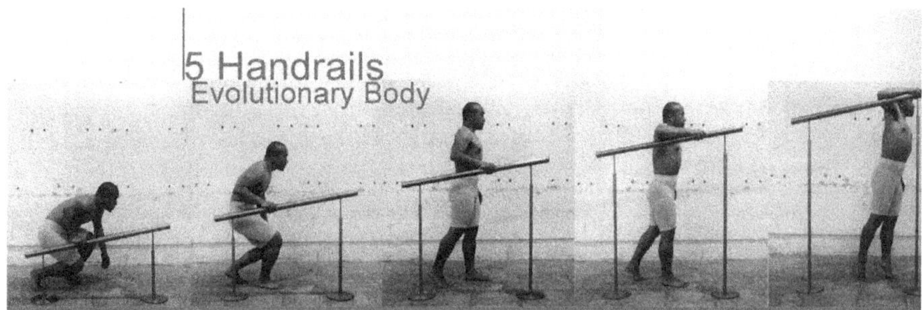

5.2 Ho Siu Kee, *Golden Proportion*, 2001, video installation, Venice Biennale, 49th Exposition International d'arte

his own Chinese body as a figure of artistic idealism. Examining what he calls the 'evolutionary body,' the artist cites concepts of artistic integration with those of body symmetry, using the formula 'Head: Body = 1:6.833.'[100] *Phi* measures the body according to the ratio of five – five appendages to the torso, of two arms, two legs, and one head; five fingers and toes; and five openings in the face. The ideal body is a proportional and mathematical, establishing the person who 'counts' as a whole and democratic participant in society. But in the unspoken valuation of constituents of industrialized nations, the worth of an individual is always measured according to a money-class system.

Ultimately, Ho's anatomy lesson asserts the significance of the human individual through the impermanence of the video projection. As emphasized by the viewing experience, the audience become more cognizant of their own 'real' bodies through the evanescence of the projection of Ho's life-sized image. The question of the 'real' and the 'unreal' was at the forefront of issues regarding the constituent's role in the social body after Hong Kong's 1997 handover to China's sovereignty – a question that remained in people's consciousness in the four years leading up to the 2001 Biennale. The proof of the rights of an individual as one who 'counts' is measured by citizenship and the right to vote, and residents of Hong Kong for so long questioned their rights to citizenship under British lease-occupation. The aim of the official British policy for Hong Kong residents by 1997 was to end their dual citizenship as passport holders of British Dependent Territories. As Bryan Turner explains, 'citizenship in Hong Kong was never intended to be a nation-building exercise. Successive British administrations had denied basic citizenship rights in the colony, and it was not until the final stages of the process of the transfer of sovereignty that the conditions for citizenship arose.'[101] Hong Kong residents were initially deemed ineligible for residency in the UK. Under Margaret Thatcher, the 1990 immigration policy granted 50,000 Hong Kong residents the opportunity to apply for British citizenship based on restrictive criteria reviewed by age, education, and occupational status. In other words, obtaining British Hong Kong citizenship required the fulfilment of an unpredictable and evasive criteria. But after the handoff to China in 1997, the right to vote placed the Hong Kong constituent under the same constraints. By 2002, the Chief Executive of the new Special Administrative Region Tung Chee-hwa, who was a shipping magnate seen as Beijing's choice, secured a second five-year term without receiving a single vote from the Hong Kong public.

Ho's expression of the Hong Kong figure puts into question the borders of the self as an object defined by the borders of the city-state. When shown at the Biennale, the practice of comparison is natural for viewing art objects and their national affiliations. Ho foregrounds the scientific practice of comparing and idealizing the figurative object by looking at functional objects in relation to the body.[102] One part of his video projection emulates the film-strip style, as each frame shows Ho moving along a handrail with five sets of frames showing handrails raised to five different heights. For instance, Ho crouches to walk along the short, lowest handrail in the first frame whereas in the final shot, he reaches above his head to grasp the tallest handrail. What kind of norm could exist to serve the most 'evolved' body at the highest level of the staircase in relation to the lowest, shortest body, and who gets to determine the 'normal' body on the scientific scale? For the citizen-consumer, the commodified spectacle of the new ideal body replacing the 'real' body would eventually become the norm for images that could sell cars, clothes, and magazines in the shopping capital of the world.

China

While Taiwan's representation of Chineseness at the Biennale expresses a cultural identity premised on Confucian and Buddhist concepts, and Hong Kong's representation expresses a nationalist identity premised on the citizen-consumer, China's artists Zhang Huan and Cai Guo-Qiang provide a representation of both cultural and national identities, as emphasized by their performative bodily-oriented works at the 1999 Biennale. Included in the *Aperto* international group show, Zhang Huan explains how body art enables the exposure of the 'shift between the mind and the body' as well as the 'conflict between the body and the external environment' as the distinct 'way to prove the existence of the self.'[103] Like Stanley Wong, he had also identified with Bada Shanren as the historical model for artistic innovation during the tumultuous times in China's past. But the complex nature of ascribing national identity in the 1990s amidst the political challenges in China was exemplified by the mobility of contemporary artists who began to work and exhibit outside of the country. Cai Guo-Qiang's efforts during this time were perhaps the most transparent in terms of creating artworks that challenged the representation of 'nation.' In his performance for the *1995* Venice Biennale, *Bringing to Venice What Marco Polo Forgot*, Cai sailed a Chinese junk vessel 'from Piazza San Marco down the Grand Canal to the Giustinian Lolin Palazzo' with the help of two Italian boatmen.[104] This Biennale exhibition titled *TransCulture* in 1995 was funded by the Japan Foundation – Cai was a native of Fujian province, who moved to Japan in 1986 and later to New York in 1995.[105] The complexities of national identity and representing China at the 1999 Venice Biennale can therefore be explored through analyses of two iconic works selected for the international group show.[106]

As a global event, the very site of the Biennale changes the dynamics for viewing artistic production that represents China as a 'nation,' since it provides the perfect situation for staging the concept of the embodied 'self' of an elusive Chineseness through bodily-oriented art. But the conditions of change in 1999 underlie Harald Szeemann's selection of artists for the *Aperto* section

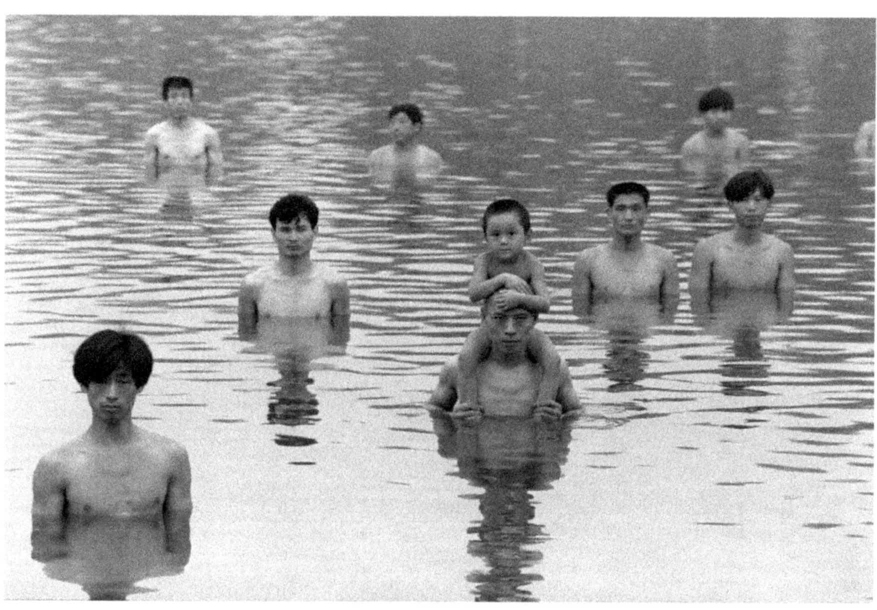

5.3 Zhang Huan, *To Raise the Water Level in a Fishpond*, 1997, performance document

of the Biennale, and while the curator/director was interested in the experimental media that artists were adopting in China, their use of performative and bodily-oriented expression was one that greatly expanded artistic subjectivity in contemporary art. As clarified by Amelia Jones, body art's 'apparent or unconscious identifications' enable the artist to place 'the body/self within the realm of the aesthetic as a political domain.'[107] Since the 1980s in China, artists have taken an interest in the body as an artistic medium because of its ability to introduce a new kind of self-reflexivity.

At the 1999 Biennale, Zhang exhibited the video documentation of his now-famous 1997 collaborative performance in Beijing titled *To Raise the Water Level in a Fishpond* (see figure 5.3). Zhang had hired forty workers and fishermen to stand immersed up to their bare torsos in a pond. As in many of Zhang's early works, the consolidation of bodies becomes a marker for indicating measurable difference according to the 'water level' of the pond. The performance served as a metaphor for the cumulative effect of change to the social environment, one that was created by China's rapid economic transition from socialist methods to capitalist semi-privatization.[108] In reviewing this transitional period at the end of the 1990s, *To Raise the Water Level* renews the function of the *Shuihu zhuan*, the classic literary tradition that 'literally means "a story that happened on the water margin,"' according to theorist Liangyan Ge, who traces its origins to the Confucian *Shijing (Classic of Poetry – the Book of Songs).*[109] The *Tale of the Water Margin (Shuihu zhuan*) refers specifically to a metaphorical place as the hideout of the bandit-rebels located on the side of the lake. One of the most famous novels of the vernacular tradition in Chinese literary history, Ge explains that the '"water margin" indeed seems to be where the rebels belong, for as outlaws they are marginalized from society – politically as well as geographically.'[110] The bandit was a heroic character whose defiant spirit of rebellion could express for the common folk a resistance against authority and the official court. The folk genre was distinguished by stories about the adventures of a group of bandits that were handed down through generations of popular storytelling in the oral tradition.[111] The tales were eventually established as literature during the Ming period (1368–1644). The bandit, throughout Chinese history, was a signifier for the artists and poets who were often in the position of exile because they would inevitably offend the emperor's court and were then banished from society. Designated as the fringe of society by location at the outskirts, the water margin represents the de-socialized space that painters and poets have mythologized throughout history. Zhang's performance reminds the Chinese viewer, who is accustomed to some folk version or other of the *Shuihu zhuan*, about the way in which social status has always been a matter of belonging to a particular place – geographically or metaphorically – and in this way, Zhang's performance connects to past artistic performances in the vernacular tradition of the *Shuihu zhuan.*

The different narratives underwriting *Raise the Water Level* will therefore include alternative forms of discursivity in addition and/or related to those associated with collective memory. Reading body artworks through the mediation of photographic documentation requires, among other things, the acknowledgment of its production as a text, emphasizing the premise for the Biennale as a *performing archive.* As Roland Barthes might explain it, the photograph of Zhang's *Raise the Water Level* can be understood as a 'recording' of a literal message which 'reinforces the myth of photographic "naturalness": the scene *is there*, captured mechanically, not humanly (the mechanical is here a guarantee of objectivity).'[112] In other words, the photographic document of *Raise the Water Level* is a record of its existence – a confirmation of its 'having-been-there,' which is foundational to the transcription of live performance art events beyond the moment of their actual performance. Perhaps more than any other post-1980s artists, Zhang's 'being there' at the Biennale in the documentary form of the body expresses movements across borders and the transgressing of nationalist margins in the most poignant and effective way. As opposed to a representative 'art object,' performance art's bodily-oriented expression could reveal the meaning of the human individual as identified by nationality but ultimately as representative of a culturally ethnic Chinese artist.

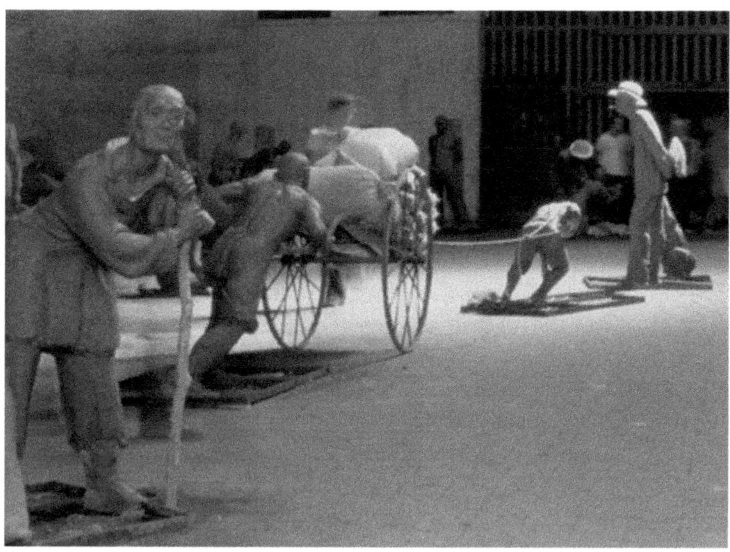

5.4 Cai Guo-Qiang, *Venice's Rent Collection Courtyard*, 1999, installation, realized at Deposito Polveri, Arsenale, Venice, 108 life-sized sculptures created on site by Long Xu Li and nine guest artisan sculptors, 60 tons of clay, wire, and wood armature, commissioned by 1999 Venice Biennale, artwork not extant, installation view

In an entirely different kind of performative act, Cai Guo-Qiang had reproduced the infamous sculptural installation titled *The Rent Collecting Courtyard* for presentation in the 1999 international group show[113] (see figure 5.4). The enormous clay sculpture was a replica of the historical monument of the same title still exhibited in Dayi county west of Sichuan, and the original 1960s' government-commissioned Social-Realist tableau depicted the narrative of the cruel feudal landlord who exploited the peasants.[114] A symbol of the Maoist era, Jiang Qing, Mao Zedong's wife, had toured around the country exhibiting duplicates of the sculpture at a time when many other works of art were deemed 'bourgeois' and destroyed during the Red Guard purges of the Cultural Revolution. The iconoclasm of the era functioned on behalf of the revolutionary frenzy that dictated the Social Realist genre for visual representation. Emulating the original act of making multiple copies, Cai's reinvention of the sculpture added new figures of workers and students to the *Rent Collecting Courtyard* model that originally consisted of 114 clay sculptures.[115] According to Eric Eckholm, after Cai presented his reproduction at the Venice Biennale in 1999, some of the sculptors of the original monument, such as Wang Guanyi, a sixty-four-year-old professor at the Sichuan Academy, believed that Cai 'violated our creative rights' since he 'did this without our approval.'[116] Threats were made to bring a lawsuit against the artist and the Biennale institution for copyright infringement. The work stirred a debate among the art community in China with discussion that ranged from criticism to appreciation of Cai's 'mockery' or homage to China's embattled past, as well as the artist's co-optation into Western forms of expression, denying an 'authentic' Chinese tradition. Cai's method of pastiche-copy was often understood as a Western style of expression rather than emulating Jiang Qing's redoubling of the socialist realist cause.

The patriotic sentiment in the 1990s expressed by those in China who defended the original function of the art of the Cultural Revolution can be viewed cross-culturally as the social acceptance of national monuments as works of cultural memory – the longstanding function of public art in the West also aligns with the Biennale's monumentalizing of art by nation. The heroic works from the Maoist past were easily manipulated by the State; but nonetheless, Cai's rehabilitation of the anti-feudalist memorial is a gesture that requires acknowledgment of Cai's original intent in 1999, which was to address 'multiple factors,' according to Yvonne Zhao, 'including the creative process and the inescapable effects of time, and commenting on the fate of art under the manipulation of political ideology.'[117] In the end, however, the Party approved of the work on the basis that *Venice's Rent Collection Courtyard* represents the nation of China since its exhibition at the Biennale makes this mission very clear. As noted by Fan Di'an, the Biennale commissioner of the 2005 China pavilion, 'Ever since Mr. Cai won the Golden Lion (the top Venice prize) the government has realized that art can be a good ambassador for China.'[118] The aesthetic institution of the artfair continues to promote national progress through the long-standing formula for displaying the arts as the example of national innovation. However, the avant-gardism of an art (defined by either Mao's 1942 *Talks at Yan'an* or Peter Bürger's 1984 *Theory of the Avant-Garde*) that challenges China's political policies will lose its radical component as soon as the work becomes the 'good ambassador for China' in the function of national production.

Cai provides some insight into his aims in recreating *Rent Collecting Courtyard* for the 1999 Biennale when he noted in a press release promoting the 2005 show that he organized: 'The Chinese pavilion should not be another national symbol of power and style, rather it should respond to its time and space, and serve as a new model for national pavilions of the 21st century.'[119] Creating a new model for a global exhibition based on national representation, however, could prove to be a rather complex task when thinking about the increasing transnationalism of migrating societies – of which Cai is one of the original qualifying members. The idea that artists represent China, Taiwan, and Hong Kong simply because their works are exhibited in assigned pavilions begins to lose meaning when considering that Cai and Zhang Huan who represented China, and Lin Shumin representing Taiwan, all resided in

New York at the time of their Biennale shows. In this way, the Biennale functions as the archive documenting the slow process of the change to a transnational Chineseness wherein the migration of the artists themselves becomes a project of 'undoing nationalism' when they represent as members of the *Zhongguo ren gongtong ti*.[120]

Every myth can have its history and geography

Under the classificatory terms of the museum, the art institution presides over the art object in a history of Chineseness that can be visualized by the sixteenth-century Ming vase, whether from the imperial dynastic court or for export to Borneo and the nomadic places. The Sarawak vase represents Malaysian Chinese culture, revealing the diversities of the multivalent identity of Chineseness, the term that signifies a rejection of the authenticity of culture under the modern nation-statist claim. The Sarawak vase carries the nomadic life outside of the Ming dynasty while embodying a history of colonialism. But to view the world art object as a mere symbol of the colonial past, based on the provenance from the British Rajah's collection, would re-inscribe the judgments made against the object and thus against Sarawak culture itself. In the writing of the vanishing history of Malaysian Chineseness, the museum is a repository of the visual text of both the colonizer and the colonized.

On the other hand, the ability to review the Biennale as an archive for both cultural and national Chinese identities maintains the history of empire in a different way, as a source of knowledge that continues on in the structures for the biennial display. The late recognition of Chinese states, having shown for the first time between 1993 and 2005 at the Venice Biennale, provides evidence of the colonialist structures determining the complex ways in which cultures are represented at the exhibition. The *performative* representations of the inaugural Chinese artists at the Biennale, however, reveal a completely different expression of Chineseness than the conventions of 'nationality.' Taiwanese artists Lee Ming-Sheng, Wu Mali, and Lin Shu-min's portrayal of Confucian and Buddhist identities convey an enduring Chinese culture that had little to do with the politics of *Sheng Jieyan Ling* in the 1990s aftermath of Taiwan's martial law. In contrast, Stanley Wong and Ho Siu Kee's representation of Hong Kong's citizen-consumer can be conceived more conventionally as a nationalist identity; but ultimately, their expression of the association between citizenship and consumption poses an important question about the future of the *Zhongguo ren gongtong ti* and its development according to *yiguo liangzhi* 'one country, two systems.'

In acknowledging the past, Zhang Huan and Cai Guo-Qiang remind us of the social collective of Chineseness that extends from modern history. Their artworks reveal how culture itself is an act of performance, especially during periods of political transformation – from the memory of socialism's emergence in Cai's *Venice's Rent Collection Courtyard* to the immersive change from socialism to capitalism in Zhang's *Raise the Water Level*. As a whole, all of the Biennale artists represent Chineseness as a variable and fluid form of Chinese cultural identity. Still, their role in representing the political states of Taiwan, Hong Kong and China remains central to their exhibition at the Biennale. Neither the museum nor the biennial can escape the impact of the classificatory order of the past. The legitimating processes for the perceptual organization based on the myth of 'nations' is one that has insured the Biennale's institutional longevity. As Roland Barthes once wrote, 'every myth can have its history and its geography; each is in fact the sign of the other,' a statement that can be taken quite literally as the organizing principle of nationalism at the Venice Biennale.[121]

Notes

1 Amy Qin, 'Contemporary Art Sizzles in Shanghai,' *New York Times* (30 December 2014), C1.

2 Nikos Papastergiadis, 'A Breathing Space for Aesthetics and Politics: An Introduction to Jacques Rancière,' *Theory, Culture & Society*, vol. 31, no. 7/8 (2014), 6.

3 Gunhild Borggreen and Rune Gade, eds, *Performing Archives/Archives of Performance* (Copenhagen: Museum Tusculanum Press, 2013), 25–6.

4 Manthia Diawara, 'Édouard Glissant's Worldmentality: An Introduction to One World in Relation,' *South as a State of Mind, No. 6* [Documenta 14 #1, 2016], www.documenta14.de/en/south/34 (accessed 19 January 2018).

5 Wu Hung, 'Introduction: A Decade of Chinese Experimental Art (1990–2000),' in Wu Hung, Huang Zhuan and Feng Boyi, eds, *The First Guangzhou Triennial: Reinterpretation: A Decade of Experimental Chinese Art (1990–2000)* (Guangzhou: Guangdong Museum of Art, 2003), 17.

6 Ibid., 490.

7 'Deng Xiaoping's South China tour (January 1992),' *China.org.cn* (19 April 2011), www.china.org.cn/china/CPC_90_anniversary/2011-04/19/content_22392494.htm (accessed 10 December 2017).

8 Lu Peng, *Passage to History: 20 Years of La Biennale di Venezia and Chinese Contemporary Art* (Venice: Biennale Arte, 2013), foreword.

9 Ibid.

10 Achille Bonito Oliva, *La Biennale di Venezia: 45 Esposizione Internationale d'Arte 1993* (Venice: Marsilio Editiori, 1993).

11 Peng, *Passage to History*.

12 Wu Hung, 'Introduction,' 17.

13 Barbara Pollock, 'Shanghai's Tricky Museum Transformation,' *ARTnews* (March 2014), 70.

14 See also Franziska Koch, '"China" on Display for European Audiences? The

Making of an Early Travelling Exhibition of Contemporary Chinese Art: China Avantgarde (Berlin/1993),' *Transcultural Studies*, vol. 2 (2011).

15 Wu Hung, 'Introduction,' 17.

16 Ibid., 10.

17 Ibid., 16.

18 Ibid.

19 See the announcement presented on *E-flux*.com, www.e-flux.com/announce ments/39014/farewell-to-post-colonialism (accessed 25 October 2017).

20 Enwezor, 'The Black Box,' 42.

21 Ibid., 44.

22 Maharaj, *Farewell to Postcolonialism*, 13.

23 Theodor W. Adorno, *Negative Dialectics*, tr. E.B. Ashton (London: Routledge, 1973), 320.

24 Susan Buck-Morss, *The Origin of Negative Dialectics: Theodor W. Adorno, Walter Benjamin, and the Frankfurt Institute* (New York: The Free Press, 1977), 61. Emphasis in original. For the last phrase, the author cites Max Horkheimer and Theodor W. Adorno, *Dialectic of Enlightenment*, tr. John Cumming (New York: Herder and Herder, 1972), 26.

25 Johnson Chang Tsong-Zung, 'Fare Well, The Third Guangzhou Triennial,' in Sarat Maharaj, ed., *Farewell to Postcolonialism: Querying the Guangzhou Triennial 2008* (Dublin: Visual Artists Ireland, 2009), 14.

26 Ibid.

27 See Jean-Hubert Martin, 'The Whole Earth Show,' interview with Benjamin Buchloh, *Art in America* (July 1989), 158.

28 Ibid.

29 Ibid., 14.

30 Gertrud Sandqvist, 'Some Notes on the Road to the GZ3,' in Maharaj, ed., *Farewell to Postcolonialism*, 61.

31 Ibid.

32 Hans Belting, 'Contemporary Art as Global Art: A Critical Estimate,' in Hans Belting and Andrea Buddensieg, eds, *The Global Art World: Audiences, Markets, and Museums* (Ostifildern: Hatje Cantz, 2009).

33 Ibid., 4–5.

34 Ibid.

35 In discussions with the artist.

36 See Maris Gillette, 'Copying, counterfeiting, and capitalism in contemporary China: Jingdezhen's porcelain industry,' *Modern China*, vol. 36, no. 4 (2010) and also Jane Chin Davidson, 'Affirmative Precarity: Ai Weiwei and Margarita Cabrera,' *Journal of Visual Culture*, vol. 12, no. 1 (2013).

37 See John F. Burns, 'This Old Thing? It's Worth Only, Oh, Close to $70 Million,' *New York Times* (13 November 2010), A4.

38 See Amarjit Kaur, 'The Babbling Brookes: Economic Change in Sarawak 1841–1941,' *Modern Asian Studies*, vol. 29, no. 1 (February 1995), 65–109. Incidentally, the title of the Raj was always subject to the Orientalist naming of the 'petty dig-natory' by the British who originally used it as a title for the rule of India.

39 Steven Runciman, *The White Rajahs: A History of Sarawak from 1841 to 1946* (Cambridge: Cambridge University Press, 1960), 9.

40 Ibid.

41 Kaur, 'The Babbling Brookes,' 73.

42 See Adam T. Kessler, *Song Blue and White Porcelain on the Silk Road* (London: Brill, 2012), 287. Kessler cites Stacey Pierson, *Collectors, Collections and Museums: The Field of Chinese Ceramics in Britain, 1560–1960* (Bern: Peter Lang, 2007).

43 Belting, 'Contemporary Art as Global Art,' 5.

44 Constance Classen and David Howes, 'The Museum as Sensescape: Western Sensibilities and Indigenous Artifacts,' in Elizabeth Edwards, Chris Gosden and Ruth Phillips, eds, *Sensible Objects: Colonialism, Museums and Material Culture* (Oxford: Berg, 2006), 209.

45 'Working with Artists,' *The Pitt Rivers Museum Handbook*, www.prm.ox.ac.uk/sites/default/files/imported/basic/pdf/edweb/workingwithartists.pdf (accessed 18 December 2017).

46 See Donald Judd, 'Specific Objects,' *Arts Yearbook*, vol. 8 (1964), 184.

47 Hou Hanru, 'Wong Hoy Cheong, Wrapping Up History,' *Flash Art* (November/December 2008), 69.

48 Ibid.

49 Ibid.

50 Ibid.

51 Hanru, 'Wong Hoy Cheong,' 69.

52 Nikos Papastergiadis, 'Space/Time: Matter and Motion in On Kawara,' *Afterall: A Journal of Art, Context and Enquiry*, vol. 41 (spring/summer 2016), 129.

53 Édouard Glissant, *Poetics of Relation,* tr. Betsy Wing (Ann Arbor: University of Michigan Press, 1997), 90.

54 Ibid.

55 Okwui Enwezor, 'The Postcolonial Constellation: Contemporary Art in a State of Permanent Transition,' *Research in African Literatures*, vol. 34, no. 4 (winter 2003), 58.

56 Ibid., 59.

57 Ibid., 58.

58 A shorter version of this chapter was published in 'The Body of the Archive: Chineseness at the Venice Biennale (1993–2005), *Journal of Contemporary Chinese Art*, vol. 3, no. 1&2 (2016), 27–46.

59 Diana Taylor, *The Archive and the Repertoire: Performing Cultural Memory in the Americas* (Durham, NC: Duke University Press, 2003), 19.

60 Ibid.

61 Borggreen and Gade, *Performing Archives/Archives of Performance*, 10.

62 Wang Jingwei, 'Minzudi guomin (Citizens of a Nation),' in Nan Zhang and Renzhi Wang, eds, *Xin hai ge ming qian shi nian jian shi lun xuan ji (A collection of Discussions of Issues in the Ten Years Before the 1911 Revolution)* (Hong Kong: Sanlian shudian, 1962), 82–114.

63 Zeng Zi, *Xiao Jing: The Classic of Xiao,* tr. Feng Xin-ming (馮欣明英語譯解 2007 年五月譯, 2008 年二月及五月修改), 2.

64 The Four Olds, 'old ideas, old culture, old customs and old habits,' was recorded in Lin Biao's editorial in *People's Daily* (1 June 1966).

65 'The Practice of the "One Country, Two Systems" Policy in the Hong Kong Special Administration Region,' Information Office of the State Council, The People's Republic of China (Beijing: June 2014).

66 The old filial nationalism concept was articulated anew as the Chinese cultural rim in Wang Yichuan, Zhang Fa, Tao Dongfung, Zhang Rongyi, and Sun Jing, 'Bianyuan, Zhongxin, Dongfang, Xifang' (Periphery, center, east, and west), *Dushu*, vol. 1 (January 1994).

67 Wu Hung, Wang Huangsheng, and Feng Boyi, *Reinterpretation: A Decade of Experimental Chinese Art, 1990–2000* (Guangzhou: Guandong Museum of Art, 2002).

68 Oliva, *La Biennale di Venezia.* See also Meiqin Wang, *Confrontation and Complicity: Rethinking Official Art in Contemporary China* (New York: Binghamton, 2007).

69 Lu Peng, *Passage to History: 20 Years of La Biennale di Venezia and Chinese Contemporary Art* (Venice: Biennale Arte, 2013), foreword.

70 Chao-yi Tsai, *Macro Vision, Micro Analysis, Multiple Reflections: Contemporary Art in Taiwan in the Post-Martial Law Era* (Taichung: National Taiwan Museum of Fine Arts, 2007), preface.

71 See Hsin-Yi Yeh, 'A Sacred Bastion? A Nation in Itself? An Economic Partner of Rising China? Three Waves of Nation-Building in Taiwan after 1949,' *Studies in Ethnicity and Nationalism*, vol. 14, no. 1 (2014).

72 Lee Ming-Sheng (2015), 台灣當代藝術資料庫介紹/Taiwan Contemporary Archives, Curriculum Vitae of Works, Taipei.

73 See the chapter on 'The Age of Ritual Art' in Wu Hung, *Monumentality in Early Chinese Art and Architecture* (Palo Alto: Stanford University Press, 1995).

74 Thomas J. Berghuis, *Performance Art in China* (Hong Kong: Timezone 8, 2006), 66.

75 Glissant, *Poetics of Relation,* 150.

76 Ibid.

77 Jan W. Walls, 'Twenty-First-Century Taiwan Culture: Internationalization with Local Characteristics,' in Leo Y. Liu, ed., *Taiwanese Polity in the Twenty-First Century: Politics and Culture in a Global Context* (Lewiston, NY: Edwin Mellen Press, 2004), 40.

78 Jean Clair, *La Biennale Di Venezia: 46 Esposizione Internazionale D'arte: Identity and Alterity, Figures of the Body 1895–1995* (Venice: Marsilio Editiori, 1995). To emphasize her assertion of this institutional critique, Wu's second installation, also titled *Library,* was exhibited at the 1997 Biennale exhibition.

79 Wu Mali, 'Artist Statement,' *The Journalist, Taipei,* no. 478 (5 May 1996).

80 See, for instance, Michael Nylan, *Wujing: The Five 'Confucian' Classics* (New Haven: Yale, 2001). The *Four Books* of the Confucian canon were the *Analects,* the *Classic of Filial Piety,* the *Great Learning,* and the *Doctrine of the Mean,* which were formally dated to the fourth century BC, as well as the *Five Classics* of

Change, Poetry, History, the Record of Rites, and the Spring and Autumn Classics as they were organized during the Han dynasty (206 BC–220 AD)

81 Linda Jaivin, 'Consuming Texts: The Work of Mali Wu,' *N. Paradoxa*, no. 5 (November 1997).

82 Ibid.

83 Mali, 'Artist Statement.'

84 Germano Celant, ed., *47th International Art Exhibition* (Venezia: La Biennale di Venezia, 1997), 681.

85 The other artists were Chang Chien-chi, Michael Ming-hong Lin, Liu Shih-ten, and Wang Wen-chih. *La Biennale di Venezia: 49 Esposizione Internazionale D'arte*, vol. 2 (Venezia: 2001), 166.

86 Betsy Di Julio, *Forces 'the Glass Ceiling,'* Virginia Beach: Contemporary Art Center (1998).

87 I am paraphrasing from the Altar Sūtra. Lu K'uan Yü, *Ch'an and Zen Teaching*, 2nd ed. (London: Rider & Co., 1969), 69.

88 Ibid.

89 Pat Binder and Gerhard Haupt, *Shu-Min Lin: Interview* (Universes in Universe, 2001).

90 Ibid.

91 Janet Ng, *Paradigm City* (New York: SUNY Press, 2009), 89.

92 See Rey Chow, 'King Kong in Hong Kong Watching the "Handover" from the U.S.A.,' *Social Text*, no. 55 (summer 1998), 95.

93 Ng, *Paradigm City*, 119.

94 Interview with Stanley Wong. *La Biennale Di Venezia: 51 International Art Exhibition, Participating Countries/Collateral Events* (Venezia: Fondazione La Biennale di Venezia, 2005).

95 Interview with Stanley Wong and Sabrina Fung and other members of Hong Kong Development Council, 11 June 2005.

96 Stanley Wong, 'Artist Statement' (2002) www.anothermountainman.com/about-anun/?q_cat=5 (accessed 6 October 2016).

97 Wang Fangyu, *Master of the Lotus Garden: The Life and Art of Bada Shanren (1626–1705)* (New Haven: Yale University Press, 1990).

98 Mao Zedong, 'Talks at the Yan'an Conference on Literature and Art,' tr. Bonnie S. McDougall (Ann Arbor: University of Michigan Press, 1980), 75.

99 La Biennale Venezia, *49 Esposizione Internazionale D'arte*, vol. 2 (Venezia: La Biennale di Venezia, 2001).

100 La Biennale Venezia, *49 Esposizione Internazionale D'arte*, 164.

101 Bryan S. Turner, 'Making and Unmaking Citizenship in Neo-liberal Times,' in Agnes S. Ku and Ngai Pun, eds, *Remaking Citizenship in Hong Kong* (London: Routledge, 2004), preface. See also Kabir Chhibber, 'Timeline: Hong Kong,' *Guardian* (Monday 1 July 2002).

102 Ibid., 162.

103 Interview with Zhang Huan, 2001. Qian Zhijian, 'Performing Bodies: Zhang Huan, Ma Liuming, and Performance Art in China,' *Art Journal* (summer 1999), 68.

104	See Xiaoping Lin, 'Globalism or Nationalism? Cai Guoqiang, Zhang Huan, and Xu Bing in New York,' *Third Text*, vol. 18, no. 4 (2004), 285.

105	*TransCulture* la Biennale di Venezia 1995, exhibition catalogue (Japan Foundation, Tokyo, 1995), 162.

106	See Chang Tianle, 'Masterminding the Rare Occasion,' *Shanghai Star* (18 October 2001).

107	Amelia Jones, *Body Art: Performing the Subject* (Minneapolis: University of Minnesota Press, 1998), 13–14.

108	Gao Minglu, *Inside Out: New Chinese Art* (San Francisco Museum of Modern Art and Asia Society, 1999), 4.

109	Liangyan Ge, *Out of the Margins: The Rise of a Chinese Vernacular Fiction* (Honolulu: University of Hawai'i Press, 2001), 8.

110	Ibid., 9.

111	*Yibai Ershi Hui De Shuihu* (Hong Kong: Commercial Press, 1969).

112	Roland Barthes, *Image – Music – Text*, tr. Stephen Heath, 3rd ed. (London: Fontana, 1982), 44. Emphasis in original.

113	See Chang Tianle, 'Masterminding the Rare Occasion,' *Shanghai Star* (18 October 2001).

114	Julia F. Andrews and Kuiyi Shen, *The Art of Modern China* (Berkeley: University of California Press, 2012), 185.

115	La Biennale di Venezia, *48 Esposizione Internazionale D'arte* (Venice: La Biennale di Venezia, 1999).

116	Erik Eckholm, 'Cultural Revolution, Chapter 2; Expatriate Artist Updates Maoist Icon and Angers Old Guard,' *New York Times* (17 August 2000), Sec E.

117	Yvonne Zhao, author's correspondence with Cai Guo-Qiang Archives, Los Angeles, 17 May 2016.

118	Fan Di'an, 'Commissioner's Statement, China Pavilion, Venice Biennale,' (2005).

119	Fan Di'an, 'Press Release: China Pavilion at 51st Biennale Di Venezia, Virgin Garden: Emersion,' (2005).

120	Dean Chan, ed., 'Undoing Nationalism, Fabricating Transnationalism,' *Third Text*, vol. 28, no. 1 (2014).

121	Roland Barthes, *Mythologies* (New York: Hill and Wang, 1973), 149.

Select bibliography

Abrams, Kerry. 'Polygamy, Prostitution, and the Federalization of Immigration Law.' *Columbia Law Review*, vol. 105, no. 3 (April 2005).

Alaimo, Stacy. *Exposed: Environmental Politics and Pleasures in Posthuman Times.* Minneapolis; London: University of Minnesota Press, 2016.

Althusser, Louis. *For Marx.* Translated by Ben Brewster. London: Verso, 1990.

———— *Lenin and Philosophy and Other Essays.* Translated by Ben Brewster. New York and London: Monthly Review Press, 1971.

Anderson, Benedict. *Imagined Communities: Reflections on the Origin and Spread of Nationalism.* London: Verso, 2006.

Andrews, Julia F. and Kuiyi Shen. *The Art of Modern China.* Berkeley: University of California Press, 2012.

Badiou, Alain and Bosteels, Bruno. 'The Cultural Revolution: The Last Revolution?' *Positions: East Asia Cultures Critique*, vol. 13, no. 3 (winter 2005).

Balibar, Etienne. *Race, Nation, Class Ambiguous Identities.* New York: Verso, 1991.

Belting, Hans, Andrea Buddensieg, and Peter Wiebel. *The Global Contemporary and the Rise of New Art Worlds.* Cambridge, MA: MIT Press, 2013.

Benjamin, Walter. *Selected Writings.* Volume 3, 1935–1938. Edited by Howard Eiland and Michael W. Jennings. Cambridge, MA: Harvard University Press, 2002.

———— *The Arcades Project.* Translated by Howard Eiland and Kevin McLaughlin. Cambridge, MA: Harvard University Press, 1999.

———— *Illuminations.* London: Pimlico, 1999.

———— *Understanding Brecht.* Translated by Anna Bostock. London: Verso, 1998.

———— *Selected Writings*, Volume 1, 1913–1926. Edited by Marcus Bullock and Michael W. Jennings. Cambridge, MA: Harvard University Press, 1996.

———— 'Gespräch mit Anne May Wong.' *Die literarische Welt*, no. 27 (July 1928).

Binghua, Wang. *Xinjiang gu shi: gu dai Xinjiang ju min ji qi wen hua, The Ancient Corpses of Xinjiang: The Peoples of Ancient Xinjiang and their Culture.* 新疆人民出版社 Wulumuqi-shi: Xinjiang ren min chu ban she, 2001.

Bishop, Claire. 'Digital Divide.' *Artforum* (September 2012): 434–42.

Bourdieu, Pierre. *Pascalian Meditations.* Cambridge: Polity Press, 2000.

Brecht, Bertolt. *Diaries 1920–1922.* Reprinted in Jacques Rancière, *The Politics of Literature.* Cambridge: Polity, 2011.

_______ *The Good Person of Szechwan*. Translated by John Willett. London: Bloomsbury, 1985.

_______ 'On Chinese Acting.' *The Tulane Drama Review*, vol. 6, no. 1 (September 1961).

Breitz, Candice and Allan Bower, eds, *Africus: Johannesburg Biennale 20 February–30 April 1995: But is it Art?* Johannesburg: Transitional Metropolitan Council, 1995.

Brown, Melissa, ed. *Negotiating Ethnicities in China and Taiwan*. Berkeley: University of California Press, 1996.

Butler, Judith, Ernesto Laclau, and Slavoj Žižek. *Contingency, Hegemony, Universality: Contemporary Dialogues on the Left*. London and New York: Verso, 2000.

_______ *The Psychic Life of Power: Theories in Subjection*. Stanford: Stanford University Press, 1997.

_______ 'Performative Acts and Gender Constitution: An Essay in Phenomenology and Feminist Theory.' *Theatre Journal*, vol. 40, no. 4 (December 1988).

Chan, Anthony B. *Perpetually Cool: The Many Lives of Anna May Wong (1905–1961)*. Lanham: Scarecrow Press, 2007.

Chan, Wing-Tsit. *A Source Book in Chinese Philosophy*. Princeton: Princeton University Press, 1963.

Chang, Patty. *Patty Chang: The Wandering Lake*. New York: Queens Museum, 2017.

Chen, Elsa Hsiang-chun. 'Wu Mali: My Skin is my Home/Nation.' *Contemporary Chinese Art – Another Kind of View. DSL Collection*. 2008. www.g1expo.com/fiche.php?id=26 (accessed 18 July 2017).

Chen, Jinhua. 'More than a Philosopher: Fazang (643–712) as a Politician and Miracle Worker.' *History of Religions*, vol. 42, no. 4 (May 2003).

Chen Been-lon, 'Inside the Taiwan Miracle,' *Taiwan Review*, 1 June 2011. http://tai wantoday. tw/news.php?unit=8,8,29,32,32,45&post=13965 (accessed 18 November 2017).

Cheng, Meiling. *Beijing Xingwei: Contemporary Chinese Time-Based Art*. London: Seagull Books, 2013.

Chin, Gabriel. 'Preserving Racial Identity: Population Patterns and the Application of Anti-Miscegenation Statutes to Asian Americans, 1910–1950.' *Journal of Asian Law* (May 2002).

Chin Davidson, Jane. 'Displacements of the Desiring Machine.' *Interventions: International Journal of Postcolonial Studies*, vol. 14, no. 3 (2012).

_______ 'De-Territorializing Bodies: Body Art and the Colonial World Expositions,' in Jonathan Harris, ed., *Dead History, Live Art? Spectacle, Subjectivity and Subversion in Visual Culture since the 1960s*. Liverpool: Liverpool University Press, 2007

_______ and Esslinger, Sandra, eds, *Global and World Art in the Practice of the University Museum*. New York and London: Routledge, 2017.

'China Diverts 10 Billion Cubic Meters of Water From South to North.' *China Daily* (4 October 2017). www.chinadaily.com.cn/china/2017–10/04/content_32830449.htm (accessed 7 January 2017).

Chin-Chin Yap. 'The Virtual Muse and her Taxman.' *Art Asia Pacific Magazine*, no. 57 (March/April 2008).

Chou Hui-ling. 'Striking Their Own Poses: The History of Cross-Dressing on the Chinese Stage.' *TDR (1988–)*, vol. 41, no. 2 (summer 1997).

Chow, Peter C.Y. *Economic Integration Across the Taiwan Strait: Global Perspectives.* Northampton, MA: Edward Elgar Publishing, 2013.

Chow, Rey. *Entanglements, or Transmedial Thinking about Capture.* Durham, NC: Duke University Press, 2012.

_______ 'On Chineseness as a Theoretical Problem.' *boundary 2*, vol. 25, no. 3 (fall 1998).

_______ *Primitive Passions: Visuality, Sexuality, Ethnography, and Contemporary Chinese Cinema.* New York: Columbia University Press, 1995.

Dalberg-Acton, John Emerich Edward. *The History of Freedom and Other Essays.* London: Macmillan and Co., 1909.

Danielsson, Sarah K. *The Explorer's Roadmap to National-Socialism: Sven Hedin, Geography and the Path to Genocide.* London: Routledge, 2016.

Davis, Heather and Etienne Turpin, eds, *Art in the Anthropocene: Encounters Among Aesthetics, Politics, Environments and Epistemologies.* London: Open Humanities Press, 2015.

Deepwell, Katy. 'Mali Wu: A Profile.' *n.paradoxa*, no. 5 (November 1997).

Deleuze, Gilles. *Difference and Repetition.* Translated by Paul Patton. London and New York: Continuum, 1994.

Demos, T.J. 'Contemporary Art and the Politics of Ecology.' *Third Text*, vol. 27, no. 1 (2013).

Eiland, Howard and Michael W. Jennings. *Walter Benjamin: A Critical Life.* Cambridge MA: Belknap Press, Harvard University Press, 2014.

Eley, Geoff and Ronald Grigor Suny, eds, *Becoming National: A Reader.* New York and Oxford: Oxford University Press, 1996.

Eveleth, Rose. 'China is Opening Around 100 Museums Every Year.' *Smithsonian.com.* 21 May 2013. www.smithsonianmag.com/smart-news/china-is-opening-around-100-museums-every-year-74842851/ (accessed 11 January 2018).

Ferguson, Russell. *Patty Chang, Shangri-La.* Los Angeles: Hammer Museum, 2005.

Foucault, Michel. 'The Subject and Power.' *Critical Inquiry,* vol. 8, no. 4 (summer 1982).

Fukuyama, Francis. 'The End of History.' *The National Interest,* no. 16 (summer 1989).

Glissant, Édouard. *Poetics of Relation.* Translated by Betsy Wing. Ann Arbor: University of Michigan Press, 1997.

Goto, Reiko, Margaret Shiu, and Wu Mali. 'Ecofeminism: Art as Environment – A Cultural Action/WEAD.' *Bamboo Curtain Studio Newsletter,* 3 December 2014.

Grewal, Inderpal and Caren Kaplan. 'Global Identities: Theorizing Transnational Studies of Sexuality.' *GLQ: A Journal of Lesbian and Gay Studies.* vol. 7, no. 4 (2001).

Groys, Boris. 'Politics of Installation.' *e-flux journal,* no. 2 (January 2009).

Guang Lu. *Modern Revolutionary Beijing Opera: Context, Contents, and Conflicts.* Kent, Ohio: Kent State University, 1997.

Haas, Benjamin. 'Where the Wind Blows: How China's Dirty Air Becomes Hong Kong's Problem.' *Guardian.* 16 February 2017. www.theguardian.com/cities/2017/feb/16/hong-kong-death-trap-dirty-air-pollution-china (accessed 16 October 2017).

Hall, Stuart. *Race, The Floating Signifier Featuring Stuart Hall*, DVD transcript, Media Education Foundation, 1997.

Hedin, Sven. *The Wandering Lake: Into the Heart of Asia.* London: Tauris, 2009.

Hegel, Georg W.F. *The Philosophy of History.* New York: Prometheus, 1991.

Hernandez, Javier C. 'Climate Change May Be Intensifying China's Smog Crisis.' *New York Times*. 25 March 2017.

'HK Crowned World's Most Competitive Economy.' *South China Morning Post* (1 June 2017).

Hodges, Graham Russell Gao. *Anna May Wong: From Laundryman's Daughter to Hollywood Legend*. New York: Palgrave Macmillan, 2004.

Hou Hanru. 'Politics of Intimacy – On Cao Fei's Work.' Interview. San Francisco. 25 February 2008, republished online at www.caofei.com/texts.aspx?id=17&year=2008&aitid=1 (accessed 8 August 2017).

Hsiao-peng Lu, Sheldon. *Transnational Chinese Cinemas*. Honolulu: University of Hawai'i Press, 1997.

Hu Fang. 'Contemplating the City,' in Renate Wiehager, ed., *Cao Fei: I Watch That Worlds Pass By*. Gent: Snoeck, 2016.

Huang, Yiju. 'On Transference: Badiou and the Chinese Cultural Revolution.' *Comparative Literature Studies*, vol. 52, no. 1 (2015).

Huenemann, Ralph W. 'Economic Reforms, 1978–Present,' in *Oxford Bibliographies: Chinese Studies* edited by Timothy Wright. New York: Oxford University Press.

Irigaray, Luce. *This Sex Which is Not One*. Translated by Catherine Porter. Ithaca: Cornell University Press, 1985.

Johnson, Ken. 'Art in Review.' *New York Times* (23 November 2001).

Jones, Amelia. *Seeing Differently: A History and Theory of Identification and the Visual Arts*. New York and London: Routledge, 2013.

_______ *Body Art/Performing the Subject*. Minneapolis: University of Minnesota Press, 1998.

_______ and Adrian Heathfield, eds, *Perform, Repeat, Record: Live Art in History*. London: Intellect, 2012.

Jose, Nicholas and Yang Wen-I. *Art Taiwan: The Contemporary art of Taiwan*. Sydney: Museum of Contemporary Art, 1995.

Juan Mei-shu, *Yionan chiaolou te ch'isheng: hsunchao 2–28 sanluo te yitzu (Sound of Weeping in a Dim Corner: Looking for the Dispersed February 28 Victim's Families)*. Taipei: Ch'ien-wei, 1992.

Kolås, Åshild. *Tourism and Tibetan Culture in Transition: A Place Called Shangrila*. New York and London: Routledge, 2007.

Krauss, Rosalind. 'Sculpture in the Expanded Field.' *October*, vol. 8 (spring 1979).

Lau, Emily. 'Paper Lion: Howe's Visit Fails to Placate the British Territory.' *Far Eastern Economic Review* (13 July 1989).

Lau, Lawrence J. 'The Long-Term Economic Growth of Taiwan,' working paper for the Institute of Global Economics and Finance. The Chinese University of Hong Kong (December 2012).

Li, Chunxiang, Hongjie Li, Yinqiu Cui, Chengzhi Xie, Dawei Cai, Wenying Li, Victor H. Mair, Zhi Xu, Quanchao Zhang, Idelisi Abuduresule, Li Jin, Hong Zhu, and Hui Zhou. 'Evidence that a West-East Admixed Population Lived in the Tarim Basin as Early as the Early Bronze Age.' *BMC Biology*, vol. 8, no. 15 (February 2010).

Lieberenz, Paul and Rudolf Biebrach, directors. *Mit Sven Hedin durch Asiens Wüsten*

(With Sven Hedin Across the Deserts of Asia). Film. Sweden: Svensk Filmindustri (SF), 1928.

Lim, Shirley Jennifer. '"Speaking German Like Nobody's Business": Anna May Wong, Walter Benjamin, and the Possibilities of Asian American Cosmopolitanism.' *Journal of Transnational American Studies*, vol. 4, no. 3 (2012).

Lin, Xiaoping. 'Globalism or Nationalism: Cai Guoqiang, Zhang Huan and Xu Bing in New York.' *Third Text*, vol. 18, no. 4 (2004).

Liu Kang. 'The Frankfurt School and Chinese Marxist Philosophical Reflections since the 1980s.' *Journal of Chinese Philosophy*, vol. 40, no. 3/4 (September/December 2013).

______ *Aesthetics and Marxism: Chinese Aesthetic Marxists and Their Western Contemporaries*. Durham, NC: Duke University Press, 2000.

______ 'The Problematics of Mao and Althusser: Alternative Modernity and Cultural Revolution.' *Rethinking Marxism*, vol. 8, no. 3 (1995).

Lo, Kwai-Cheung. 'Sinicizing Žižek? The Ideology of Inherent Self-Negation in Contemporary China.' *Positions: East Asia Cultures Critique*, vol. 19, no. 3 (winter 2011).

______ *Excess and Masculinity in Asian Cultural Productions*. New York: SUNY Press, 2010.

Lu Tonglin, ed. special volume. 'The Chinese Perspective On Žižek And Žižek's Perspective On China.' *Positions: Asia Critique*, vol. 19, no. 3 (winter 2011).

Mao Tse-Tung. *Let a Hundred Flowers Bloom: The Complete Text on the Correct Handling of Contradictions Among the People*. New York: Tamiment Institute, 1957.

Mao Zedong. 'Talks at the Yan'an Conference on Literature and Art: A Translation of the 1943 Text with Commentary,' ed. Bonnie McDougall. Ann Arbor: University of Michigan Press, 1980.

______ *Selected Works of Mao Tse-tung* (14 July 1956), www.marxists.org/reference/archive/mao/selected-works/volume-5/mswv5_52.htm (accessed 18 July 2017).

Martin, Carol. 'Brecht, Feminism, and Chinese Theatre.' *TDR (1988–)*, vol. 43, no. 4 (winter 1999).

McDonough, Tom, ed. *Guy Debord and the Situationist International: Texts and Documents*. Cambridge, MA: MIT Press, 2004.

Mercer, Kobena. *Exiles, Diasporas & Strangers*. London: Iniva, 2008.

Merchant, Carolyn. *Radical Ecology: The Search for a Livable World*. New York: Routledge, 1992.

Minh-Ha, Trinh T. 'Documentary Is/Not a Name.' *October*, vol. 52 (spring 1990).

Mitchell, Timothy. *Carbon Democracy: Political Power in the Age of Oil*. London: Verso, 2011.

______ *Questions of Modernity*. Minneapolis: University of Minnesota Press, 2000.

______ 'Orientalism and the Exhibitionary Order,' in Donald Preziosi, ed., *The Art of Art History: A Critical Anthology*. Oxford and New York: Oxford University Press, 1998.

______ *Colonising Egypt*. Cambridge: Cambridge University Press, 1988.

Moderation(s): Yuk King Tan tour. Incidents of Travel. Website for Witte de With Center for Contemporary Art, Rotterdam, www.wdw.nl/en/our_program/events/

moderation_s_yuk_king_tan_tour_incidents_of_travel_hong_kong (accessed 15 August 2017).

Nancy, Jean-Luc and John Paul Ricco. 'The Existence of the World is Always Unexpected,' in Heather Davis and Etienne Turpin, eds, *Art in the Anthropocene: Encounters Among Aesthetics, Politics, Environments and Epistemologies.* London: Open Humanities Press, 2015.

Napack, Jonathan. 'An Art Market with Chinese Characteristics.' *Yishu: Journal of Chinese Contemporary Chinese Art* (March 2007).

Oliva, Achille Bonito. *La Biennale di Venezia, 45 Esposizione Internationale d'Arte 1993.* Venice: Marsilio Editiori, 1993.

Ong, Aihwa. *Flexible Citizenship: The Cultural Logics of Transnationality.* Durham, NC: Duke University Press, 1999.

Papastergiadis, Nikos. 'A Breathing Space for Aesthetics and Politics: An Introduction to Jacques Rancière,' *Theory, Culture & Society*, vol. 3, no. 7/8 (2014).

_______ *Spatial Aesthetics: Art, Place, and the Everyday.* Amsterdam: Network Cultures Institute, 2010.

Pecora, Vincent P., ed. *Nations and Identities: Classic Readings.* Oxford: Blackwell, 2001.

Peffer, George Anthony. 'Forbidden Families: Emigration Experiences of Chinese Women Under the Page Law, 1875–1882.' *Journal of American Ethnic History*, vol. 6, no. 1 (fall 1986).

Peng, Lu. *Passage to History: 20 Years of La Biennale di Venezia and Chinese Contemporary Art.* Venice: Biennale Arte, 2013.

Phelan, Peggy. *Unmarked: The Politics of Performance.* New York: Routledge, 1993.

Pollock, Barbara. 'Shanghai's Tricky Museum Transformation.' *Artnews.* March 2014.

Qian, Sima. *Records of the Grand Historian: Han Dynasty II.* Translated by Burton Watson. New York: Columbia University Press, 1993.

Railton, Ben. *The Chinese Exclusion Act.* New York: Palgrave Macmillan, 2013.

Rancière, Jacques. *Althusser's Lesson.* Translated by Emiliano Battista. London and New York: Continuum, 2011.

_______ *The Politics of Literature.* Cambridge: Polity, 2011.

_______ 'The Emancipated Spectator.' *Artforum* (March 2007).

_______ *Film Fables.* Translated by Emiliano Battista. Oxford: Berg, 2006.

Robcis, Camille. '"China in Our Heads": Althusser, Maoism, and Structuralism.' *Social Text 110*, vol. 30, no. 1 (spring 2012).

Ross, Eleanor. 'What's the History Behind China's Current Obsession with Xinjiang?' *Newsweek* (10 March 2017), www.newsweek.com/protest-xinjiang-china-muslim-central-asia-terrorism-559161 (accessed 15 August 2017).

Said, Edward W. *Orientalism.* New York: Penguin, 1995.

Scott, Izabella. 'Interview with Cao Fei.' *The White Review* (June 2016), www.thewhiter-eview.org/interviews/interview-with-cao-fei (accessed 15 August 2017).

Scott, Joan Wallach, ed. *Feminism and History.* Oxford: Oxford University Press, 1996.

Shao, Larry. 'Interview with Wu Mali.' *Asia Art Archive* (1 November 2010). www.aaa.org.hk/en/ideas/ideas/interview-with-wu-mali (accessed 18 January 2018).

Shih, Shu-mei. *Visuality and Identity: Sinophone Articulations Across the Pacific.* Berkeley: University of California Press, 2007.

Shimizu, Celine Parreñas. *The Hypersexuality of Race: Performing Asian/American Women on Screen and Scene.* Durham, NC: Duke University Press, 2007.

Solomon, Alisa. *Re-Dressing the Canon: Essays on Theater and Gender.* London: Routledge, 1997.

Song, Aly. 'The Women of China's Workforce.' *Reuters* (4 March 2014). https://wider-image. reuters.com/story/the-women-of-chinas-workforce (accessed 1 January 2018).

Song, Xianlin. 'Re-gendering Chinese History: Zhao Mei's Emperor Wu Zetian.' *East Asia,* vol. 27 (2010).

Spivak, Gayatri Chakravorty. *An Aesthetic Education in the Era of Globalization.* Cambridge, MA: Harvard University Press, 2012.

______ 'Nationalism and the Imagination.' *Lectora*, vol. 15 (2009).

Stanway, David. 'Beijing Bans High-Emission Vehicles in Anti-Smog Move: Xinhua.' *Reuters* (13 February 2017). www.reuters.com/article/us-china-pollution-autos-idUSKB5T00V (accessed 17 August 2018).

Storr, Robert. 'Prince of Tides: Interview with 1999 Venice Biennale Visual Arts Director Harald Szeemann.' *Artforum*, vol. 37, no. 9 (1999).

Sui, Cindy. 'Taiwan Kuomintang: Revisiting the White Terror Years,' *BBC News Taipei* (13 March 2016). www.bbc.com/news/world-asia-35723603 (accessed 20 December 2018).

Tatlow, Antony and Tak-Wai Wong. *Brecht and East Asian Theatre.* Hong Kong: Hong Kong University Press, 1982.

Toscano, Alberto and Kinkle, Jeff. *Cartographies of the Absolute.* Alresford: Zero Books, 2015.

Vasari, Giorgio. *Lives of the Most Eminent Painters, Sculptors and Architects. Volume 1, Cimabue to Agnolo Gaddi.* Translated by Gaston Du C. De Vere. London: Macmillan and the Medici Society, 1912–14.

Vogel, Carol. 'China Celebrates the Year of the Art Market.' *New York Times* (24 December 2006).

______ 'Sotheby's Bets on a Windfall for Today's Chinese Art.' *New York Times* (29 March 2006).

'Vroom Vroom: Cao Fei's BMW Car Unveiled.' *The Art Newspaper* (1 June 2017). http://theartnewspaper.com/news/vroom-vroom-cao-feis-bmw-car-unveiled (accessed 30 June 2017).

Wiehager, Renate, ed. *Cao Fei: I Watch That Worlds Pass By.* Gent: Snoeck, 2016.

Wong, Edward. 'Rights Groups Ask China to Free Tibetan Education Advocate,' *New York Times* (18 January 2017). www.nytimes.com/2017/01/18/world/asia/china-tibetan-education- advocate.html?_r=0 (accessed 3 January 2018).

______ 'Nearly 14,000 Companies in China Violate Pollution Rules.' *New York Times* (13 June 2017). www.nytimes.com/2017/06/13/world/asia/china-companies-air-pollution-paris-agreement.html (accessed 15 August 2018).

______ 'On Scale of 0 to 500, Beijing's Air Quality Tops "Crazy Bad" at 755.' *New York Times* (12 January 2013).

______ 'The Dead Tell a Tale China Doesn't Care to Listen To.' *New York Times* (18 November 2008), A6.

Wu, Dunfu, ed. (吴敦夫f) *Footprints of Foreign Explorers on the Silk Road* (丝绸之路上的外国探险家的足迹英). Beijing: China Intercontinental Press, 2007.

Wu Hung, ed. *The First Guangzhou Triennial, Reinterpretation: A Decade of Experimental Art, 1990–2000*. Guangzhou: Guangdong Museum of Art, 2002.

Wu Mali. 'Who's Listening to Whose Story?' *World Art*, vol. 5, no. 1 (2015).

Wu Zuguang, Huang Zuolin, and Mei Shaowu. *Peking Opera and Mei Lanfang*. Beijing: New World Press, 1981.

Yeh, Emily T. and Christopher R. Coggins. *Mapping Shangrila: Contested Landscapes in the Sino-Tibetan Borderlands*. Seattle: University of Washington Press, 2014.

Yu, Enoch. 'From Bullets to Cash machines, HSBC's 151-Year History is Closely Aligned with the Evolution of Hong Kong.' *South China Morning Post*. 24 April 2016.

Zhang, Jianping, Houyuan Lu, Naiqin Wu, Xiaoguang Qin, and Luo Wang, 'Palaeoenvironment and Agriculture of Ancient Loulan and Milan on the Silk Road.' *The Holocene*, vol. 23, no. 2 (2012).

Zhang Yiwu and Jon Solomon. 'Žižek's China, China's Žižek.' *Positions: East Asia Cultures Critique*, vol. 19, no. 3 (winter 2011).

Zhao Mei. *Nuren: Wu Zetian*. Beijing: Tuanjie chubanshe, 2007.

Zheng Bo. 'An Interview with Wu Mali.' *Field: A Journal of Socially Engaged Art Criticism* (winter 2016).

Žižek, Slavoj. *Mao on Practice and Contradiction*. London: Verso, 2007.

______ *On Belief*. New York and London: Routledge, 2003.

Index

EU authorised representative for GPSR:
Easy Access System Europe, Mustamäe tee 50,
10621 Tallinn, Estonia
gpsr.requests@easproject.com

www.ingramcontent.com/pod-product-compliance
Ingram Content Group UK Ltd.
Pitfield, Milton Keynes, MK11 3LW, UK
UKHW062135150726
7214IPUK00024B/417